# The Creative Power Of Mind

## Daily Meditations For A Better Life

Complied By David Allen

A compilation from the archives of some of the best authors on how we create our lives by design

Metaphysics / Law of Attraction Edition

Copyright © 2019

Copyright © 2019 by David Allen / Shanon Allen

All rights reserved. No part of this publication may be reproduced, distributed, or transmitted in any form or by any means, including photocopying, recording, or other electronic or mechanical methods, without the prior written permission of the publisher, except in the case of brief quotations embodied in critical reviews and certain other noncommercial uses permitted by copyright law.
Printed in the United States of America

February 2019

ISBN: 978-0-9995435-6-6

Visit Us At **NevilleGoddardBooks.com** for a complete listing of all our books and **1000's of Free Books to Read online and download.**

## Foreword

How do I introduce a book like this? It is a book on the creative powers of the mind of man(kind). It outlines principles that will bring happiness, joy, success to all areas of life for the one who can see those principles and apply them. It is packed with Gold that has taken the form of Words that the reader can turn back into Gold if he/she will only take the time to understand what he/she is reading and applies it to his or her life. It is life transforming information. May this book bless you for the remainder of your long healthy and prosperous life.

I give you water by telling you how the law operates. Now you must turn it into wine by application. - Neville Goddard

All anyone can do for us is give us the truth of how the law operates, which I have found that the excerpts you find in this book do. It is up to the reader to take this information and turn it into wine by application of these truths. When you do, you will find that the truth does indeed set you free.

David Allen

## Acknowledgements

The Creative Power of Mind is a compilation from the archives of the following authors

James Allen, Bruce Maclelland, Charles F. Haanel, Charles Fillmore, Charles Wesley Kyle, Christian Larson, Emmett Fox, Ernest Holmes, Eugene Del Mar, Fay Adams, Floyd B Wilson, Genevieve Behrend, George Schubel, Helen Wilmans, Henry Harrison Brown, Henry Thomas Hamblin, Jeanie P. Owens, John Seaman Garns, Joseph Murphy, Mrs. Evelyn Lowes Wicker, Orison Swett Marden, Prentice Mulford, R. C. Douglass, Robert Collier, Shirley Bell Hastings, Uriel Buchanan, Venice J. Bloodworth, W. J. Colville, Wallace Wattles, Walter C Lanyon, William Walker Atkinson

## Contents

Legal
Foreword
Acknowledgements
January      -  6
February     -  30
March        -  53
April        -  76
May          -  96
June         -  120
July         -  141
August       -  162
September    -  184
October      -  204
November     -  225
December     -  247

Metaphysical / Law of Attraction Books - 269

# January

## January 1st

### Ernest Holmes

Every person is surrounded by a thought atmosphere. This mental atmosphere is the direct result of thought which in its turn becomes the direct reason for the cause of that which comes into our lives. Through this power we are either attracting or repelling. Like attracts like and we attract to us just what we are in mind. It is also true that we become attracted to something that is greater than our previous experience by first embodying the atmosphere of our desire. Every business, every place, every person, everything has a certain mental atmosphere of its own. This atmosphere decides what is to be drawn to it. For instance, you never saw a successful man who went around with an atmosphere of failure. Successful people think about success. A successful man is filled with that subtle something which permeates everything that he does with an atmosphere of confidence and strength. In the presence of some people we feel as though nothing were too great to undertake; we are uplifted; we are inspired to do great things, to accomplish; we feel strong, steady, sure. What a power we feel in the presence of big souls, strong men, noble women!

## January 2nd

### Orison Swett Marden

The great trouble with those of us who are living in a world of unfulfilled desires and ambitions is that we do not hold the right consciousness. Dr. Perry Green rightly says that Job's lament — "The thing which I feared is come upon me" — should be changed to "The thing 'which I was greatly conscious of is come upon me." In other words, it is the thing we hold in our consciousness that comes out of the invisible world of realities and takes visible form in our lives according to its nature, — poverty or prosperity; health or disease; happiness or misery. The whole secret of individual growth and development is locked up in our consciousness, for this is the door of life itself. Every experience whether of joy or sorrow, of health or disease, of success or failure, must come through our consciousness. There is no other way by which it can enter and become a part of the life. You cannot have what you are not conscious of; you cannot do what you are not conscious of being able to do. In short, it is an immutable law that, whatever you hold in mind, believe that you can do or get, is the thing that will manifest itself in your life.

## January 3rd

### Charles F. Haanel

That much gathers more is true on every plane of existence and that loss leads to greater loss is equally true. Mind is creative, and conditions, environment and all experiences in life are the result of our habitual or predominant mental attitude. The attitude of mind necessarily depends upon what we think. Therefore, the secret of all power, all achievement and all possession depends upon our method of thinking. This is true because we must "be" before we can "do," and we can "do" only to the extent which we "are," and what we "are" depends upon what we "think." We cannot express powers that we do not possess. The only way by which we may secure possession of power is to become conscious of power, and we can never become conscious of power until we learn that all power is from within. There is a world within – a world of thought and feeling and power; of light and life and beauty and, although invisible, its forces are mighty. The world within is governed by mind. When we discover this world we shall find the solution for every problem, the cause for every effect; and since the world within is subject to our control, all laws of power and possession are also within our control. The world without is a reflection of the world within. What appears without is what has been found within. In the world within may be found infinite Wisdom, infinite Power, infinite Supply of all that is necessary, waiting for unfoldment, development and expression. If we recognize these potentialities in the world within they will take form in the world without.

## January 4th

### Ernest Holmes

It is hard to get a clear concept of this great Ceaseless Cause, this something from which all things come; at times we get into a maze of confusion when we attempt to realize what the Spirit means. It is then that we should think of It as the great reason behind everything. Being all-knowledge It must know Itself, and must know everything It creates; so It knows us and It knows everyone. Since It is All-Presence we can contact anywhere and will never have to go to some particular spot to find It. As It is All-Knowing and operates through the power of the Word, It know everything we think. Just how It creates we cannot know and need not attempt to understand, for whatever this process of creation is, we find it is always an inner thought process. We should keep this in mind — the Spirit makes all things out of Itself. Everything comes into being without effort, and when we exert ourselves we are not in accord with the Creative Spirit in the way in which It works. The impulse of the Spirit to move must be caused by a desire to express what It feels Itself to be — Beauty, Form, Color, Life, Love and Power. All things else we find in the manifest universe are attributes of the Spirit, and are caused to spring into being through the Word, because the Spirit wants to enjoy Itself.

## January 5th

### Wallace Wattles

To set about getting rich in a scientific way, you do not try to apply your will power to anything outside of yourself. You have no right to do so, anyway. It is wrong to apply your will to other men and women in order to get them to do what you wish done. It is as flagrantly wrong to coerce people by mental power as it is to coerce them by physical power. If compelling people by physical force to do things for you reduces them to slavery, compelling them by mental means accomplishes exactly the same thing; the only difference is in methods. If taking things from people by physical force is robbery, them taking things by mental force is robbery also.

There is no difference in principle. You have no right to use your will power upon another person, even "for his own good," for you do not know what is for his good. The science of getting rich does not require you to apply power or force to any other person, in any way whatsoever. There is not the slightest necessity for doing so. Indeed, any attempt to use your will upon others will only tend to defeat your purpose. You do not need to apply your will to things in order to compel them to come to you. That would simply be trying to coerce God and would be foolish and useless. You do not have to try to compel God to give you good things, any more than you have to use your will power to make the sun rise. You do not have to use your will power to conquer an unfriendly Deity, or to make stubborn and rebellious forces do your bidding. Substance is friendly to you, and is more anxious to give you what you want than you are to get it. To get rich, you need only to use your will power upon yourself. When you know what to think and do, then you must use your will to compel yourself to think and do the right things. That is the legitimate use of the will in getting what you want — to use it in holding yourself to the right course. Use your will to keep yourself thinking and acting in the certain way.

## January 6th

### Robert Collier

Initiative, plus imagination, will take you anywhere. Imagination opens the eyes of the mind, and there is nothing good you can image there that is not possible of fulfillment in your daily life. Imagination is the connecting link between the human and the Divine, between the formed universe and formless energy. It is, of all things human, the most God-like. It is our part of Divinity. Through it we share in the creative power of Universal Mind. Through it we can turn the most drab existence into a thing of life and beauty. It is the means by which we avail ourselves of all the good which Universal Mind is constantly offering to us in such profusion. It is the means by which we can reach any goal, win any prize. What was it gave us the submarine, the airplane, wireless, electricity? Imagination. What was it that enabled man to build the Simplon Tunnel, the Panama Canal, the Hell Gate span? Imagination. What is it that makes us successful and happy, or poor and friendless? Imagination — or the lack of it. It was imagination that sent Spanish and English and French adventurers to this new world. It was imagination that urged the early settlers westward — ever westward. It was imagination that built our railroads, our towns, our great cities. Parents foolishly try to discourage imagination in their children, when all it needs is proper guidance. For imagination forms the world from which their future will take its shape. Restrain the one and you constrict the other. Develop the one in the right way, and there is no limit to the other. Uncontrolled, the imagination is like a rudderless ship. Or even, at times, like the lightning. But properly controlled, it is like the ship that carries riches from port to port. Or like the electric current, carrying unlimited power for industry and progress. Do you want happiness? Do you want success? Do you want position, power, riches? Image them! How did God first make man? "In his image created He him." He "imaged" man in His Mind. And that is the way everything has been made since time began. It was first imaged in Mind. That is the way everything you want must start — with a mental image.

### January 7th

Prentice Mulford

If our minds are, from what is falsely called economy, ever set on the cheap–cheap lodgings, cheap food and cheap fares, we get in the thought current of the cheap, the slavish and the fearful. Our views of life and our plans will be influenced and warped by it. It paralyzes that courage and enterprise implied in the old adage "Nothing ventured nothing gained." Absorbed in this current and having it ever acting on you, it is felt immediately when you come into the presence of the successful and causes them to avoid you. They feel in you the absence of that element which brings them their relative success. It acts as a barrier, preventing the flow to you of their sympathy. Sympathy is a most important factor in business. Despite opposition and competition, a certain thought current of sympathy binds the most successful together. The mania for cheapness lies in the thought current of fear and failure. The thought current of fear and failure, and the thought current of dash, courage and success will not mingle nor bring together the individuals who are in these respective streams of thought. They antagonize, and between the two classes of mind is built a barrier more impenetrable than walls of stone.

### January 8th

Uriel Buchanan

Hold ever in mind an image of the ideal you are seeking to make manifest. That image will become a central living magnet which will begin to draw to you the experiences that must be encountered and the conditions that must be overcome before the ideal can be attained. Concentrate all the forces of your being on the undoubted duty of the moment; then the numberless wants will be forgotten, and the troubles and uncertainties of life will pass away. The pathway of today is illumined by the experience you have gained from the yesterdays; and the light that dispels the mystery surrounding the present gives greater knowledge, which will shine with increased brightness tomorrow. The things that are true, the things that are good, and all that is helpful, will gravitate to you only in proportion to the degree that you desire and invite them. Though the unwelcome duties of the hour may cause unrest, and the barren outlook of the future discourage, have faith in your power to triumph over all things which would wrest from your grasp the glorious heritage. Have faith in the harmony, the love and the goodness of the immutable laws which govern life and destiny and change.

### January 9th

Venice J. Bloodworth

The best and quickest way to bring about reform in our thinking is by the use of a strong affirmation, to be repeated in the Silence and any time the need arises. The following: "I AM healthy, strong, young, powerful, loving, harmonious, successful, and happy" is constructive and may be used with good results. Your present character is made up of countless thoughts, beliefs, habits, entertained and formed by you in the past. This character is expressed on your subconscious mind and is the cause of your present health, your present state of mind, and your present financial status. If you wish to change all or any one of them the affirmation just given will be effective. This is true because any statement continuously made by the conscious mind is accepted by the subconscious mind as a pattern by which to weave your future. Your present conditions are the results of your past thinking. You will be what you are thinking today.

### January 10th

### W. J. Colville

"In the beginning was the word." Words are necessarily forms for the expression of ideas. There is vastly more meaning in them than the majority of people attach to words. A condition is made by the speaking of a word. The spoken words "I AM glad," attract gladness. We can attract to us whatsoever we demand. Whenever we wish a thing, we should voice it — just as a master calls a dog. Every person and every thing answers to his, her, or its name. Putting power on the basis of immutable law, we may call for what we wish. Whatever we call upon in the universe answers the call. The statement "Wherever two or three are gathered together in My name [in the name of any good] there am I [the object sought] in the midst of them," is in accordance with the Law of Attraction. If gathered together in the name of Truth, there is Truth. We are responsible for every word we speak; there is limitless power in the spoken word. Every word carries power and conviction with it. There is no chance, and there are no accidents.

### January 11th

### Shirley Bell Hastings

You have within you a mighty kingdom (area, state) of mind. You have it within you and by moving into this kingdom, into mind, you find it filled with tremendous force which seems to work with your idea and bring it into manifestation. To put it in another way, there is a great divine activity within you which runs according to your thinking, according to your ideas. You are a part of this activity, this force. You are one with it, unified with it. This activity or force is the creator of all things, the father of all things, the source of all things, the very life of all things. It acts according to the principle involved in the thinking. If we set ourselves to judge others we get a boomerang — we are judged. So we must judge with love and wisdom. We must be just in our judgments, see all things in their right relations. We find that love — love in the highest sense — love or good will, is the ideal emotion in which to indulge, good will for our neighbor, good will for our friend, good will for our foe. Good will is a principle. Endeavor to feel good will, forgiveness, justice and faith. Use your equipment of mind with its force. Do your best today in outer activities. Make the effort to work over the ideas you desire to be creative. You will surely get results.

## January 12th

### Charles Fillmore

"Thou shalt decree a thing, and it shall be established unto thee." We are always decreeing, sometimes consciously, often unconsciously, and with every thought and word we are increasing or diminishing the threefold activity of substance. The resulting manifestation conforms to our thought, "As he thinketh within himself, so is he." There is no scarcity of the air you breathe. There is plenty of air, all you will ever need, but if you close your lungs and refuse to breathe, you will not get it and may suffocate for lack of air. When you recognize the presence of abundance of air and open your lungs to breathe it deeply, you get a larger inspiration. This is exactly what you should do with your mind in regard to substance. There is an all-sufficiency of all things, just as there is an all-sufficiency of air. The only lack is our own lack of appropriation. We must seek the kingdom of God and appropriate it aright before things will be added to us in fullness. There is a kingdom of abundance of all things, and it may be found by those who seek it and are willing to comply with its laws. Jesus said that it is hard for a rich man to enter into the kingdom of heaven. This does not mean that it is hard because of his wealth, for the poor man gets in no faster and no easier. It is not money but the thoughts men hold about money, its source, its ownership, and its use, that keep them out of the kingdom. Men's thoughts about money are like their thoughts about all possessions; they believe that things coming out of the earth are theirs to claim and control as individual property, and may be hoarded away and depended on, regardless of how much other men may be in need of them. The same belief is prevalent among both rich and poor, and even if the two classes were suddenly to change places, the inequalities of wealth would not be remedied. Only a fundamental change in the thoughts of wealth could do that.

## January 13th

### Bruce Maclelland

Improve the character of your thoughts and you will naturally gravitate towards a better class of friends. Their association will put you in touch with opportunities that never would have been yours under the old conditions. But you say, "How am I to change the character of my thoughts?" Just keep the thought of courage, peace, strength, power, justice, good will, decision, force, confidence, determination, etc., before you; live in it, dwell on it, demand it, pray for it, and these qualities will come to you, slowly at first, but every atom gained gives you increased strength to draw more until at last the added strength attracts a cleaner, stronger class of thoughts and they bring you in touch with successful men. So with money and continued prosperity. The attractive force of your mentality will bring you the opportunity. You need not seek it. It will seek you, and your mind will be in condition to recognize the value, will have the decision to force you to act and the courage to carry you through. Using your thought powers to seek an avenue to lead you to wealth is an error, and a useless expenditure of energy. No great success was ever planned but came naturally from following an idea, working on it quietly, steadily and courageously, and usually with little fear of future success or failure. Choose the occupation you like. If it were something that you consider beyond you, and it probably will be, develop yours into a successful mind by the methods to be given you, when it will be commonplace and natural. One of the first requisites is a condition of calmness or peace. Many people are today in a chaotic condition; they cannot hold their thoughts to one subject for ten seconds, cannot prevent their darting around with lightning-like rapidity. If a successful thought comes they cannot grasp it firmly enough or hold it long enough to act on it. This condition of mind weakens both mental power and physical strength, renders sleep fitful and subject to fantastic imagining, and prevents the inflow of strength and destroys all prospect of health and success. You are what you think; not what you think you are.

### January 14th

John Seaman Garns

There is a Law of Mind which we ought to consider together before we touch the creative technique which I have promised to unfold to you. It has been called by some the "first law of mind," — meaning that it is of primary importance in all creative work, whether in the making of money, the building of a cathedral or the writing of a poem. This Law seems to recognize that there is a very definite mental attitude which "holds over" all our activities, making them succeed or fail. Mr. A. K. Mozumdar has stated this Law as follows, "Mind operates under its own conception of itself." If this statement is really true, we can see the reason why we do so often limit ourselves. Whenever I believe that I cannot, my whole mind is operating under this concept of its own impotence. When I believe that I can, and accept the fact deeply enough to involve all levels of my mind, both conscious and subconscious, I seem to release super-powers and often actually accomplish the impossible.

### January 15th

Orison Swett Marden

Multitudes of people are attracting the wrong things because they do not know the law. They have never learned that the great secret of health, happiness, and success lies in holding the mental attitude which builds, which constructs, the mental attitude which draws to us the good things we desire. They have never learned the difference between building and tearing down thoughts; the difference between success and failure thoughts; in fact, they do not know that whatever comes to us in life, in our undertakings, great or small, is largely a question of the kind of thoughts we hold in the mind. We can attract the thing we desire as easily as we can attract the thing we hate and despise and long to get rid of. It is simply a matter of holding the image of the thing in the mind. That is the model which the life processes will build into our environment and which we will objectify. Like attracts like, failure more failure, poverty more poverty. Hatred attracts more hatred, envy more envy, jealousy more jealousy, and malice more malice. Everything has power to attract its kind. The feeling of jealousy or hatred is a seed sown in the great cosmic soil all about us, and the eternal laws return to us a harvest the same in kind. What we sow we reap, just as the soil will return to us exactly what we put into it. Nothing has the power to reproduce anything but itself. There is no exception to this law.

### January 16th

Walter C. Lanyon

Do you see, beloved, the gift — the complete — wholeness? For this Is (right here and now) Life Eternal, that they might know me. To know the ME — the I AM — and to identify yourself with this, is to experience the Life Eternal which needs nothing. Can you conceive of Spirit being burned, drowned, killed, aided or assisted in any way by matter? To know yourself as the Son is to experience the freedom of the Son of God — to experience the power of decreeing a thing and seeing it come to pass. The recognition —recognition — cognizing again that which has always been true — the Divine remembrance of your rightful heritage, is what will restore to you the lost substance of life, is what will bring to you the robe, the ring, and the fatted calf. To him that hath shall be given, and to him that hath not shall be taken away. You have into manifestation exactly what you have in consciousness — good, bad, or indifferent. Why waste any further time trying to change the outside condition, when it is held in manifestation by the inner state of consciousness? To him that hath shall be given because he will take, be this good, bad, or indifferent manifestation. A man with a consciousness full of troubles always gets more troubles, and he finds them everywhere. It is what he finds to be true, and so he must find it into manifestation. No wonder the prophet asked, "What have you in your house?" What have you in your house, your consciousness? You have just what you conceive the Father within to be, and you cannot increase this until you begin to recognize the nature of the pure substance of Spirit from which all things come into manifestation. Until you recognize the True Self, and stop trying to doctor up an old body or condition, you cannot know the glory of the Son of God.

## January 17th

Christian Larson

When things are not to your liking, be glad nevertheless, for the glad heart can cause all things to be as we wish them to be. When things do not give you pleasure, proceed instead to create pleasure in your own heart and soul. And you can if you will always be glad. Besides, things will soon change for the better if you continue in the spirit of rejoicing. It is the law that all good things will sooner or later come and be, where the greatest happiness is to be found. Therefore, be happiness in yourself, regardless of times, seasons or circumstances. When things do not please you, resolve to please yourself by being glad, and you can add immeasurably to your happiness in this simple manner. Then you must remember that the fountain of joy within your own soul is infinitely greater than all external sources of joy combined. But as far as we can, we should add the joys from without to the joys from within, and in all things be glad. Rejoice in your strength, rejoice in your talents and powers, rejoice in the wonders of your own nature. For there is far more in you than you ever dreamed. So whatever may come, you are greater than it all, richer than it all. And knowing this, why should you not be glad. When evil befalls you, consider the fact that the good that is yet in your possession is many times as great as all the evil you could ever know. Consider this stupendous fact and be glad. Then remember, with rejoicing, that neither evil nor wrong can exist very long in the radiant sunshine of a glad triumphant soul. If you have lost anything, have no regrets. Be glad and begin again. Be glad that you can begin again. Be glad to know that the future is always richer and better than the past if we only try to make it so. Then forget the loss, and rejoice in the fact that you have the power to secure something far better in return. You know that you have this power; then you can never be otherwise than glad.

## January 18th

### Henry Thomas Hamblin

I want you to affirm the following: "The old life is dead and buried. I have severed myself from it once and for all. Henceforth I live the new life of success and power, of self mastery and all accomplishment." First of all memorize these words. Keep repeating them over until they sink deeply into your memory, and their meaning finds a place in your consciousness. If you can get a few moments to yourself during the day, practice making the affirmations. The right way is as follows: Go into a quiet place, whether you sit, stand, or lie down is immaterial. Now close your eyes and say the words over very earnestly. Strive to realize all that they mean and address the words to your inner mind. It is your submerged mind that you are influencing, so address the affirmation very earnestly to it. Do this for several minutes, and finish by making the affirmation into space. Hurl it out as a message to the Universe and by so doing you will come into harmony with innumerable invisible forces, who will help and strengthen you. Do not make the affirmation while in a state of strain and nervous tension. Relax yourself, take a deep breath, and as you exhale let your muscles go limp; smooth out your nerves until your whole body is in a peaceful easy state. Concentrate your thoughts on what you are doing. If they wander bring them back and begin again. The more you concentrate the better will be the result. The most important, in fact the time above all times for making the affirmation is just as you are falling to sleep. There is a great psychological reason for this. If you can fall asleep while making the affirmation, or while visualizing it, so much the better. Therefore take no food or stimulants (it is better to avoid the latter altogether) just before retiring. The reason cannot be given here because it would take too long, but it is an important one.

## January 19th

### Genevieve Behrend

Once you really believe that your mind is a center through which the unformed substance of all there is in your world, takes involuntary form, the only reason your picture does not always materialize is because you have introduced something antagonistic to the fundamental principle. Very often this destructive element is caused by the frequency with which you change your pictures. After many such changes, you decide that your original desire is what you want after all. Upon this conclusion, you begin to wonder why it (being your first picture) has not materialized. The Substance with which you are mentally dealing is more sensitive than the most sensitive photographer's film. If, while taking a picture, you suddenly remembered you had already taken a picture on that same plate, you would not expect a perfect result of either picture. On the other hand, you may have taken two pictures on the same plate unconsciously. When the plate has been developed, and the picture comes into physical view, you do not condemn the principle of photography, nor are you puzzled to understand why your picture has turned out so unsatisfactorily. You do not feel that it is impossible for you to obtain a good, clear picture of the subject in question. You know that you can do so, by simply starting at the beginning, putting in a new plate, and determining to be more careful while taking your picture next time. If these lines are followed out, you are sure of a satisfactory result. If you will proceed in the same manner with your mental picture, doing your part in a correspondingly confident frame of mind, the result will be just as perfect. The laws of visualizing are as infallible as the laws governing photography. In fact, photography is the outcome of visualizing.

## January 20th

### William Walker Atkinson

There are more people on the negative plane of thought than on the positive plane, and consequently there are more negative thought vibrations in operation in our mental atmosphere. But, happily for us, this is counterbalanced by the fact that a positive thought is infinitely more powerful than a negative one, and if by force of will we raise ourselves to a higher mental key we can shut out the depressing thoughts and may take up the vibrations corresponding with our changed mental attitude. This is one of the secrets of the affirmations and autosuggestions used by the several schools of Mental Science and other New Thought cults. There is no particular merit in affirmations of themselves, but they serve a twofold purpose: (1) They tend to establish new mental attitudes within us and act wonderfully in the direction of character-building — the science of making ourselves over. (2) They tend to raise the mental keynote so that we may get the benefit of the positive thought waves of others on the same plane of thought. Whether or not we believe in them, we are constantly making affirmations. The man who asserts that he can and will do a thing — and asserts it earnestly — develops in himself the qualities conducive to the well doing of that thing, and at the same time places his mind in the proper key to receive all the thought waves likely to help him in the doing. If, on the other hand, one says and feels that he is going to fail, he will choke and smother the thoughts coming from his own subconscious mentality which are intended to help him, and at the same time will place himself in tune with the Failure-thought of the world — and there is plenty of the latter kind of thought around, I can tell you.

## January 21st

Charles Wesley Kyle

The axiom, "As a man thinketh in his heart so is he," is the most startling truth ever uttered of man. What an amazing statement! Power! Self-mastery! A being of Life, Love, and Intelligence, possessed of the power to create and rule himself and his environment by the choice and mastership of thought! A realization of the meaning of the above aphorism awakens a power in man that transforms him into a new being. The wonderful fascination of this saying lies in the all-embracing statement which it so directly makes. It covers every possible act of man and clearly states that he is capable of exercising unlimited powers. Look which way we will we cannot escape from the finality of this decree. The beauty of this saying is that it is true, just as it is written. Man is a world within himself, and he is master of himself, it matters not how well or ill he may exercise his powers of mastership. He is the unquestioned thinker of his own thoughts, which are the tools of his workmanship. He is the master workman of his own designs, and he builds constructively or destructively as he wills. He makes himself sick or well, rich or poor, strong or feeble, sorrowful or joyous by the character of the thoughts he thinks. "Thought in the mind hath made us. What we are by thought was wrought and built. If a man's mind hath evil thoughts, pain comes to him as comes the wheel the ox behind. If one endure in purity of thought, joy follows him as his own shadow — sure."

## January 22nd

R. C. Douglass

"Give us truth for authority, not authority for truth," said Leucretia Mott. Nothing short of truth will satisfy the hunger of our souls. Nothing else will remove the "burdens" which these counterfeit words have bound upon us, and under which we groan. " Every man's word is his only burden." This is a statement of fact under the law of sowing and reaping, " What a man soweth, that shall he also reap." Every thought is a seed sown in the soil of the subconscious mind which is sure, in due time, to bring forth its harvest for our reaping. If we have sown the seeds of error, we must reap its bitter fruit. This is the universal law of cause and effect operating everywhere, on every plane throughout the universe. Thus my thoughts are my own burden. I AM always receiving my own. My good thoughts which I have sent forth return to bless me, and my evil thoughts return to curse me. Not only do "curses like chickens come home to roost," but all my thoughts return to me their legitimate fruitage. I AM always receiving what belongs to me. If I sow the seeds of covetousness, coveting my neighbor's beautiful things, I need not think it a strange fatality if a veritable thief breaks into my house and steals my purse. Covetousness was the thief-thought I sent out, and it brought me the thief. I AM only receiving what belongs to me. I AM always environed by myself. All the burdens I bear are therefore of my own making. I AM the sower, and I AM the reaper.

### January 23rd

Jeanie P. Owens

If you want to know just how to prove the power of your own thought, here is a very practical experiment which you may try. Is there any one person whom you specially dislike? It may be merely some person whom you look upon as shallow and contemptible, or it may perhaps be someone who has deliberately tried to injure you; it does not matter at all whether you feel yourself justified in your dislike or not. For five minutes each day (no one is so busy as not to have that much leisure) sit down quietly and send out thoughts of good-will to this person. Close your eyes, call up a mental picture of him or her, and, no matter what you may feel, say over and over, " I am not your enemy; I want to like you better than I do; I want to help you in whatever way I can." Repeat this again and again very slowly, until the time is up, keeping your mind fixed on what you are saying. If you have enough perseverance to keep it up five minutes every day for a month, you will find at the end of that time that your feelings toward that person are considerably altered.

## January 24th

### Charles Fillmore

It is found by the use of these mind forces that man can dissolve things by denying their existence, and build them up by affirming their presence. This is a simple statement, but when it is applied in all the intricate thought-forms of the universe, it becomes complex. Yet when one knows it to be the key to mental power, and persistently uses it, its truth becomes axiomatic. This power of the mind to build or destroy, through affirmation and denial, is exemplified most strikingly in the human body. Whatever we persistently affirm as true of us, in due season manifests itself somewhere in the organism. Whatever we persistently deny, is taken away, when the law has had time to work itself out. The body is made up of cells; some in a radiant state, and some crystallized into form. The visibility of these radiant thought-forms is the result of an affirmation of the ponderability of substance, or, we might say, that it is the belief in man's mind that his body is material instead of spiritual. The affirmative state of mind is a binding, holding process, and it involves all thoughts, and their manifestations, that come within its scope. If man affirms his unity with the life, substance and intelligence of God, he lays hold of these spiritual qualities, but if he affirms the reality of matter and the physical body, he attaches his Ego to the gross instead of the spiritual.

## January 25th

### Henry Harrison Brown

Our thoughts and prayers must be sent forth with confidence in the Spirit doing the work. If you send me down town, you do not pull me back to see if I am going. If you send a letter to the post office, you do not pull it back; but you do often start the thought and then pull it back. You should send your thought out and know that you have accomplished all you can; it completes the circle itself. I have a friend who does her work in this way. She sends forth the thought, and then forgets about it and it works for her. She wanted some apples, and soon a neighbor sent to ask if she did not want some of the nice apples they had, as they had more than they could use. She wanted some milk for her cooking, and before she got ready to use it some milk was sent in to her. Let the thought go, and it will return loaded with what you desire. Do not run after it, do the duty at hand and the work is done for you. Shall you wish for things? As you please. You can, but it may not be wise. I never call for things. "Seek ye first the kingdom of God, and all these things shall be added unto you." Deal with principle and it will take care of detail. I AM health, and I do not ask how to cure my pocket, etc. God is Supply. "The Lord is my shepherd I shall not want." Let that thought go out as a ray from the sunlight, and it will bring that which you need. My word is sent out, and it cannot return to me void, for the I AM within me is bringing my own to me, and nothing else can come. I do not worry, I do not doubt, I trust the Infinite. The universal supply brings me all that I need, and I AM content. Let us send out the true word, the strong word, the healing word, the word of peace, and know that they will accomplish the mission to which we send them, and then return with blessings of added power. "My word shall not return to me void, but shall accomplish that whereunto I send it."

### January 26th

Eugene Del Mar

It is the purpose of Life that the conscious should dominate and direct the steady progress of growth, development, and unfoldment; and that it should cooperate with the subconscious, so that what has been attained and achieved shall be made habitual, automatic, and readily responsive only to continually higher inspirations of conscious thought. If not directed or controlled, the subconscious tendencies will prevail, and one will be bound fast by tradition, convention, and conservatism — habit-bound, thought-bound, sectarian, and superstitious. Yes; and be proud of his servitude! Instead of living Life, he will have permitted Life to live him, frozen and crystallized at a low average of human attainment! Control of the subconscious involves thinking for oneself, which seems to most people to be the most unusual and tiresome thing there is. Why go to this trouble and exertion, when the priests, doctors, lawyers, politicians, and all the many other pillars of society are willing to do it for us, at the usual rate? It is much easier to leave one's thinking to others. It has been left to them, speaking generally, and a sorry mess they have made of it. What has been the result? The result has been a world bound by tradition and convention, by habits and customs, all inherited readymade, and cut on such a pattern that no amount of mere patching will make it fit the thought-form of humanity of the present day. The result has been that the individual has become the slave of his environment, when he might command and control it. He has become thought-blind, quoting the dead wisdom of others, when he might be alive with the wisdom of his own.

## January 27th

James Allen

Good thoughts and actions can never produce bad results. Bad thoughts and actions can never produce good results. This is but saying that nothing can come from corn but corn, nothing from nettles but nettles. Men understand this law in the natural world, and work with it. But few understand it in the mental and moral world (though its operation there is just as simple and undeviating), and they, therefore, do not cooperate with it. Suffering is always the effect of wrong thought in some direction. It is an indication that the individual is out of harmony with himself, with the Law of his being. The sole and supreme use of suffering is to purify, to burn out all that is useless and impure. Suffering ceases for him who is pure. There could be not object in burning gold after the dross had been removed, and perfectly pure and enlightened being could not suffer.

## January 28th

Ernest Holmes

When we behold a beautiful sunset we should see the wonderful thought of God, the radiance of his presence. In the strength of the hills we should see the strength of the Spirit; and seeing all things as spiritual ideas, we should learn to love them, because God has made them and given them to us to use. The soul who in ecstasy can rush up to a tree and embrace it realizes more of God than all the bigoted priests who have ever lived. The one who can sniff the ocean breeze with delight feels the presence of the divine being more keenly than does the one who kneels in despair before an awful God of Justice. Learn then how to appreciate Nature and Nature's God. Spend much time in the out of doors; look up at the stars; let them be your companions; tread the pathless ways of the trees and the giant forests and see God in everything that you look upon, the God of the everywhere.

## January 29th

Joseph Murphy

Feed the "poor" within you; clothe the naked ideas, and give them form by believing in the reality of the idea, trusting the great Fabricator within to clothe it in form and objectify it. Now your word (idea) shall become flesh (take form). When you are hungry (poor states), you seek food. When worried, you seek peace. When you are sick, you seek health; when you are weak, you seek strength. Your desire for prosperity is the voice of God in you telling you that abundance is yours; therefore, through your poor state, you find the urge to grow, to expand, to unfold, to achieve, and to accomplish your desires. A pain in your shoulder is a blessing in disguise; it tells you to do something about it at once. If there were no pain and no indication of trouble, your arm might fall off on the street. Your pain is God's alarm system telling you to seek His Peace and His Healing Power, and move from darkness to Light. When cold, you build a fire. When you are hungry, you eat. When you are in lack, enter into the mood of opulence and plenty. Imagine the end; rejoice in it. Having imagined the end, and felt it as true, you have willed the means to the realization of the end.

### January 30th

Ernest Holmes

The man who can control his thought can have and do what he wishes to have and to do; everything is his for the asking. He must remember that whatever he gets is his to use but not his to hold. Creation is always flowing by and we have as much of it as we can take and use; more would cause stagnation. We are relieved of all thought of clinging to anybody or anything. Cannot the Great Principle of Life create for us faster than we can spend or use? The universe is inexhaustible; it is limitless; it knows no bounds and has no confines. We are not depending on a reed shaken by the wind, but on the principle of life itself, for all that we want, have or ever shall have. It is not some power, or a great power, we affirm again; it is ALL POWER. All that we have to do is to believe this and act as though it were so, never wavering, not even once, no matter what happens. As we do this we shall find that things are steadily coming our way, and that they are coming without that awful effort that destroys the peace of the majority of the race. We know that there can be no failure in the Divine Mind, and this Mind is the Power on which we are depending.

### January 31st

Wallace Wattles

You do not need to pray repeatedly for things you want. It is not necessary to tell God about it every day. Your part is to intelligently formulate your desire for the things which make for a larger life and to get these desire arranged into a coherent whole, and then to impress this whole desire upon the formless substance, which has the power and the will to bring you what you want. You do not make this impression by repeating strings of words; you make it by holding the vision with unshakable PURPOSE to attain it and with steadfast FAITH that you do attain it. The answer to prayer is not according to your faith while you are talking, but according to your faith while you are working. You cannot impress the mind of God by having a special Sabbath day set apart to tell him what you want, and then forgetting him during the rest of the week. You cannot impress him by having special hours to go into your closet and pray, if you then dismiss the matter from your mind until the hour of prayer comes again. Oral prayer is well enough, and has its effect, especially upon yourself, in clarifying your vision and strengthening your faith, but it is not your oral petitions which get you what you want. In order to get rich you do not need a "sweet hour of prayer;" you need to "pray without ceasing." And by prayer I mean holding steadily to your vision, with the purpose to cause its creation into solid form, and the faith that you are doing so. "Believe that ye receive them."

# February

## February 1st

Robert Collier

Whatever thought, whatever problem you can get across to your subconscious mind at the moment of dropping off to sleep, that "Man Inside You," that Genie-of-your-Mind will work out for you. Of course, not everyone can succeed in getting the right thought across to the subconscious at the first or the second attempt. It requires understanding and faith, just as the working out of problems in mathematics requires an understanding of and faith in the principles of mathematics. But keep on trying, and you WILL do it. And when you do, the results are sure. If it is something that you want, VISUALIZE it first in your mind's eye, see it in every possible detail, see yourself going through every move it will be necessary for you to go through when your wish comes into being. Build up a complete story, step by step, just as though you were acting it all out. Get from it every ounce of pleasure and satisfaction that you can. Be thankful for this gift that has come to you. Then relax; go on to sleep if you can; give the "Man Inside You" a chance to work out the consummation of your wish without interference. When you waken, hold it all pleasurably in thought again for a few moments. Don't let doubts and fears creep in, but go ahead, confidently, knowing that your wish is working itself out. Know this, believe it — and if there is nothing harmful in it, IT WILL WORK OUT!

## February 2nd

Helen Wilmans

If a man believes himself sick, I treat him for his belief. His belief is his real condition. He is sick. Being all mind he is, therefore, a series of beliefs, and "as he thinketh so is he." The man is sick and his sickness is unmistakable evidence of his negative condition, and this must be overcome, else growth would stagnate in him, and he might as well have never been born. How would a man know he was negative unless he had some unpleasant evidence of it? If there were never a ripple to break our negative condition and suggest an improvement, our condition would not rise above that of the brute. Indeed, it would never have risen so high. Then what is the duty of a teacher? It is to infuse the student with positive thought. All positive thought is based on the belief in absolute Life. The more strongly the teacher is ingrained in the knowledge of absolute Life, the more powerful he is as a teacher. The duty of the teacher, then, is to present all the logic he possibly can in favor of the fact that all is Life. This logic must make its indelible impression on the student's intelligence. The student must be convinced that this logic is correct. This is the teacher's duty. No teacher can do any more than to impress the fact upon the student's intellectual perceptions. And here, where the teacher's work stops, the student's work begins; for this truth needs more than a mere intellectual perception of it. It needs to enter into every part of the student's organization and to remodel him after its own pattern.

**February 3rd**

Prentice Mulford

If a medicine was found which would put in a man or woman, boy or girl, force or force of character, — power and capacity to do business, power to influence and govern, — such a medicine would have a very ready sale. Yet keeping yourself in a certain condition of mind will add continually to your force or force of character; and whatever you so add through keeping in this condition can never be lost. That condition is the keeping of the mind in the constant desire for force. Desire for a thing or a quality of mind is a power always drawing that thing or quality to you, whether that thing or quality be for good or evil. Force is an unseen substance as real as anything you see. The more of force you call to you, the more and more power do you gather to attract force to you, because like attracts like in all elements, seen or unseen. Globules of quicksilver mingle and form one mass; trees of the same species grow together; sheep herd with sheep and not with cows; tramps consort with tramps, because dejected, weak, despondent human spirit naturally runs to other dejected, despondent, unaspiring human spirit; just as men of force, push, and determination naturally drift, associate, plan, and work with other men of force, push, and determination. What is force? If you have a purpose, a project, a business, and in presenting it or pushing it on people who may at first be indifferent or hostile to it, and in so pushing and presenting it you can always keep up your spirits, your energy, your confidence, and your enthusiasm in that business, you have force. If, after a few attempts, you become discouraged, disheartened, and despondent you lack force. The peddler who goes from door to door and persists in offering his wares despite all rebuffs and snubs and doors slammed in his face, and keeps up all the while a cheerful mood, has force. That peddler is winning his way up to a larger business. It was Cyrus W. Field's force that made at last the Atlantic cable a success, despite failure after failure, and breakage after breakage, and the invectives and growls of enraged and despairing shareholders. That quality in Mr. Field is a spiritual power; and the force in any man or woman that plans a business and persists in it and pushes it into success is a spiritual power; and the very core, root, origin and cornerstone of that power lies in the quiet, persistent resolve to have force, and the constant imaging or imagining of yourself as an ever-increasing force or power.

## February 4th

### Mrs. Evelyn Lowes Wicker

Thought Currents. Every thought in the universe seeks its own kind. There is a law of attraction which permeates the thought world. "Like attracts like.' Every thought that we think, when sent out into the ether is immediately, through the force of its own law, drawn to its own kind. When we think a thought of anger it immediately joins the other thoughts of anger that have been sent out in the world and becomes a part of that thought-current. When we think a thought of impatience the same thing happens, only in a lighter degree. When you think of faith immediately that thought joins the higher plane of thought and you become connected with the thought of faith. Every thought has its own thought-current. Every mental picture that you have has a corresponding mental current in the ether. By constantly concentrating upon one type of thought, you become connected with that thought-plane of the universe, and you become a channel for those thoughts to play through. Let us suppose that thought current be hate. You have been hating someone or some thing. You are constantly thinking upon this destructive thought. You make it a part of yourself; you work your emotions up to a high pitch over the affront, or whatever it is that has brought this thought of hate to you. The more you concentrate upon it the more you become connected with the hate thought of the universe, until you become a channel for that thought-current. Not only do you suffer for your own hate thought, but you suffer from the hate thought of the whole world. When you have carried this far enough it becomes an obsession, and when hate becomes an obsession there is murder in the heart. The murders of the world have oftentimes been committed because the murderer connected up with the murder-thought of the world, and he became obsessed with the thought of murder and nothing but the doing of the deed could satisfy the obsession.

## February 5th

Uriel Buchanan

Your attitude of mind will determine your success or failure in whatever you undertake. Your mind is a magnet which will attract to you the elements you earnestly desire. If you set up thoughts of determination, strength, cheerfulness, hope and kindred attributes of success, you will establish invisible magnetic connection with those who are richly endowed and inspired by similar aims and will draw these elements to you. When you take a firm stand for justice, order and precision, when you resolve to remain steadfast, to push forward and be true to your highest leadings, you will draw to you a host of invisible thought elements which will rapidly increase your ability to control the events of your life. If your acts are inspired by your highest idea of right, if you are confident, earnest and determined you will use the finest and most subtle thought element at your command, which will go out with an irresistible constructive force that will shape things to your desire. If you fix your mind persistently upon some plan, and will allow nothing to distract you or cause you to swerve from your purpose, you can use your power to accomplish wonderful results. To hold steadfastly to the silent concentration of mind, to think of some high purpose and aim, and to persistently resolve, will bring new suggestions and easier methods for pushing your plans to completion. To have a special purpose in life and to work earnestly for its accomplishment will fill your mind with cheerful thoughts and keep you in touch with all the progressive currents of nature.

## February 6th

### Venice J. Bloodworth

You cannot teach the Creator. The power that thought the universe into expression does not need to be advised by you. "Ask and you shall receive." You must, however, supply the idea or mental picture, and you must make the image clear, and hold it, concentrate on it until it becomes the only real thing to you. Want it with all your mind and heart and strength. Expect what you want and nothing else. Give no thought to external conditions, build your IDEAL in the world within and the Law of Attraction will certainly and surely bring it to you. The law is that "like attracts like." Whatever you hold in mind for any length of time MUST come into expression for you. No matter what it is you desire — health, business, a new job, automobile, home or anything else — just make a clear mental picture of it and hold it in mind as your own; the way will be opened for you and you will have the joy of knowing you can be what you will to be, and no restriction can be placed on you, for your subconscious mind has no pattern with which to mold your future except that furnished by your conscious mind.

## February 7th

### Charles Fillmore

This law of prosperity has been proved time and time again. All men who have prospered have used the law, for there is no other way. Perhaps they were not conscious of following definite spiritual methods, yet they have in some way set the law in operation and reaped the benefit of its unfailing action. Others have had to struggle to accomplish the same things. Remember that Elijah had to keep praying and affirming for a long time before he demonstrated the rain. He sent his servant out the first time, and there was no sign of a cloud. He prayed and sent him out again and again with the same result, but at last, after repeated efforts, the servant said he saw a little cloud. Then Elijah told them to prepare for rain, and the rain came. This shows a continuity of effort that is sometimes necessary. If your prosperity does not become manifest as soon as you pray and affirm God as your substance, your supply, and your support, refuse to give up. Show your faith by keeping up the work. You have plenty of Scripture to back you up. Jesus taught it from the beginning to the end of His ministry and demonstrated it on many occasions.

## February 8th

George Schubel

It is quite natural to understand that it would be of little value for the photographer to see and comprehend his object if he had not some sort of mechanical equipment with which to project, focus and reproduce what he sees. So, too, it would be of little avail for us to be able to formulate our mental objects, and to comprehend them if we did not have some sort of mental-mechanism by means of which we could reproduce outwardly the thought images held within the mind. For photographic purposes the photographer has a well-equipped studio provided with settings, camera and all other essentials and materials. A similar inner equipment of the mind is found in what we call our objective state of consciousness serving us as an elaborate mental photographic studio provided with all the mental-mechanical essentials and materials needed to image forth and reproduce our desires— our objects of thought.

## February 9th

Charles F. Haanel

All growth is from within. This is evident in all nature. Every plant, every animal, every human is a living testimony to this great law, and the error of the ages is in looking for strength or power from without. The world within is the Universal fountain of supply, and the world without is the outlet to the stream. Our ability to receive depends upon our recognition of this Universal Fountain, this Infinite Energy of which each individual is an outlet, and so is one with every other individual. Recognition is a mental process, mental action is therefore the interaction of the individual upon the Universal Mind, and as the Universal Mind is the intelligence which pervades all space and animates all living things, this mental action and reaction is the law of causation, but the principle of causation does not obtain in the individual but in the Universal Mind. It is not an objective faculty but a subjective process, and the results are seen in an infinite variety of conditions and experiences. In order to express life there must be mind; nothing can exist without mind. Everything which exists is some manifestation of this one basic substance from which and by which all things have been created and are continually being recreated. We live in a fathomless sea of plastic mind substance. This substance is ever alive and active. It is sensitive to the highest degree. It takes form according to the mental demand. Thought forms the mold or matrix from which the substance expresses. Remember that it is in the application alone that the value consists, and that a practical understanding of this law will substitute abundance for poverty, wisdom for ignorance, harmony for discord and freedom for tyranny, and certainly there can be no greater blessing than these from a material and social standpoint.

## February 10th

Orison Swett Marden

What we most frequently visualize, what we think most about, is constantly weaving itself into the fabric of our lives, becoming a part of ourselves, increasing the power of our mental magnet to attract those things to us. It doesn't matter whether they are things we fear and try to avoid or things that are good for us, that we long to get. Keeping them in mind increases our affinity for them and inevitably tends to bring them into our lives. It is a curious fact that many people seem to think that one must spend years as an apprentice to become an expert in any line of endeavor, in business or in a profession, but that in regard to prosperity it is largely a matter of chance, of fate, something which cannot be affected very much by anything they may be able to do. They say, "Well, I was not built that way. I am not a natural money-maker, and never can be." Or they excuse themselves on the ground that their parents and those before them were never money-makers, and never did anything more than make a bare living. There is nothing at all peculiar about prosperity any more than there is about legal efficiency or expertness in law or medicine. Its realization is purely a matter of concentration and of preparation; a matter of focusing all our powers upon the prosperity law in order to attract prosperity and to make ourselves expert in attaining it. The law of prosperity, of opulence, is just as definite as the law of gravitation, and it works just as unerringly. Its first principle is mental. Wealth is created mentally first; it is thought out before it becomes a reality.

**February 11th**

Ernest Holmes

Relieve yourselves of all responsibility of making anything. You could not make anything if you tried to. The united intelligence of the human race from time immemorial summed up into one moment could not create one petal of one rose, because it does not know enough to do it, and it is good that it does not. But it can have created for it as many roses as it sees fit through using the creative principle which is, and it need not take the responsibility of that creative power at all. So when we come to our responsibility, it rests solely in providing the right atmosphere and nothing else. I am giving you a system of thought, and if you want to make a demonstration you can work it out. I would not do it for you if I could. I would be depriving you of a divine right. From the metaphysical standpoint, I say get your arms away from clinging on other people. Dare to be yourself. Where did you think anybody ever got so much that you could not know? Then and there you are foreswearing yourself. I am just as intelligent as anybody who ever lived. You have got to have a kind of a decent idea of yourself in metaphysics. Did you ever see a person succeed in business who thought it would fail? You never did and you never will. People who succeed in life are the people who know that they will. And that free knowing is creation in the mind of the Universal. You must do this all for yourself and know this for yourself. It is working for me every day I live. There is One, and not two. Never forget that. Anywhere in the universe, just One. That one life is the substance of everything. It is one in unity but multiple in manifestation. It is one substance from which an infinite variety of different things come but every one of those things is made out of the one thing. Now, that one life and intelligence and creative power operates through me, that is the next thing. It would not be of any good to us if there was one infinite life unless that life was in some way connected up with me. Many people make a mistake in thinking it is enough to claim that God is all. We must realize there is one Power, one God, one All, one Life, and that life is in me now. I AM a manifestation of that One.

### February 12th

James Allen

And as with the conduct of others, so is it with external things – with surroundings and circumstances – in themselves they are neither good nor bad, it is the mental attitude and state of heart that makes them so. A man imagines he could do great things if he were not hampered by circumstances — by want of money, want of time, want of influence, and want of freedom from family ties. In reality the man is not hindered by these things at all. He, in his mind, ascribes to them a power which they do not possess, and he submits not to them, but to his opinion about them, that is, to a weak element in his nature. The real "want" that hampers him is the want of the right attitude of mind. When he regards his circumstances as spurs to his resources, when he sees that his so-called "drawbacks" are the very steps up which he is to mount successfully to his achievement, then his necessity gives birth to invention, and the "hindrances" are transformed into aids. The man is the all-important factor. If his mind be wholesome and rightly tuned, he will not whine and whimper over his circumstances, but will rise up, and outgrow them. He who complains of his circumstances has not yet become a man, and Necessity will continue to prick and lash him till he rises into manhood's strength, and then she will submit to him. Circumstance is a severe taskmaster to the weak, an obedient servant to the strong.

## February 13th

### Christian Larson

Every circumstance you meet contains something for you; because it is made to enrich your life, to serve you, and to promote your welfare in every way possible. By meeting a circumstance in the harmony of aspiration you call forth its real possibilities, and especially if you look directly for those possibilities. When you take an active interest and a friendly interest in the constructive powers of a circumstance, those powers will place themselves in your hands, and every disagreeable element will disappear. By taking the best out of every circumstance, and by transmuting all the forces you meet so that they become your forces, you add so much to your present life that you rise readily to a higher position, where superior circumstances and still greater possibilities will be met. Any circumstance can be changed, if constantly approached in this way; or you will change so much that far better circumstances will be ready to receive you. Directly connected with the attitude of harmony is the attitude of love; and the way we love, as well as what we love, is of the highest importance in the mastery of fate. The law is that we steadily grow into the likeness of that which we love; and the reason is that what we love is so deeply impressed upon mind that it never fails to reproduce itself in thought. Anything that enters mind while mind is in the state of deep feeling, is deeply impressed; and it is the deepest impressions that serve as patterns for the creative energies. Love only that which has high worth, and never permit the common, the ordinary or the inferior to enter the world of feeling.

### February 14th

Joseph Murphy

Look upon the story in John of changing water into wine in a figurative way, and say to yourself as the above mentioned chemical salesman did: "I can make the invisible ideas, urges, dreams, and desires of mine visible, because I have discovered a simple, universal law of mind." The law he demonstrated is the law of action and reaction. It means your external world, body, circumstances, environment, and financial status are always a perfect reflection of your inner thinking, beliefs, feelings, and convictions. This being true, you can now change your inner pattern of thought by dwelling on the idea of success, wealth, and peace of mind. As you busy your mind with these latter concepts, these ideas will gradually seep into your mentality like seeds planted in the ground. As all seeds (thoughts and ideas) grow after their kind, so will your habitual thinking and feeling manifest in prosperity, success, and peace of mind. Wise thought (action) is followed by right action (reaction). You can acquire riches when you become aware of the fact that prayer is a marriage feast. The feast is a psychological one; you meditate on (mentally eat of) your good or your desire until you become one with it.

### February 15th

Prentice Mulford

It sees in such persuasive power, as you may have with tongue or pen, the only force you possess for dealing with people to accomplish results. The spiritual mind will know in time that your thought influences people for or against your interests, though their bodies are thousands of miles distant. The material mind does not regard its thought as an actual element as real as air or water. The spiritual mind knows that every one of its thousand daily secret thoughts are real things acting on the minds of the persons they are sent to. The spiritual mind knows that matter or the material is only an expression of spirit or force; that such matter is ever changing in accordance with the spirit that makes or externalizes itself in the form we call matter, and therefore, if the thought of health, strength and recuperation is constantly held to in the mind, such thought of health, strength and rejuvenation will express itself in the body, making maturity never ceasing, vigor never ending, and the keenness of every physical sense ever increasing. The material mind thinks matter, or that which is known by our physical senses, to be the largest part of what exists. The spiritual mind regards matter as the coarser or cruder expression of spirit and the smallest part of what really exists. The material mind is made sad at the contemplation of decay. The spiritual mind attaches little importance to decay, knowing in such decay that spirit or the moving force in all things is simply taking the dead body or the rotten tree to pieces, and that it will build them up again as before temporarily into some other new physical form of life and beauty. The mind of the body thinks that its physical senses of seeing, hearing and feeling constitute all the senses you possess. The higher mind or mind of the spirit knows that it possesses other senses akin to those of physical sight and hearing, but more powerful and far reaching. The mind of the body has been variously termed "the material mind," the "mortal mind" and the "carnal mind." All these refer to the same mind, or, in other words to that part of your real sell which has been educated in error by the body.

## February 16th

### Robert Collier

The impressions that enter the subconscious form indelible pictures, which are never forgotten, and whose power can change the body, mind, manner, and morals; can, in fact, revolutionize a personality. — All during our waking hours the conscious mind, through the five senses, acts as constant feeder to the subconscious; the senses are the temporal source of supply for the content of the soul mind;

therefore it is most important that we know and realize definitely and explicitly that every time we think a thought or feel an emotion, we are adding to the content of this powerful mind, good or bad, as the case may be. Life will be richer or poorer for the thoughts and deeds of today. Your thoughts supply you with limitless energy which will take whatever form your mind demands. The thoughts are the mold which crystallizes this energy into good or ill according to the form you impress upon it. You are free to choose which. But whichever you choose, the result is sure. Thoughts of wealth, of power, of success, can bring only results commensurate with your idea of them. Thoughts of poverty and lack can bring only limitation and trouble.

## February 17th

### Uriel Buchanan

There are many who live idle and useless lives, because they believe they have nothing within them worthy of attention. The fact that we possess the mysterious gift of existence is sufficient cause for lofty endeavor. In every mind are possibilities which should be recognized and unfolded. It is the duty of each to make the best possible use of his talents. We should see beneath the falsehood and weakness, we should pierce through the mask, and discover the power, the talent and the yearnings which await our encouragement and help. There is a refuge, a strength, a fountain of happiness at the summit of the inner life, to which all who are noble may go for inspiration and guidance. From the deepest recess of this refuge arises a joy which banishes sorrow and floods the heart and mind with peace. When things go contrary to every desire, and you find no cause in present events for rejoicing, there is always a refuge deep down in the consciousness where against all the opposing forces shall beat in vain. There is not a beautiful thought, or a generous deed, but had its first impulse deep down in the inner life. Back of every noble deed are countless unexpressed impulses for good which have never been brought to the surface. But every lofty desire will ennoble the character and strengthen some purpose.

## February 18th

### Venice J. Bloodworth

It has been commonly supposed that the dreamer is a failure, but he who builds his future in his imagination with faith and purpose, never fails to realize his desire. Of course, merely wishing for anything or just to let your fancy run riot is wasted effort, because when you wish you do not believe you can obtain your wishes and you are really saying to your inner power, "I certainly would like to have so and so, but it is beyond my means." To use your mental powers in this way is to sow failure. Be positive, do not say, "I'd like to have," but, "It is MINE." Whenever you claim anything by faith never go behind that statement. Let every effort of yours be mentally listed as carrying you nearer your goal. When Jesus said, "As thy faith is, so be it unto you," He made a statement that is today considered a SCIENTIFIC FACT. There are times when even the bravest want to give up; times when appearances indicate that everything is against us, and it is no use to try. At such times you should remember that it is always darkest just before the dawn; that a little more faith, a little more patience is all that we need to win. Remember, too, that all those who have reached their goal ahead of you felt tired sometimes, and wanted to give up, but they DID NOT. If they had, you would never have heard of them.

## February 19th

### Ernest Holmes

How can we hope to make the world see the right way unless we overflow with joy? The world has now too many sad faces. We see them everywhere, that resigned look that seems to say, "One rebuff more or less makes no difference; I am already so sad that nothing matters; I can bear it." This was all right when we thought everything was all wrong, but now we know that "all's well with the world" we must get over this depression which robs us of the power of attraction of the good things of life, and "enter in." The man who is always glad will surround himself with people who are happy, and life will be a continual enjoyment, This robs no one; it does not make a race of irresponsible people; it makes a world of joy, a world that is good to live in.

## February 20th

Robert Collier

We all have inspired moments when we see clearly how we may do great things, how we may accomplish wonderful undertakings. But we do not believe in them enough to make them come true. An imagination which begins and ends in daydreaming is weakening to character. Make the daydreams come true. Make them so clear and distinct that they impress themselves upon your subconscious mind. There's nothing wrong with daydreaming, except that most of us stop there. We don't try to make the dreams come true. The great inventor, Tesla, "dreams" every new machine complete and perfect in every particular before ever he begins his model for it. Mozart "dreamed" each of his wonderful symphonies complete before ever he put a note on paper. But they didn't stop with the dreaming. They visualized those dreams, and then brought them into actuality. We lose our capacity to have visions if we do not take steps to realize them. Power implies service, so concentrate all your thought on making your visions of great deeds come true. Thinking is the current that runs the dynamo of power. To connect up this current so that you can draw upon universal supply through your subconscious mind, is to become a Super-man. Do this, and you will have found the key to the solution of every problem of life.

## February 21st

Orison Swett Marden

The great trouble with most people who fail to realize their ambition is that they face life the wrong way. They do not understand the tremendous potency of the influence of the habitual mental attitude in shaping the career and actually creating conditions. It is really pitiful to see people making slaves of themselves trying to get ahead, but all the time side-tracking the good things which would come their way if they did not head them off by their conviction that there is nothing much in the world for them anyway, nothing more than a bare living at the best. They are actually driving away the very things which might flow to them in abundance if they held the right mental attitude. In every walk of life we see men and women driving away the things they want. Most people think the things they do not want. They go through life trying to build happy, prosperous, healthful lives out of negative, destructive thinking, always neutralizing the results of their hard work. They indulge in worries, in fears and envies, in thoughts of hatred and revenge, and carry habitually a mental attitude, which means destruction to health, growth, and creative possibility. Their lives are pitched to a minor key. There is always a downward tendency in their thought and conversation. Nine-tenths of the people in the world who complain of being poor and failures are headed in the wrong direction, headed right away from the condition or thing they long for. What they need is to be turned about so that they will face their goal instead of turning their backs on it by their destructive thinking and going in the other direction. The Morgans, the Wanamakers, the Marshall Fields, the Schwabs, think prosperity, and they get it. They don't anticipate poverty; they don't anticipate failure; they know they are going to be prosperous and successful, because they have eliminated all doubt from, their minds.

**February 22nd**

James Allen

A man should conceive of a legitimate purpose in his heart, and set out to accomplish it. He should make this purpose the centralizing point of his thoughts. It may take the form of a spiritual ideal, or it may be a worldly object, according to his nature at the time being. But whichever it is, he should steadily focus his thought forces upon the object which he has set before him. He should make this purpose his supreme duty, and should devote himself to its attainment, not allowing his thoughts to wander away into ephemeral fancies, longings, and imaginings. This is the royal road to self-control and true concentration of thought. Even if he fails again and again to accomplish his purpose (as he necessarily must until weakness is overcome), the strength of character gained will be the measure of his true success, and this will form a new starting point for future power and triumph.

## February 23rd

### Christian Larson

Life becomes worth the living only when the living of life makes living more worthwhile for an ever increasing number. It is only the joys we share that give happiness; it is only the thoughts we express that enrich our own minds; it is only the strength we use in actual helpfulness that makes our own souls strong. Therefore, to add to the pleasures of others, is to add to our own pleasure; to add to the wealth and comfort of others is to add in like manner to our own. This the great soul knows; and every soul is great that has learned to be glad regardless of what may come or go in the world. To be glad at all times is to be of greater service to mankind than any other thing that we can do. If we have not the power or ability to apply ourselves more tangibly in behalf of others, we can instead be glad. We can always give sunshine. And we shall find that just being glad is frequently sufficient, even when needs seem great and circumstances extreme. In most instances it is all the world wants; but it does want human sunshine so much, that those who can give it at all times need not do anything else to reap immortal fame. Surround us with an abundance of human sunshine, and the day's work will easily be done; we shall, with far less effort, overcome our obstacles; our troubles will largely be removed, and our burdens entirely laid aside. Give us the privilege to work to the music of rejoicing and our work will become a pleasure; every duty will become a privilege, and all we do will be well done. This is the way the world thinks and feels. So therefore be glad. Give an abundance of human sunshine everywhere and always, and you will please the world immensely.

## February 24th

Joseph Murphy

Our subconscious convictions and beliefs dictate and control all of our conscious actions. The secret of guidance or right action is to mentally devote yourself to the right answer, until you find its response in you. The response is a feeling, an inner awareness, an overpowering hunch whereby you know that you know. You have used the power to the point where it begins to use you. You cannot possibly fail or make one false step while operating under the direction of the subjective wisdom within you. Think of a garden; then you will understand the two-fold aspect of mind, and the subjective law by which it operates. The conscious mind plants the seed in the soil. It decides what kind of seed shall be planted. As you know the soil will grow whatever is planted, whether it is grapes or thorns. Similarly, look upon the subconscious mind as the soil; it contains all of the elements necessary and essential for growth. Again let us realize it is the nature of the soil to bring forth, but as you know, it is not the slightest bit interested in what it brings forth. It does not care whether it brings forth a pear tree or an apple tree. All of the laws of nature would be violated should the soil refuse to produce or grow poisonous plants.

## February 25th

Henry Thomas Hamblin

When you enter into the realization of the mighty Power within you, you enter into possession of all good and perfect things. You cease to strive, and squabble, and snatch, with selfish anxious hand, the bread from another's mouth. You leave off striving, with palpitating heart and careworn face, to push your way in front of the one next to you. Instead, you set your ambitions high, and sustained and carried forward by invisible forces, enter into possession of all that you desire. Work? Yes, you will work, for right thinking — and this realization of the Power within you is the result of right thinking — is the inspiration of all right action. You will work hard enough — and no one is happy who does not work —

but the difference will be that your work will be the greatest joy in your joyful life. Joy! there is no joy like the joy of work well loved and well done, and which leads to accomplishment and victory. Work! yes, you will work, but not with the feverish haste or with the fear of failure and bankruptcy ever before you. Instead, you will work with confidence and power, sure in the knowledge, that your efforts lead definitely to Success. When you have realized the inward Power, you will feel it pushing you in the back and impelling you forward, you will feel yourself borne along to the goal of your endeavor. Whereas formerly you were chasing Success, and waiting on it cap in hand; in future you will realize that you are master; that you command and Success obeys. You realize that instead of as in the past, running after fame and fortune, which, like a will o' the wisp, constantly eluded you, you have now the power to attract all desirable things to you. Instead of feverish anxiety and joyless quest, you possess calm confidence and the power to accomplish everything that you desire.

### February 26th

Wallace Wattles

To permit your mind to dwell upon the inferior is to become inferior and to surround yourself with inferior things. On the other hand, to fix your attention on the best is to surround yourself with the best, and to become the best. The creative power within us makes us into the image of that to which we give our attention. We are of thinking substance, too, and thinking substance always takes the form of that which it thinks about. The grateful mind is constantly fixed upon the best. Therefore it tends to become the best. It takes the form or character of the best, and will receive the best. Also, faith is born of gratitude. The grateful mind continually expects good things, and expectation becomes faith. The reaction of gratitude upon one's own mind produces faith, and every outgoing wave of grateful thanksgiving increases faith. The person who has no feeling of gratitude cannot long retain a living faith, and without a living faith you cannot get rich by the creative method. It is necessary, then, to cultivate the habit of being grateful for every good thing that comes to you and to give thanks continuously. And because all things have contributed to your advancement, you should include all things in your gratitude. Do not waste a lot of time thinking or talking about the shortcomings or wrong actions of those in power. Their organization of the world has created your opportunity; all you get really comes to you because of them. Do not rage against corrupt politicians. If it were not for politicians we should fall into anarchy and your opportunity would be greatly lessened.

## February 27th

Charles Haanel

The laws under which we live are designed solely for our advantage. These laws are immutable and we cannot escape from their operation. All the great eternal forces act in solemn silence, but it is in our power to place ourselves in harmony with them and thus express a life of comparative peace and happiness. Difficulties, inharmonies, and obstacles, indicate that we are either refusing to give out what we no longer need, or refusing to accept what we require. Growth is attained through an exchange of the old for the new, of the good for the better; it is a conditional or reciprocal action, for each of us is a complete thought entity and this completeness makes it possible for us to receive only as we give. We cannot obtain what we lack if we tenaciously cling to what we have. We are able to consciously control our conditions as we come to sense the purpose of what we attract, and are able to extract from each experience only what we require for our further growth. Our ability to do this determines the degree of harmony or happiness we attain. The ability to appropriate what we require for our growth, continually increases as we reach higher planes and broader visions, and the greater our abilities to know what we require, the more certain we shall be to discern its presence, to attract it and to absorb it. Nothing may reach us except what is necessary for our growth. All conditions and experiences that come to us do so for our benefit. Difficulties and obstacles will continue to come until we absorb their wisdom and gather from them the essentials of further growth. That we reap what we sow is mathematically exact.

We gain permanent strength exactly to the extent of the effort required to overcome difficulties.

## February 28th

Eugene Del Mar

Here is a Kingdom of Light which man is ever seeking. While he is conscious of darkness, intuitively he feels that there must be a realm where darkness does not exist. He flees from the darkness and he pursues the light. The light is ahead of him and the darkness behind; and the light attracts him with its warmth while the darkness repels him with its chill. As one ascends a mountain he reaches a finer atmosphere and senses a clearer light, and as one's mind develops his thought-atmosphere becomes finer and a clearer vision opens before him. One's body is lightened and refined as his thoughts ascend in quality, and one's thoughts rise in purity and ideality as he reaches the grander heights of spiritual unfoldment. Man is on his journey from the outer realm of Unconscious Light to the inner kingdom of Conscious Light. The entrance to the latter is through a labyrinth, the keys of which are physical health, mental harmony, and spiritual realization. In each of the courts of the labyrinth there are many points of vantage, where one may obtain a clear view of the road over which he has passed; and the knowledge so obtained relieves him from the necessity of again traversing it, and enables him to avoid the obstacles and obstructions that had hindered his progress. Everything that man can do consciously has already been done for him unconsciously. The light of the Infinite Intelligence radiates always in one's direction, but it does not force itself upon his attention. Its entire absorption is in Being. The Infinite Intelligence offers itself; but it is at one's option to accept or reject, and therein lies the privilege and duty of existence. One is able increasingly to accept its offers only as he grows physically, develops mentally, and unfolds spiritually, these being the steps whereby the truths of Being of which he has been unconscious are converted into facts of conscious existence.

## February 29th Leap Year

### Genevieve Behrend

"Ask, believing you have already received, And you shall receive" This is not as difficult as it appears on the surface, once you realize that: Everything has, its origin in the mind, and that which you seek outwardly, you already possess. No one can think a thought in the future. Your thought of a thing constitutes its origin. THEREFORE: The Thought Form of the Thing is already Yours As soon as you think it. Your steady recognition of this Thought Possession causes the thought to concentrate, to condense, to project itself, and to assume physical form. Remember that it should never be your intention to make yourself believe that which you know to be untrue. You are simply thinking into God or First Cause with the understanding that: "If a thing is true at all, there is a way in which it is true throughout the universe." Remember that the power of thought works by absolutely scientific principles. These principles are expressed in the language of the statement: "As a man thinketh in his heart, so is he." This statement contains a world of wisdom, but man's steady recognition and careful application of the statement itself is required to bring it into practical use.

# March

## March 1st

Charles Fillmore

In following the principles of mathematics we use rules. There is a rule of addition that we must observe when we add; other rules that must be followed when we subtract or multiply. The ideas of Divine Mind can only be expressed when we follow the rules or laws of mind, and these rules require understanding if we would follow them intelligently and achieve results. Man is given all power and authority over all the ideas of infinite Mind, and the idea of wisdom is one of them. Closely associated with the idea of wisdom in Divine Mind is the idea of love. These ideas are the positive and the negative pole of the creative Principle. "Male and female created he them." The ideas of God-Mind are expressed through the conjunction of wisdom and love. God commanded that these two ideas should be fruitful and multiply and replenish the whole earth with thoughts in expression. We have access to the divine realm from which all thoughts are projected into the world. We are constantly taking ideas from the spiritual world and forming them into our own conception of the things we desire. Sometimes the finished product does not satisfy or please us. That is because we have taken the idea away from its true parents, wisdom and love, and let it grow to maturity in an atmosphere of error and ignorance. In the matter of money or riches we have taken the idea of pure substance from the spiritual realm, then have forgotten the substance idea and tried to work it out in a material atmosphere of thought. It was a wonderful idea, but when we took it away from its spiritual parents wisdom and love, it became an unruly and disappointing child. Even if without love and understanding of substance you accumulate gold and silver, your store will not be stable or permanent. It will fluctuate and cause you worry and grief. There are many people who "don't know the value of a dollar," with whom money comes and goes, who are rich today and poor tomorrow. They have no understanding of the substance that is the underlying reality of all wealth.

## March 2nd

Walter C. Lanyon

Be still, then — I AM HERE NOW — I AM the Spirit of the Consciousness. You have always had the Consciousness of the Presence of God, no matter how little you knew it, no matter how many spiritual busybodies have told you that it has to be evolved. If you were created by God and out of God, you have had the consciousness of God always, and no lying mortal man, no matter if he have a thousand diplomas to tell of his learning, shall make this false. You have this consciousness whether someone has told you, you were consecrated or damned. You are the Son or the Living God, and you are already in possession of this consciousness, and when you recognize the Spirit of the Consciousness, the instantaneous manifestation of the Kingdom is revealed to you. Do not look for a sign. I, the I AM, descend into the stagnant pool or your human belief. I descend into the dirty waters and purify them. I free you from the prison of your own making. 'The Spirit of the Consciousness of the Presence of God is the Source of all Supply. The overflowing, unending, unlimited source of all supply. 'I come quickly.' 'In the twinkling of an eye all [not some, but all] shall be changed. '

## March 3rd

Floyd B. Wilson

If the world generally would recognize that this simple proposition in natural science, that like produces like, has as complete proof in mental science as in it, then the way would be opened for all to learn the secret of keeping good health. One cannot afford to complain and talk of aches and pains. This he must overcome, for consideration of them only establishes them more firmly. If he can overcome this habit in no other way than by reading interesting books or seeking interesting company, I commend either of these ways. Some are stronger when alone to rise above their ills with strong mental assertions which they may make. Others never speak of their illnesses when they are in company of friends, and so receive really a splendid treatment through association. In the discipline of self the truth contained in the three words that I have taken for the subject of this article, should be ever held in mind. If we send out wrong or bitter thoughts to others, they must return to us. We must reap what we. sow.

### March 4th

Mrs. Evelyn Lowes Wicker

Energizing the Body. Deep breathing also generates the energies to all parts of the body. We have at the waistline a nerve center that is called the solar plexus. This center is the reservoir of energy. When there is a continual, deep, steady breathing the solar plexus is massaged and energized. It then generates through the nervous system the energies needed for the body. Whenever the energies are congested in the solar plexus there will often be a case of "blues' ' or bad feeling. When we continually breathe deeply we are generating our energies, as well as forcing the blood to circulate. From the above stated facts you will see the necessity of lung exercise. Without right breathing your development, physiologically and spiritually, is going to be greatly hindered. I do not at any time undervalue the power of right thinking. Eight thinking is essential to our spiritual development. Just as right thinking is essential to our spiritual development, so is right breathing essential to our bodily development. You cannot be well; you cannot have perfect digestion; you cannot have a clear mind; you cannot be one hundred percent efficient until you become a hundred percent breather.

### March 5th

Shirley Bell Hastings

Love is a necessary influence and power in life, in your life, in my life. Love the Force. Love people. Love all things. Love involves forgiveness. We must forgive people and experiences. We must forgive ourselves. Love and forgiveness open doors for us through which we pass as we unfold. If you are not capable of forgiveness, then you are not capable of becoming all that you might otherwise become. We stunt our growth when we do not forgive. We stunt our growth through criticism and condemnation. Thought is the power that produces. Thought filled or colored with love and forgiveness is of a different nature than thought colored with lack of forgiveness, criticism, or condemnation. Think this over. Look at people as they think. It is easy to watch your neighbor think. Look at the ones who are hating. Then turn your attention toward one who is generous, loving, forgiving. Look at the one who is continually criticizing or condemning. Which one do you evade? Which one do you enjoy being near?

## March 6th

### Ernest Holmes

We live and move and have our being in what we call an Infinite Mind, an Infinite Creative Mind, also infinitely receptive, operative, omnipotent, and all-knowing; and we have learned that this mind presses against us on all sides, flows through us, and becomes operative through our thinking. The human race, ignorant of the laws of this mind, ignorant of the power of its own thought, has through its ignorance misused and abused the creative power of its thought, and brought upon itself the thing it feared. This is true because all thought is law, and all law is mind in action, and the word which you speak today is the law which shall govern your life tomorrow, as the word which you spoke, ignorantly or innocently, consciously or unconsciously yesterday, is absolutely governing your life today. As metaphysicians, then, we are not dealing with a material, nor denying a manifest universe, but we are claiming that the manifestation is the result of the inner activity of the mind; and if we wish for a definite manifestation, we must produce a definite inner activity. You and I, then, are not dealing with conditions, but with mental and spiritual law. We are dealing with the power of thought, the power of mind, and the more spiritual the thought the higher the manifestation. The more our reliance upon what we call God, the greater the power.

## March 7th

### Christian Larson

The spirit of gladness when combined with the spirit of strength, will enlarge the mind, expand the soul, and enrich all thought and life; it is the moving mystery from within that makes everything good in human nature grow; that makes man noble and great; that makes human existence a world of immeasurable richness and sublime worth. It is the same spirit that makes life "a thing of beauty and a joy forever;" that makes the lovely and the true become the tangible and heal; that causes all things we have loved so much come forth into our world m abundance. Therefore be glad when you feel strong, and be strong when you feel glad; and always know that you can. Whatever your present position may be there is a way from where you now stand that leads to better things and greater things for you than you ever knew. So whatever happens, just be glad. Live the spirit of gladness; think in the spirit of joy; thus you will be able to see the royal path, for the mind that is illumined with gladness is never in the dark, never under the clouds of doubt or dismay. When overtaken with calamity or tribulation, come forth undaunted and undismayed. Inspire the soul to reach for the high realms of victory and joy; and hold fast to that lofty position even though the whole world seem to disappear beneath your feet. With such a victory for your strong inspiration, your own soul will prove more than sufficient for all that life may demand of you. Then remember that mankind stands ready to welcome and exalt every soul whose strength is greater than any circumstance, whose joy is greater than any tribulation, and whose faith is greater than all doubts and failures in the world.

## March 8th

### Uriel Buchanan

Magnetism is the life of the world. Electricity is motion without life. Magnetism is life without motion. Union of the two results in the manifestation of celestial harmonies. These in a way are the manifestation of the same force; they are dual. Electricity and magnetism, uniting in the physical organism, are constantly generating the vital force, or human fire. To arouse these energies of your being and to wisely direct them, is to have opened unto you the gates of the realized ideal. Magnetism is the king. Electricity is the servant. We can say to electricity, you shall run our cars, illuminate the cities by night, and carry news from continent to continent by the lightning's flash. But we cannot say that to magnetism. It will not be ordered. We must draw it and supplicate it. We draw it by thought and love. Magnetism is produced and increased by silent meditation. Magnetism gives power to infuse new life and build new purpose. Who has not grasped the hand of a magnetic person and felt the magic influence that the touch inspires, or has been thrilled by the searching gaze of the magnetic eye. Magnetism is the key which unlocks the storehouse of nature and gives free access to an ever present and ceaseless supply of power for all the purposes and demands of life. To absorb an abundance of this force will give brilliancy to the eyes, color to the lips and cheeks, and great vitality. There are many people who work incessantly, yet their efforts are barren of results. They work without understanding. They are under the delusion that nothing can be achieved except by bodily activity. They have not learned the value of forethought. They rush blindly about, striking a blow here and one there, until physically exhausted; then they sit down and wail at the cruelty of fate; and in moments of retrospection they see what might have been done if they had only known; but the awakening comes too late. Their ways of working without a knowledge and proper use of their magnetic forces may be compared to one who might cross the continent on foot instead of taking the train. Thus they continue to struggle with adverse conditions, in perpetual conflict with the world and with themselves, all because they depend upon externalities and deal with effects while ignorant of causes.

## March 9th

### Orison Swett Marden

The time will come when the law of attraction will be known as the greatest power in creation. This is the law upon which all successes, all characters, all lives are built. Mental attraction is the only power upon which we can build anything successfully. It is an inevitable law, an inexorable principle, that everything attracts to itself everything else like itself, that air affinities tend to get together, and when you make your mind a magnet it will attract according to its quality, according to your mental vision, your thoughts, your motives, your dominant attitude. The saying "Money attracts money" is only another way of stating the law, — "like attracts like." The prosperous classes think prosperity, believe in it, work for it, never for a moment doubt their right to have all the money and all the good things they need, and of course they get them. They are living up to the very letter and spirit of the law of attraction. A Rockefeller, a Schwab, uses this law in a masterly way to amass a large fortune. The newsboy uses the same law in selling his newspapers, running a newsstand and climbing gradually to the mayoralty of his city or town. We all use this law of attraction no matter whether we know it or not. We use it every instant of our lives.

## March 10th

Prentice Mulford

The highest love for all things is for us a literal source of life. The more things in the world of Nature to which we can give the higher love, the more of their natural love and life shall we get in return. So, as we grow, refine and increase this power of recognizing and loving the bird, the animal, the insect or, in other words, the Infinite in all things, we shall receive a love, a renewed life, strength, vigor, cheer and inspiration from not only these, but the falling snow-flake, the driving rain, the cloud, the sea, the mountain. And this will not be a mere sentiment, but a great means for recuperating and strengthening the body, for this strengthens the spirit with a strength which comes to stay, and what strengthens the spirit must strengthen the body.

## March 11th

James Allen

Consider the man whose mind is suspicious, covetous, envious. How small and mean and drear everything appears to him. Having no grandeur in himself, he sees no grandeur anywhere; being ignoble himself, he is incapable of seeing nobility in any being. Even his God is a covetous being that can be bribed, and he judges all men and women to be just as petty and selfish as he himself is, so that he sees in the most exalted acts of unselfishness only motives that are mean and base. Consider again the man whose mind is unsuspecting, generous, magnanimous. How wondrous and beautiful is his world. He is conscious of some kind of nobility in all creatures and beings. He sees men as true, and to him they are true. In his presence the meanest forget their nature, and for the moment become like himself, getting a glimpse, albeit confused, in that temporary upliftments of a higher order of things, of an immeasurably nobler and happier life. That small-minded, and this large-hearted, man live in two different worlds, though they be neighbors. Their consciousness embraces totally different principles. Their actions are each the reverse of the other. Their moral insight is contrary. They each look out upon a different order of things. Their mental spheres are separate, and, like two detached circles, they never mingle. The one is in hell, the other in heaven as truly as they will ever be, and death will not place a greater gulf between them than already exists. To the one, the world is a den of thieves; to the other, it is the dwelling-place of Gods. The one keeps a revolver handy, and is always on his guard against being robbed or cheated (unconscious of the fact that he is all the time robbing and cheating himself), the other keeps ready a banquet for the best. He throws open his doors to talent, beauty, genius, goodness. His friends are of the aristocracy of character. They have become a part of himself. They are in his sphere of thought, his world of consciousness. From his heart pours forth nobility, and it returns to him tenfold in the multitude of those who love him and do him honor.

## March 12th

William Walker Atkinson

Your thoughts are either faithful servants or tyrannical masters — just as you allow them to be. You have the say about it; take your choice. They will either go about your work under direction of the firm will, doing it the best they know how, not only in your waking hours, but when you are asleep — some of our best mental work being performed for us when our conscious mentality is at rest, as is evidenced by the fact that when the morning comes we find troublesome problems have been worked out for us during the night, after we had dismissed them from our minds — apparently; or they will ride all over us and make us their slaves if we are foolish enough to allow them to do so. More than half the people of the world are slaves of every vagrant thought which may see fit to torment them. Your mind is given you for your good and for your own use — not to use you. There are very few people who seem to realize this and who understand the art of managing the mind. The key to the mystery is Concentration. A little practice will develop within every man the power to use the mental machine properly. When you have some mental work to do concentrate upon it to the exclusion of everything else, and you will find that the mind will get right down to business — to the work at hand — and matters will be cleared up in no time. There is an absence of friction, and all waste motion or lost power is obviated. Every pound of energy is put to use, and every revolution of the mental driving wheel counts for something. It pays to be able to be a competent mental engineer.

## March 13th

Ernest Holmes

The very presence of one that understands the truth will have a great power of healing. The reason for this is that we are all in Mind, and we have with us at all times our thought, and since all manifestation is the result of mind in action, and we are thinking beings and are always causing mind to act, the very presence of our thought will have some power to act upon whatever we are thinking about. We are dealing with a power which in itself is limitless. We limit it, and so it cannot become to us the bigger thing. Of itself the power is the same that made the worlds, and it cannot realize any sense of limitation. "They could not enter in because of their unbelief and because they limited the Holy one of Israel." Stop limiting things. Things are as big as we make them, no more, no less. There is room at the top. Get on top of everything, and dare to dominate the earth. All things are given us to use; make use of them. Everything is limitless, and we must see the truth that the fault is not in the Law but in ourselves when we fail. Not with God but with man. Dare, Dare, Dare.

## March 14th

### Christian Larson

When things go wrong, do not become disheartened; it is much easier to set them right when your soul is full of sunshine; so just be glad. It is the best way out. When all seems lost, remember that it requires strength to regain everything; and it is the glad heart that remains strong. When the heart saddens, weakness will overtake you, and it will not be possible to regain your position. So therefore be glad regardless of what may transpire. It is one of the royal paths to everything that life holds dear. But sadness does not merely bring weakness, it also brings illness, and age, and it shortens the length of our days. In gladness, however, there is health and youth, strength and longevity. The glad heart will not grow old, nor can illness ever enter where the spirit of joy is supreme. When in pain, be glad; and you can. Be glad that you are greater than pain. Be glad that pain has come to prevent you from going wrong. Be glad that you can prevent all pain in the future. And be glad that it is wholly impossible for pain to come any more after gladness has become the rule of your life. For your own advancement, be glad. The spirit of joy is the spirit that makes the heart kind, the soul strong and the mind brilliant. It is this spirit that makes for greatness, for nobleness, for excellence, for worth. We repeat it, therefore, just be glad.

## March 15th

Joseph Murphy

You know there is only one spiritual Power, one primal cause, and you, therefore, cease giving power to conditions, circumstances, and opinions of men. Give all Power to the Spiritual Power within you, knowing that It will respond to your thought of abundance and prosperity. Recognizing the supremacy of the Spirit within, and the Power of your own thought or mental image, is the way to opulence, freedom, and constant supply. Accept the abundant life in your own mind. Your mental acceptance and expectancy of wealth has its own mathematics and mechanics of expression. As you enter into the mood of opulence, all things necessary for the abundant life will come to pass. You are now the judge arriving at a decision in the courthouse of your mind. You have, like Quimby, produced indisputable evidence showing how the laws of your mind work, and you are now free from fear. You have executed and chopped the heads off all the fear and superstitious thoughts in your mind. Fear is the signal for action; it is not really bad; it tells you to move to the opposite, which is faith in God and all positive values.

## March 16th

Orison Swett Marden

If we could only see a picture of the mental processes of whatever is held in the mind, pulling the things which correspond to our thought; if we could see more failure, more bad business, more debts, more losses starting towards us because we have contacted with these things in our thought, we would quit worrying about the things we don't want and think the things we do want, attracting more instead of less, attracting abundance instead of poverty, prosperity instead of failure. Oh, how often we make our mind a magnet to attract all sorts of enemy thoughts, poverty thoughts, sick thoughts, fear thoughts, and worry thoughts, and then somehow we expect that a miracle will be performed, and that out of these negative causes we will be sure in some way to enjoy positive results. No miracle could perform such a change as this. Results correspond with causes. Before we can be conquered by poverty, we must, first of all, be poor mentally. The poverty thought, the acceptance of a poverty-stricken environment as an inevitable condition from which you cannot get away, keeps you in the poverty current and draws more poverty to you. It is the operation of the same law which attracts good things, a better environment, to those who think abundance, prosperity, who are convinced that they are going to be well off, and work confidently, hopefully, toward that end.

## March 17th

### Henry Thomas Hamblin

Man cannot create a planet, but he can consciously form an image or picture in his creative mind, a picture of better circumstance, different environment or definite achievement, and holding that image persistently compel it to materialize in his life and circumstances. This is not a fairy tale — it is a hard, common sense fact. There is nothing that has ever been accomplished by man that has not first been created and imaged in his mind. It is always the vision first, and afterwards the accomplishment. The difference between men is a difference of vision. The difference between their vision is the difference between their accomplishment. Some men create more than others — it is because theirs is a greater vision. All the great ones of the earth, leaders of men and nations, artists, poets, inventors, financiers, have been what they were because of their "vision," because they were men of "imagination." People who pride themselves on being "practical" look askance at imagination, thinking it to be something impractical and shadowy; something belonging to the realm of dreams. They confuse constructive imagery with daydreaming. Now, the imagination of which I am speaking is the very antithesis of daydreaming. Daydreaming is the aimless frittering away of the mental powers; creative imagination, on the other hand, gathers together the mental forces, and by focusing the powers of the hidden mind bring into being a definite image. This definite image is the vision which all men of accomplishment possess.

## March 18th

Venice J. Bloodworth

Everything that has ever been accomplished has been done by visualization. Every building was first in the architect's mind; every picture painted was the brain child of an artist; every invention was first an idea in the inventor's mind. The law of cause and effect is absolute and undeviating. Thought precedes and determines every action and manifestation, so when we fix any goal, and concentrate on that purpose we may be sure of our results. That is the law and it always has been the law, and is still the law. Even if you should try to do something and seem to fail, try again and keep on trying. If a building or bridge falls we do not think the law of gravity has failed. We know the building or bridge was not strong enough. A hundred years ago we had as much electricity as we have now, but it did not do us any good until someone found the law by which to make it serve us. It will prove so with you when you have established the consciousness of your oneness with the Universal Mind and your power to use the Law. Your needs will not even reach the stage of needs. You will find the way prepared before you realize the desire. "Before they call I will answer them and while they are yet speaking I will hear."

## March 19th

Charles F. Haanel

People say that they desire abundant life, and so they do, but so many interpret this to mean that if they will exercise their muscles or breathe scientifically, eat certain foods in certain ways, drink so many glasses of water every day of just a certain temperature, keep out of drafts, they will attain the abundant life they seek. The result of such methods is but indifferent. However, when man awakens to the truth, and affirms his oneness with all Life, he finds that he takes on the clear eye, the elastic step, the vigor of youth; he finds that he has discovered the source of all power. All mistakes are but the mistakes of ignorance. Knowledge gaining and consequent power is what determines growth and evolution.

The recognition and demonstration of knowledge is what constitutes power, and this power is spiritual power, and this spiritual power is the power which lies at the heart of all things; it is the soul of the universe. This knowledge is the result of man's ability to think; thought is therefore the germ of man's conscious evolution. When man ceases to advance in his thoughts and ideals, his forces immediately begin to disintegrate and his countenance gradually registers these changing conditions. Successful men make it their business to hold ideals of the conditions which they wish to realize. They constantly hold in mind the next step necessary to the ideal for which they are striving. Thoughts are the materials with which they build, and the imagination is their mental workshop. Mind is the ever-moving force with which they secure the persons and circumstance necessary to build their success structure, and imagination is the matrix in which all great things are fashioned.

## March 20th

### Robert Collier

It is the first step in making your dreams come true. You are creating the model in mind. And if you don't allow fear or worry to tear it down, Mind will recreate that model for you in your everyday life. "All that the Father hath is yours," said Jesus. And a single glance at the heavens and the earth will show you that He has all riches in abundance. Reach out mentally and appropriate to yourself some of these good gifts. You've got to do it mentally before you can enjoy it physically. "'Tis mind that makes the body rich," as Shakespeare tells us. See the things that you want as already yours. Know that they will come to you at need. Then LET them come. Don't fret and worry about them. Don't think about your LACK of them. Think of them as YOURS, as belonging to you, as already in your possession. Look upon money as water that runs the mill of your mind. You are constantly grinding out ideas that the world needs. Your thoughts, your plans, are necessary to the great scheme of things. Money provides the power. But it needs YOU, it needs your ideas, before it can be of any use to the world. The Falls of Niagara would be of no use without the power plants that line the banks. The Falls need these plants to turn their power to account. In the same way, money needs your ideas to become of use to the world.

### March 21st

Prentice Mulford

This idea of the body's regeneration is for you a benefit now, if you can accept it. It cannot be displaced from your mind. It will first, as a tiny seed, stay there. It may for months or years show no sign of life and seem to be forgotten. But it will grow and have more and more of a place in your thought. It will gradually change the quality of your thoughts. It will gradually force out an old and false interpretation of life and bring in a new one. It will impel you to look ever forward to newer joys and make you cease groping among regrets and sad remembrances of your past, when you know that such thoughts bring decay and death to the body. We are built literally of our thoughts. When we realize that our regrets, our envyings and jealousies, our borrowings of trouble, or our morbid contemplations of subjects ghastly and sickly, are literally things, and bad things, actually put in our bodies, as such thoughts, materializing themselves from invisible to visible element, turn into flesh and blood, and that as so built into ourselves they bring us pains, aches, weakness, sickness, wrinkles, bowed backs, weak knees and failing powers, we have a good and tangible reason for getting rid of them. The body of a person given over to melancholy will be literally built of gloomy thoughts materialized into flesh and blood.

### March 22nd

Uriel Buchanan

The act of thinking increases the capacity of the brain. The tendency of the mind to wander, to yield to cares and disappointments, to be easily distracted, is the direct cause of so many failures. If you do not concentrate your mind on what you are doing, your efforts will be barren of results. You should learn to fix your whole attention on one thing at any given moment to the exclusion of all other thoughts. There are two kinds of attention: passive and active. In the passive attention you still the senses and place yourself in a receptive mood; not in a state of anxious expectancy, but of quiet repose. In the active attention you place your mind in a positive receptive attitude. You listen with concentration. You send out suggestions at the same time you are receiving them. There is a dual action of the mind. You are listening to what is being said, and at the same time are forming conclusions and sending back a silent mental answer. You should never give your passive attention to one who seeks a favor, or would take advantage of you. While you should be receptive to the suggestions of another, you should at the same time be in that positive state which will make you impervious to any influence that is undesirable. You should stand guard at the threshold and permit no unworthy or harmful suggestion to enter your mind. Every thought sent out should be under the control of the will. Every word should be carefully weighed until the habit of right speaking is well established. And every deed should be done from the center of the higher self. You should breathe your very life into everything you do.

## March 23rd

### Wallace Wattles

The whole process of mental adjustment and attunement can be summed up in one word: Gratitude. First, you believe that there is one intelligent substance, from which all things proceed. Second, you believe that this substance gives you everything you desire. And third, you relate yourself to it by a feeling of deep and profound gratitude. Many people who order their lives rightly in all other ways are kept in poverty by their lack of gratitude. Having received one gift from God, they cut the wires which connect them with him by failing to make acknowledgment. It is easy to understand that the nearer we live to the source of wealth, the more wealth we shall receive, and it is easy also to understand that the soul that is always grateful lives in closer touch with God than the one which never looks to him in thankful acknowledgment. The more gratefully we fix our minds on the supreme when good things come to us, the more good things we will receive, and the more rapidly they will come. And the reason simply is that the mental attitude of gratitude draws the mind into closer touch with the source from which the blessings come. If it is a new thought to you that gratitude brings your whole mind into closer harmony with the creative energies of the universe, consider it well, and you will see that it is true. The good things you have already have come to you along the line of obedience to certain laws. Gratitude will lead your mind out along the ways by which things come, and it will keep you in close harmony with creative thought and prevent you from falling into competitive thought.

## March 24th

### Charles Fillmore

That part of the Lord's Prayer which reads, "Give us this day our daily bread," is more correctly translated, "Give us today the substance of tomorrow's bread." By prayer we accumulate in our mind ideas of God as the substance of our supply and support. There is no lack of this substance in infinite Mind. Regardless of how much God gives, there is always an abundance left. God does not give us material things, but Mind substance not money but ideas — ideas that set spiritual forces in motion so that things begin to come to us by the application of the law. It may be that you solve your financial problem in your dreams. Men often think over their problems just before going to sleep and get a solution in their dreams or immediately upon awakening. This is because their minds were so active on the intellectual plane that they could not make contact with the silent inner plane where ideas work. When the conscious mind is stilled and one makes contact with the Superconsciousness, it begins to show us how our affairs will work out or how we can help to bring about the desired prosperity. This is the law of mind. The principle is within each one of us, but we must be spiritually quickened in life and in understanding before we can successfully work in accord with it. However we must not discount the understanding of the natural man. The mind in us that reasons and looks to the physical side of things has also the ability to look within. It is the door through which divine ideas must come. Jesus, the Son of man, called Himself "the door" and "the way." It is the divine plan that all expression or demonstration shall come through this gateway of man's mind. But above all this are the ideas that exist in the primal state of Being, and this is the truth of which we must become conscious. We must become aware of the source of our substance. Then we can diminish or increase the appearance of our supply or our finances, for their appearance depends entirely on our understanding and handling of the ideas of substance.

### March 25th

Fay Adams

Since desire is prayer the meaning of the statements of Jesus, "Man ought always to pray," and "Ask that your joy may be full," is clear. In other words, to DESIRE continually is to express abundantly. To work according to law is easy and harmonious. The reason people fail to realize wishes is because they desire something that belongs to somebody else, instead of desiring that their own should manifest. "You ask and receive not because ye ask amiss." Speak your desires into the original substance instead of longing for the things of your neighbor. Anything you can name you can possess. If you can ask the same for the rest of the world it is not only your right but your duty to bring it into expression. Desire is the promissory note payable on demand.

### March 26th

Ernest Holmes

Knowing that Mind is, we have a principle that is absolute; it is exact; it is going to correspond to our thinking about it. The first great necessity is to believe this; without belief we can do nothing. This is the reason Jesus said "It is done unto you even as you have believed." Always it is done unto people as they believe, and there is Something that does it which never fails. We must believe that our word is formed upon and around by this creative Mind; for instance, we wish to create activity in our business; we believe that our word is law about that thing, and there is something that takes our thought and executes it for us. If we have accepted the fact that all is mind and that the thought is the thing, we shall see at once that our word is the power behind the thing, and that it depends upon the word or thought that we are sending out. So plastic is mind, so receptive, that the slightest thought makes an impression upon it. People who think many kinds of thought must expect to receive a confused manifestation in their lives. If a gardener plants a thousand kinds of seeds, he will get a thousand kinds of plants; it is the same in mind.

## March 27th

Orison Swett Marden

It was never intended that God's children should ever want for anything. We live in the very lap of abundance; there is plenty of everything all about us, the great cosmic universe is packed with all sorts of beautiful, marvelous things, glorious riches, ready for our use and enjoyment. Everything the human heart can crave, the great creative Intelligence offers us. We can draw from this vast ocean of intelligence everything we wish: all that it is necessary for us to do is to obey the law of attraction, — like attracts like. To realize prosperity and abundance does not depend upon man's own little brain, his own little one-sided efforts. It is a question of his making his mind a magnet to attract the things he wants, to attract his desires. Everything that the race enjoys has been attracted out of the great ocean of intelligence according to a law. All inventions, all discoveries, all the marvelous facilities of civilization, — our hospitals, our schools, our churches, our libraries, and other institutions, our homes, with their comforts and luxuries, — have all been attracted from this great cosmic storehouse of intelligence by the same law.

## March 28th

### James Allen

A man only begins to be a man when he ceases to whine and revile, and commences to search for the hidden justice which regulates his life. And as he adapts his mind to that regulating factor, he ceases to accuse others as the cause of his condition, and builds himself up in strong and noble thoughts. He ceases to kick against circumstances, but begins to use them as aids to his more rapid progress, and as a means of discovering the hidden powers and possibilities within himself.

## March 29th

### Robert Collier

There is a woman in one of the big Eastern cities whose husband died a year or two ago and left her nearly $100,000,000. She has unlimited power in her hands — yet she uses none of it. She has unlimited wealth — yet she gets no more from it than if it were in the thousands instead of millions. She knows nothing of her power, of her wealth. She is insane. You have just as great power in your hands — without this poor woman's excuse for not using it. You have access to unlimited ideas, unlimited energy, unlimited wealth. The "Open, Sesame!" is through your subconscious mind. So long as you limit yourself to superficial conditions, so long as you are a mere "hewer of wood or carrier of water" for those around you who do use their minds, you are in no better position than the beasts of burden. The secret of power is in understanding the infinite resources of your own mind. When you begin to realize that the power to do anything, to be anything, to have anything, is within yourself, then and then only will you take your proper place in the world.

## March 30th

Ernest Holmes

So when you say, "I am poor, sick or weak; I am not one with the Creative Mind," you are using that creative power to keep yourself away from the Infinite; and just as soon as you declare that you are one with God, there is a rushing out to meet you, as the Father rushed out to meet the prodigal son. "The Spirit seeketh," but as long as your mind thinks in the terms of conditions you cannot overcome. The difficulty comes from our inability to see our own Divine nature, and its relation to the Universe. Until we awake to the fact that we are one in nature with God, we will not find the way of life; until we realize that our own word has the power of life we will not see the way of life; and this brings us to the consideration of the use of the Word in our lives.

## March 31st

Christian Larson

No selfish heart can really be glad. No soul that acts solely for personal gain can enter the spirit of joy; and no man who seeks only his own pleasure and comfort can ever take part in the music of rejoicing. And yet, the glad heart receives far more of everything of worth in life than does the one who forgets gladness in pursuit of gain for self alone. And again the answer is simple. For all things respond to the call of rejoicing; all things gather where life is a song. Be glad for the things you have, and you will find you have far more than you thought. Then you will not miss, in the least, the things you have not. Besides, the happier you are over what has come to you, the more and the more will come to you in the future. This is indeed a great secret, and if universally applied would cause want to disappear from the face of the whole earth. Be glad, for nothing is as serious as it seems to be. Then remember that sunshine can banish any gloom; and you can create in yourself all the sunshine you need; so just be glad. When trouble and misfortunes surround you, just be glad. The glad heart and the cheerful soul always make things better. It is the happy heart that has the most courage; it is the joyous soul that has the greatest power; and it is the presence of sunshine that keeps darkness and gloom away.

# April

## April 1st

Robert Collier

Psychologists have discovered that the best time to make suggestions to your subconscious mind is just before going to sleep, when the senses are quiet and the attention is lax. So let us take your desire and suggest it to your subconscious mind tonight. The two prerequisites are the earnest DESIRE, and an intelligent, understanding BELIEF. Someone has said, you know, that education is three-fourths encouragement, and the encouragement is the suggestion that the thing can be done. You know that you can have what you want, if you want it badly enough and can believe in it earnestly enough. So tonight, just before you drop off to sleep, concentrate your thought on this thing that you most desire from life. BELIEVE that you have it. SEE YOURSELF possessing it. FEEL yourself using it. Do that every night until you ACTUALLY DO BELIEVE that you have the thing you want. When you reach that point, YOU WILL HAVE IT!

## April 2nd

Ernest Holmes

"The Word was with God and the Word was God." "The Word is nigh thee, even in thy own mouth that thou shouldst know it and do it." What does this mean? It clearly states that whatever power there is in the Word (and it says it is All Power) is also in our own mouths. There is no avoiding the fact that the Bible claims for man the same power in his own life and his own world that it claims for God. In the lives of the majority, men do not realize that the Word is in their own mouths. What Word? Little do we realize that this Word which they are so earnestly seeking is every word they hear, think or speak. Do we who are endeavoring to realize the greater truths of life always govern our words? If any word has power, it follows that all words have power. It is not in the few moments of spiritual meditation that we demonstrate, but we bring out the possibilities of the hidden word when we are allowing our thoughts to run in any direction; not in the short time spent in silence, but in the long hours stretching themselves into days, months, and years, are we always using the word. An hour a day spent in silent meditation will not save us from the confusion of life; the fifty-one percent of a man's thinking is what counts. It is easy when we are alone to brave the storms of life; surrounded by our own exalted atmosphere we feel the strength of the Infinite; we rise in Spirit, we think we are experiencing the ultimate of truth, that all things are ours. These moments in a busy life are well spent, but must unavoidably be brief. But what of the rest of the day; what of the busy street, of the market place, and of all the daily contact with life? Do we then obtain? Do we keep on in the same even way? Or do we fall before the outer confusion of our surroundings? We are still creating the word and setting it afloat in the great ethers of life. Are these words creating for us? Yes! How necessary, then, to "keep the independence of the solitude"; how seldom we do this!

## April 3rd

Prentice Mulford

All of us believe in many untruths today. It is an unconscious belief. The error is not brought before our minds. Still we go on acting and living in accordance with our unconscious error, and the suffering we may experience comes from that wrong belief. Demand, then, every day ability to see our wrong beliefs. We need not be discouraged if we see many more than we think we have at present. They cannot be seen and remedied all at once. Don't take a "tired feeling" or one of languor in the day time for a symptom of sickness. It is only your mind asking for rest from some old rut of occupation. If your stomach is disordered make your mind responsible for it. Say to yourself, "This disagreeable feeling comes of an error in thought." If you are weak or nervous, don't lay the fault on your body. Say again, "It is a state of my mind which causes this physical ailment, and I demand to get rid of such state and get a better one." If you think any medicine or medical advice will do you good, by all means take it, but mind and keep this thought behind it: " I am taking this medicine not to help my body but as an aid to my spirit,"

## April 4th

### Uriel Buchanan

Keep yourself positive, and banish all unwelcome thoughts that seek entrance. Study yourself, your relation to environment, your desires and possibilities. Surround yourself by those who have kindred desires and talents. Strengthen your forces by keeping in touch with those who can help you to realize your ideals. There is no one thing in life, within the range of possibility, which you cannot accomplish, if you will recognize the power and efficiency of well directed thought, supported by an unwavering faith, resolution and persistent desire. You should recognize every permanent desire as being a prophecy of its final fulfillment. To say, "Impossible, I cannot reach the goal of my ambition" is to erect the only real barrier between you and ultimate success. When you say, "I can and I will," you have already achieved victory within your mind. And this thought, if continually held, will insure its final realization on the objective plane. Keep in touch with the thought current of all that is helpful and inspiring. Keep the mind filled with bright and cheerful thoughts. Avoid selfish and sordid people, and all surroundings which have a depressing influence. Do not dwell on the past with its mistakes and disappointments, and have no fear concerning the future; for your life is in the keeping of a faithful power, and if you are true to the highest and best, in the light of the knowledge that if given you, all will be well.

## April 5th

### Ernest Holmes

If you wish to demonstrate prosperity, begin to think and talk about it, and to see it everywhere. Do nothing that contradicts this thought either mentally or physically. The world is full of good; take it and forget all else. Rise above depression and be glad that you are saved from adversity; the human mind needs to be cleansed from the morbid thoughts that bind through its false beliefs. No living soul can demonstrate two things at the same time, if one contradicts the other. There is no way except to let go of all that you do not wish to come into your experience, and, in mind, take all that you do wish.

## April 6th

### Christian Larson

A great many people imagine that they can promote their own success by trying to prevent the success of other, but it is one of the greatest delusions in the world. If you want to promote your own success as thoroughly as your capacity will permit, take an active interest in the success of everybody, because this will not only keep your mind in the success attitude and cause you to think success all along the line, but it will enlarge your mind so as to give you a greater and better grasp upon the fields of success. If you are trying to prevent the success of others, you are acting in the destructive attitude, which sooner or later will react on others, but if you are taking an active interest in the success of everybody, you are entertaining only constructive attitudes, and these will sooner or later accumulate in your own mind to add volume and power to the forces of success that you are building up in yourself. In this connection, we may well ask why those succeed who do succeed, why so many succeed only in part, and why so many fail utterly. These are questions that occupy the minds of most people, and hundreds of answers have been given, but there is only one answer that goes to rock bottom. Those people who fail, and who continue to fail all along the line, fail because the power of their minds is either in a habitual negative state, or is always misdirected. If the power of mind is not working positively and constructively for a certain goal, you are not going to succeed. If your mind is not positive, it is negative, and negative minds float with the stream.

## April 7th

### Venice J. Bloodworth

Thought is the connecting link between us and the Universal Mind, and considering this marvelous fact, we arrive at the conclusion that we ourselves are channels through which the Universal Mind pours itself into expression, and that thoughts are causes and conditions are effects. Thought being the cause, we cannot help realizing that if we control our thoughts, we control effects; then it follows that our health, happiness, and prosperity are under our control also. When you understand this glorious truth, and realize the wondrous possibilities open to you through your connection with Omnipotence you will have found "the Kingdom of Heaven within you."

## April 8th

### Charles F. Haanel

The law of attraction will certainly and unerringly bring to you the conditions, environment, and experiences in life, corresponding with your habitual, characteristic, predominant mental attitude. Not what you think once in a while when you are in church, or have just read a good book, BUT your predominant mental attitude is what counts. You cannot entertain weak, harmful, negative thoughts ten hours a day and expect to bring about beautiful, strong and harmonious conditions by ten minutes of strong, positive, creative thought. Real power comes from within. All power that anybody can possibly use is within man, only waiting to be brought into visibility by his first recognizing it, and then affirming it as his, working it into his consciousness until he becomes one with it.

## April 9th

### Ernest Holmes

We often wonder why it is that we are not making better demonstrations. We look about and observe that some are getting wonderful results, they are speaking the word and people are being healed. We see others struggling along with the word, and nothing seems to happen; and when we inquire into the reason for all this we find it to be very plain indeed. All is mind and we are mental, we are in mind and can only get from it what we first think into it. We must not only think but we must know. We have to provide within ourselves a mental and spiritual likeness for the thing desired. The reason why so few succeed, then, must be because they have not mentally really believed to the exclusion of all that would deny the thing which they believe in. And the reason why others do succeed must also be because they have absolutely believed and allowed real power to flow through and out into expression. They must have a real concept of life. Hold an object in front of a mirror and it will image in the mirror the exact size of the object. Hold a thought in mind and it will image in matter the exact likeness of the thought. Let us take this image which we hold before a mirror and change it ever so slightly and there will be a corresponding change in the reflection. It is just the same in the mental world; whatever is imaged is brought forth from mind into manifestation.

## April 10th

W. J. Colville

Thought is the magnet that attracts everything to itself. Everything originates in the thought world. Every material thing springs from the mind of some individual. We bring upon ourselves an immense amount of trouble because we act without thought; we take the consequences of our own ignorant actions. People express what they express in consequence of their chronic habits of thought. We must learn to live always in the best and highest thought; to take note of our thoughts; to encourage only those thoughts which, when manifested in external forms, express in forms of beauty. As every thought you think about yourself comes back to you, every time you call yourself "a poor creature," it will come back to you. The "worm" theology has made worms of vast numbers of people. "According to thy word, be it unto thee," is universally the case.

## April 11th

Fay Adams

The Word

The life cell contains both male and female principle. "Male and female created he them," written in Genesis, means that the double nature was contained in each. With this thought in mind, mentally take a trip back to the beginning of creation. Starting with your mother, back through her mother and so on, letting each generation fall away one at a time like husks until you are Adam. Pause here a moment while you realize that you are still male and female, then take another step back into God or the original Principle and ask yourself the question, "Who is left?" and if you answer, "I AM," then you are in a position to make the acquaintance of your Divinity. From this high point in consciousness you can realize that you and God are one. God being the principle (life), and you, the life principle individualized. Hitherto you have been unaware of your Godhood. You have regarded yourself as being alone, separated in thought from God.

## April 12th

Orison Swett Marden

The majority of people are in the position of a man who went out to water his garden, but inadvertently stepped on the hose, shutting off the water supply. He had a big hose and was very much annoyed, very much disappointed, because he was getting only a mere dribble of water when he had every right to expect — and should get — a liberal flow. Water was at the source in abundance, ready to supply his needs; only one thing was at fault, the man himself was pinching his supply, limiting it to a miserable drizzle. He was standing on the hose and didn't know it. That is literally what all who are living in grinding poverty are doing. They are pinching their supply by stepping upon the hose through which plenty would come to them. They are stopping the flow of abundance that is their birthright, by their doubts, their fears, and their unbelief; by visualizing poverty, thinking poverty, acting as if they never expected to have anything, to accomplish anything, or to be anything. Everything in man's life, everything in God's universe, is based upon principle — follows a divine law; and the law of prosperity and abundance is just as definite as the law of gravitation, just as unerring as the principles of mathematics. It is a mental law. Only by thinking abundance can you realize the abundant, prosperous life that is your birthright; in other words, according to your thought will be your life, your supply, or your lack. Your mental attitude will be flung back to you, every time, in kind. A poverty-stricken mental attitude will bring only poverty-stricken conditions to you.

### April 13th

Ernest Holmes

We must turn from all human thought and experience. We are not down trodden, depraved and miserable sinners, born in sin and conceived in iniquity and shame, some to go to heaven and some to hell and all to the eternal glory of God. This is a lie, it always was and always will be. But as long as we believe in a lie it seems to be present with us. Man is born of the Spirit of God Almighty, is pure, holy, perfect, complete and undefiled; is at one with his eternal principle of being. Many people are finding this out and as a monument to its truth millions are daily proving it for themselves. Somewhere down the path of human experience we will all awake to the realization that we ourselves are heaven or hell. We live in Spirit awaiting the touch of thought that believes. All people look, a few see.

### April 14th

Walter C. Lanyon

Thousands of sincere souls, seeking the light, have spent years trying to better the condition of the "worm in the dust" — trying to make "John Smith" a better man, healthier, richer, or happier — but have accomplished little. The caterpillar cannot change except from within. No good trying to make a caterpillar fly; it is impossible. a complete change has to take place, a transformation. Jesus the carpenter becomes the Christ, the Son of the Living God, with all power. The caterpillar becomes the butterfly. Certain laws have to be heeded. If the caterpillar fails to close itself within its cocoon, it might have the desire and the capacity to become a butterfly, but would be utterly unable to do so, because it failed to heed the law of secrecy. To lose the personality, secrecy is necessary. The change would be too great for the prying, doubting Thomas to participate in the glory of it. "See that ye tell no man" wraps a cloak about the one who suddenly begins the process of ASSUMPTION, just as the cocoon is built around the grub that is to become the butterfly. Later, that which acts as a cloak of protection becomes a hindrance and is cast off. The scaffolding is torn down finally, in order that the perfect structure can be seen. The secrecy gives up its perfect manifestation, then man may say, "Go and show John." The change that is made between the grub and the butterfly is tremendous, but it is nothing as compared to the change that takes place in the one who evolves from the "John Smith" personality (the worm of the dust) into the Son of the Living God. What was impossible to "John Smith" is divinely natural to the New Idea.

## April 15th

### Joseph Murphy

Riches are of the mind. Let us suppose for a moment that a physician's diploma was stolen together with his office equipment. I am sure you would agree that his wealth was in his mind. He could still carry on, diagnose disease, prescribe, operate, and lecture on Materia medica. Only his symbols were stolen; he could always get additional supplies. His riches were in his mental capacity, knowledge to help others, and his ability to contribute to humanity in general. You will always be wealthy when you have an intense desire to contribute to the good of mankind. Your urge for service — i.e., to give of your talents to the world — will always find a response in the heart of the universe.

## April 16th

James Allen

A man may be honest in certain directions, yet suffer privations. A man may be dishonest in certain directions, yet acquire wealth. But the conclusion usually formed that the one man fails because of his particular honesty, and that the other prospers because of his particular dishonesty, is the result of a superficial judgment, which assumes that the dishonest man is almost totally corrupt, and honest man almost entirely virtuous. In the light of a deeper knowledge and wider experience, such judgment is found to be erroneous. The dishonest man may have some admirable virtues which the other does not possess; and the honest man obnoxious vices which are absent in the other. The honest man reaps the good results of his honest thoughts and acts; he also brings upon himself the sufferings which his vices produce. The dishonest man likewise garners his own suffering and happiness.

## April 17th

Ernest Holmes

Learn to see God in all manifestation, in all people, through all events. The ordinary person sees only the lump of matter. Not so with the awakened soul. He sees in all things the Divine Mind at work molding out into expression what it feels itself to be of life, of color, of form and beauty. There are some illusioned ones who claim that what we see is all false, and that the so-called material universe is an unreality. What a mistake! What we see is the body of God, full, free, complete, whole.

## April 18th

Uriel Buchanan

To live in sympathy with nature's moods and in harmony with her changeless laws will lead to the unfoldment of all that is great and good. The beautiful earth and radiant heavens will inspire the mind with visions of hidden truths. An unbroken affinity with nature will keep aglow the fire of enthusiasm in the human heart and give renewed courage for lofty endeavor. There is a force in nature which awakens in man a feeling of kinship with the Infinite. Unless the finer sensibilities are dead man yearns for occasional solitude and for the renewal of strength which comes from the hidden life of nature. In the midst of native forests or mountains, surrounded by all that is wild and natural, man feels an exhilaration and freedom which gives renewed life. The trees and the waving grass, the rocks and rills, the birds and wild flowers, the earth and sky and all visible things unite in a living picture that is eloquent with love. And giving to nature our love in return, we may draw nearer in consciousness to the source of being and hold communion with the Infinite Mind.

## April 19th

### Venice J. Bloodworth

I had studied it and concentrated on the creative power of thought and knew it intellectually, but not until my emotional center was brought into play did I made any progress. When my subconscious mind grasped the import of my thoughts it then set about to help me. It was not all plain sailing then, but I was fortified with the wisdom to understand why certain things happened. With understanding came the courage to go right along. I saw the light ahead and I knew I would reach it, because my arrival depended absolutely on myself. The glory of that moment will never leave me. My future depended on the use I made of my own indwelling power. I was the master of my fate, the captain of my soul. There was no real evil to beset me, and God was a just, loving Father who had placed at my disposal His boundless, limitless good, and all I had to do was to set aside all limitations, decide what I wanted, and think it into being. I found that we must build our consciousness or faith step by step. When we make certain impressions on our subconscious mind and live for years by those impressions we cannot expect to destroy them in a few days. We must patiently substitute constructive, loving, harmonious thoughts for destructive, critical ones. The more you realize your freedom, the happier you become. Faith, joy, health, contentment, you just bubble over with these wonderful attributes and they attract the best people and environment. I do not claim that it is easy to change our habits of thought and action, and it is harder still to disregard race thought and the evidence of the five senses, but I say emphatically that it can be done by anyone who will systematically and patiently keep on. It takes courage, determination, patience, loving kindness, and careful attention as to thought and motive. It is worth every effort for the REWARD IS SO GREAT.

## April 20th

Orison Swett Marden

Prosperity flows only through channels that are wide open to receive it. It does not flow through channels pinched by the poverty thought, by discouragement, doubt, or fear, or by a strangling narrow-visioned policy. A generous expenditure is often the wisest economy, the only thing that brings a generous success. If a great manufacturer like Henry Ford, a great merchant like John Wanamaker, a big railroad manager, or other business man, should lose his broad vision and wide outlook; should begin to skimp on necessary output; should substitute inferior goods and men and service for the best; should reverse his policy, changing from a broad, generous one to a narrow, stingy one, he would soon find his business dwindling away to nothing. There is no changing the principle of the law of supply. Whatever your business, your profession or occupation, or your circumstances, your mental attitude will determine your success or failure. A pinched mind means a pinched supply. It means that you try to tap the great fountainhead of supply with a gimlet and then expect to get an abundant supply. That is impossible. Your mental attitude gauges the How of your supply.

## April 21st

Ernest Holmes

Thought can attract to us only that which we first mentally embody. We cannot attract to ourselves that which we are not. We can attract in the outer only that which we have first completely mentally embodied within, that which has become a part of our mental make-up, a part of our inner understanding. A man going into business will attract to himself that which he thinks about the most. If he is a barber he will attract people who want to be shaved or have their hair cut. If he sells shoes he will attract people who want to buy shoes. So it is with everything; we will not only do this, but we will also attract as much of anything as we mentally embody. This is apt to be overlooked in the study of metaphysics. It is not enough to say that we attract what we think; we become what we think, and what we become we will attract.

## April 22nd

Christian Larson

The principal reason why a man who is down, remains there, and continues to appear as ordinary as his environment, is because he permits his mind to be impressed with everything that his environment may suggest. His thoughts are therefore the reflections of his surroundings, and he is like his thoughts. Therefore, the man who would become different from his environment must learn the art of original thinking, and must enter the attitude of self-supremacy. The principal reason why a man is underpaid is because he does not value himself, and therefore hides behind personal inferiority the greater part of his ability. Another reason is because he works only for the wages that are coming to himself. He refuses to do more than is absolutely necessary, lest someone might be benefited. This attitude produces the cramped condition, which in turn reacts upon the purse. The man who is afraid to do too much, usually fails to do enough; at any rate, he produces that impression, and his recompense is lowered accordingly. On the other hand, the man who does his best at all times, regardless of the scale of wages, not only produces an excellent impression everywhere, but makes those in authority feel that he wants the enterprise to succeed. He is therefore better paid, because such men are valuable. They are wanted everywhere, not because they do more than they are paid for, but because they are a living power for success wherever they are called upon to act. The spirit of success breeds success; and the man who takes a living interest in the enterprise for which he works, even doing more than he is expected to do when the occasion demands, is creating the spirit of success, and will soon share in the greater success that follows.

## April 23rd

### Emmet Fox

Life is a reflex of mental states. As far as you are concerned, the character that things will bear will be the character that you first impress upon them. Bless a thing and it will bless you. Curse it and it will curse you. If you put your condemnation upon anything in life, it will hit back at you and hurt you. If you bless any situation, it has no power to hurt you, and even if it is troublesome for a time it will gradually fade out — if you sincerely bless it. We are told, you remember, that whatever name Adam gave to an animal — that was its name; and of course you know that the name of a thing means its character. Adam said to one animal, "You are a tiger, ferocious," and so it was. To another, he said, "You are a gazelle, gentle and kind," and so it was. Now, Adam is Everyman, and until we learn to give good names, to "christen" everything, we shall have enemies of various kinds to deal with. Bless your body. If there is anything wrong with a particular organ, bless that organ. (Of course, you must bless the organ and not the disease.) Bless your home. Bless your business. Bless your associates. Turn any seeming enemies into friends by blessing them. Bless the climate. Bless the town, and the state, and the country. Bless a thing and it will bless you.

## April 24th

Genevieve Behrend

Your desire to be your best has expanded your faith into the faith of the Universe which knows no failure, and has brought you into conscious realization that you are not a victim of the universe, but a part of it. Consequently you are able to recognize that there is that within yourself which is able to make conscious contact with the Universal Law, and enables you to press all the particular laws of Nature, whether visible or invisible, into serving your particular demand or desire. Thereby you find yourself Master, not a slave, of any situation. Troward tells us that this Mastering is to be "accomplished by knowledge, and the only knowledge which will afford this purpose in all its measureless immensity is the knowledge of the personal element in universal spirit," and its reciprocity to our own personality. In other words, the words you think, the personality you feel yourself to be, are all reproductions in miniature of God, "or specialized universal spirit." All your word-thoughts were God word-forms before they were yours. The words you use are the instruments — channels — through which the creative energy takes form. Naturally, this sensitive Creative Power can only reproduce in accordance with the instrument through which it passes. All disappointments and failures are the result of endeavoring to think one thing and produce another. This is just as impossible as it would be for an electric fan to be used for lighting purposes, or for water to flow through a crooked pipe in a straight line. The water must take the shape of the pipe through which it flows. Even more truly this sensitive, invisible Substance must reproduce outwardly the shape of the thought-word through which it passes. This is the law of its Nature; therefore, it logically follows, "As a man thinketh, so is he." Hence, when your thought or word-form is in correspondence with the Eternal constructive and forward movement of the Universal Law, then your mind is the mirror in which the Infinite Power and Intelligence of the Universe sees itself reproduced, and your individual life becomes one of harmony.

## April 25th

### Ernest Holmes

We should speak right out into mind all that we desire, and believe that it will be done unto us. Never take the time to listen to those who doubt. We observe that their philosophy has done but little to save the world or themselves. here again let the dead bury the dead and see to it that you maintain in your own thought what you want, letting go of all else. Think only what you want to happen and never let yourself get mentally lazy and sluggish taking on the suggestions of poverty and limitation. See yourself as being in the position that you desire, mentally dwell upon it and then speak with perfect assurance that it is done; and then forget it and trust in the law. This will answer all needs. If you want to do this for someone else, all that you will need to do is to think of them and go through the same process of mind action. You will be sending out the truth for them, and mind being always active will not contradict what you have said. Remember that you cannot hope to get results unless you keep but the one idea and do not mix thoughts in your mind. All is yours, but you must take it. The taking is always a mental process; it is believing absolutely. This is divine principle.

## April 26th

### William Walker Atkinson

The confident, fearless, expectant, "I Can and I Will" man is a mighty magnet. He attracts to himself just what is needed for his success. Things seem to come his way, and people say he is "lucky." Nonsense! "Luck" has nothing to do with it. It's all in the Mental Attitude. And the Mental Attitude of the "I Can't" or the "I'm Afraid" man also determines his measure of success. There's no mystery whatsoever about it. You have but to look about you to realize the truth of what I have said. Did you ever know a successful man who did not have the "I Can and I will" thought strong within him? Why, he will walk all around the "I Can't" man, who has perhaps even more ability. The first mental attitude brought to the surface latent qualities, as well as attracted help from outside; whilst the second mental attitude not only attracted "I Can't" people and things, but also kept the man's own powers from manifesting themselves. I have demonstrated the correctness of these views, and so have many others, and the number of people who know these things is growing every day. Don't waste your Thought-Force, but use it to advantage. Stop attracting to yourself failure, unhappiness, inharmony, sorrow — begin now and send out a current of bright, positive, happy thought. Let your prevailing thought be "I Can and I Will;" think "I Can and I Will;" dream "I Can and I Will;" say "I Can and I Will;" and act "I Can and I Will". Live on the "I Can and I and Will" plane, and before you are aware of it, you will feel the new vibrations manifesting themselves in action; will see them bring results; will be conscious of the new point of view; will realize that your own is coming to you. You will feel better, act better, see better, BE better in every way, after you join the "I Can and I Will" brigade.

## April 27th

### Charles Fillmore

First of all, remember that prosperity does not depend upon condition or environment wholly. Poverty is a condition brought about by certain ideas ruling in consciousness. Change those ideas, and the condition changes in spite of environment. Those who come suddenly into riches without the consciousness of riches as a balance-wheel, soon part with their money. Those who are born and bred to riches usually have plenty, though they never make an effort to earn a dollar themselves. This is because the idea of plenty is so interwoven in their thought-atmosphere that it is part of their very lives. They have no concept of a condition where the necessities of life are lacking. Like Queen Elizabeth who, when told that the poor had no bread, said, "Let them eat cake," these children of luxurious ideas give no place in their thought to the poverty possibility. And it is woe unto them if they through sympathy or study enter into the contemplation of a condition where there is lack. They invariably reap the result in a slipping away of their financial resources.

## April 28th

Jeanie P. Owens

We can use this power of Thought for either good or ill, just as one man may throw himself in front of a railway engine and let it crush him, while another uses its power to convey him to where he wants to go. And one thing or another we must do. As thoughts are continually passing through our minds, so are they continually working for our weal or woe. Each day that passes fixes our minds more firmly on lines of thought that will ultimately lead us either into the glorious liberty of the sons of God or into the bondage of darkness and ignorance. The power within us manifests itself by its effects on both our physical and spiritual conditions, on both our bodies and souls. It may, perhaps, be a new idea to some of you that what we think has any real or lasting effect on our physical bodies. Nevertheless it is a scientific fact. Our bodies can be poisoned by thought. I mean literally poisoned, just as surely, if not as quickly, as if by anything we can eat or drink.

## April 29th

Ernest Holmes

Always remember that Spirit makes things out of itself; it manifests in the visible world by becoming the thing that it wills to become. In the world of the individual the same process takes place. It is given to man to use creative power, but with the using of this power comes the necessity of using it as it is made to be used. If God makes things out of His thought before they come into manifestation, then we must use the same method. You can attract only that which you first mentally become and feel yourself to be in reality, without any doubting. A steady stream of consciousness going out into creative mind will attract a steady manifestation of conditions; a fluctuating stream of consciousness will attract the corresponding manifestation or condition in your life. We must be consistent in our attitude of mind, never wavering.

## April 30th

Charles Wesley Kyle

The supreme lesson of life is that of self-realization. You are living in a world of magic. You have more power within you than that ever recorded of any genii of whom you have ever read or dreamed. Wake up! Learn who you are before you condemn yourself to a further life of inaction and inefficiency. To come to recognize yourself is the best elixir of life you will ever know. It will take a psychological operation to rid you of your self-imposed limitations. Well, here it is. Words have a magic power. The greatest event in all the record that infinite intelligence has made, was manifest by the power of the Word. "In the beginning was the Word and the Word was with God and the Word was God." What is the meaning of that? It means that God pictured in Mind all that is, and then spoke it into actuality, creating man in His own image, an individualized center of His every attribute — consciousness, creative power and love. Did you never pause to think that man is the only instrument God has fashioned through which His word may be most fitly spoken? The man who has not come to realize this truth is apt to find that most of the paths of life lead down to the bottom of the hill, where those who have taken them lie bound by their own thoughts of limitation, which are more powerful to imprison than those made of steel. If you are there, awake and burst your bonds! Stand forth free and rejoice in your strength, for you are the ruling Prince in the House of the King of Kings. To come to recognize yourself is to experience the greatest event you will ever know. Though you may be presented at court and dine with the king, that event will be as nothing of importance to you beside it; though the king should bestow all honors upon you within his power, they will prove inconsequential, compared to the wonderful honors you will find awaiting you, when you come to know yourself.

# May

## May 1st

R. C. Douglass

Not only are my thoughts expressed in physical conditions, but my mental state may, and does express itself in my environment, so that I AM always environed by myself. My world as well as my body is the out-picturing of my mind; therefore I need not complain of either. Whether I suffer, then, in body, mind or estate, my remedy is within; as the causes of my sufferings are all to be found there. If my bodily conditions do not suit me, I may go to work and change them; by correcting my thought I shall correct my body; by reforming my mind I shall reform my body, and this is my healing. If my environing world does not please me, I may change it by reforming myself. When I have redeemed and regenerated my thought I shall have redeemed my body. As I have one sure remedy for my suffering body, so I have one sure remedy for my offending world. When I have transformed myself, my world will be transformed to me — I shall have a "new heaven and a new earth," for the world is to me according to my thought of it. This thought' the Great Metaphysician expressed in a very striking metaphor: " Why beholdest thou the mote that is in thy brother's eye, and considerest not the beam that is in thine own eye?" Thy " brother " is a factor in thy environment. How would this great philosopher have thee proceed to reform thy brother? Simply by reforming thyself, because "thy neighbor is thyself," as the wise ones say, and thy environment is thyself also. Listen to his remedy: "Thou hypocrite! first cast the beam out of thine own eye; then shalt thou see clearly to cast the mote out of thy brother's eye." Thus the fault was in me, while I thought it was in my brother.

## May 2nd

Eugene Del Mar

When man dares to believe himself a creator, the Law will accept him at his higher estimation, and respond accordingly. When man claims boldly his divine inheritance, he will enter into its possession. When man divests himself of inherited and acquired limitations, knows himself to be divine, and places himself in harmony with the Law, all that he shall desire will be his, and both the visible and invisible will pay tribute to their lord and master.

## May 3rd

### Ernest Holmes

When we realize that life is not fundamentally physical, but mental and spiritual, it will not be hard for us to see that by a certain mental and spiritual process we can demonstrate what we want. We are not dealing with conditions but with causes. Causes originate only from the unseen side of life. This is not strange as the same might be said of electricity, or even of life itself. We do not see life, we only see what it does. This we call a condition. Of itself it is simply an effect. We are living in the outer world of effects and in the inner world of causes. These causes we set in motion by our thought, and, through the power inherent within the cause, expresses the thought as a condition. It follows that the cause must be equal to the effect and that the effect always evaluates with the cause held in mind. Everything comes from One Substance, and our thought qualifies that Substance and determines what is to take place in our life.

## May 4th

### William Walker Atkinson

The attraction of THE ABSOLUTE is drawing man upward, and the vibratory force of the Primal Impulse has not yet exhausted itself. The time of evolutionary development has come when man can help himself. The man who understands the Law can accomplish wonders by means of the development of the powers of the mind; whilst the man who turns his back upon the truth will suffer from his lack of knowledge of the Law. He who understands the laws of his mental being, develops his latent powers and uses them intelligently. He does not despise his Passive mental functions, but makes good use of them also, charges them with the duties for which they are best fitted, and is able to obtain wonderful results from their work, having mastered them and trained them to do the bidding of the Higher Self. When they fail to do their work properly he regulates them, and his knowledge prevents him from meddling with them unintelligently, and thereby doing himself harm. He develops the faculties and powers latent within him and learns how to manifest them along the line of Active mentation as well as Passive. He knows that the real man within him is the master to whom both Active and Passive functions are but tools. He has banished Fear, and enjoys Freedom. He has found himself. HE HAS LEARNED THE SECRET OF THE I AM.

## May 5th

### Henry Thomas Hamblin

One who realizes and really believes that there is abundance and plenty for him, puts into operation a powerful law which will surely bring opportunity to him, sooner or later. Many, however, ruin their hopes by not knowing that for a time they must live a kind of double life They must be opulent in consciousness, but careful and thrifty in actual practice. The time will come when their means will largely increase, then, if they are wise they will live on part of their income, instead of living up to it. This will give them a wide margin for charitable purposes, for the taking up of further opportunities and for extensions. Many business men have to let golden opportunities pass, simply because they have saved little or nothing, owing to lavish private expenditure, or they have to let other people in to share their schemes who, in addition to taking a large share of the profits, may prove a serious handicap and hindrance in other ways. While in its essence, the Source of Supply is spiritual, it comes to us through material channels, and, in order to have a share in it, it is necessary to earn it. We have to give something in exchange for what we draw from life in the way of supply. We must give in order to receive, and what we give must be something that the world wants or needs. The secret of supply is, then, to realize that there is unlimited abundance and to live in the consciousness of it, as completely as though no material channels existed, but at the same time, to work as zealously and be as careful as though there were no such thing as spiritual supply. At the same time we must give the world something that it wants, or otherwise serve in some useful capacity, exercising honesty, probity and justice in all our affairs. It is folly to expect abundance to drop ready-made in our lap; it must be earned by intelligent and faithful service.

## May 6th

### Christian Larson

The possibilities of constructive and persistent desire are simply amazing. We have hardly begun to use this marvelous thing. Many have been afraid of it; multitudes have misused it; and as a race we have had too many desires that were either useless or detrimental. Too many desires have drawn the mind out into the smallness of material existence, instead of up into the immensity of the great life. That is why desire has been looked upon with suspicion. But once we begin to use this mighty force for constructive purposes only, and to the full, we shall appreciate what a marvel it is. We shall then be ready to say that desire, when deep, intensive and persistent, can get us practically anything. Another startling statement, but actually true; and the reason is that the creative power within can act with greater capacity through desire than through any other channel. And, to repeat, for emphasis, this power is able to do anything — when a large enough outlet is provided. The creative power of the mind will work for that which we look forward to; and here we discover why the great law determines what the future is to be. We cannot predict the future because it has not been made; we are making our own future day by day; but we can look forward to the future we would like to have — or any kind of a future — be it a poor one or a great one; and what we look forward to, that is what the creative power within will work for and build for — gradually causing such a future to come to pass. These things being true, we should never accept nor believe adverse predictions — nor anything detrimental regarding the future. If we deeply believe that dark days are coming, the creative power within will create dark days for us. If we are looking forward to troubled times, this same power will produce troubled conditions in our own lives. That power always produces for us what we continue to keep in mind. We should keep in mind the very best, therefore and look forward to the most perfect, the most ideal and the most wonderful future that we can possibly vision; and that is what will be worked out for us from within as the months and the years pass.

## May 7th

### Ernest Holmes

What if at times we attract something that we do not want? What about all the things that we have already attracted into our lives? Must we still suffer until the last farthing be paid? Are we bound by Karma? Yes, in a certain degree we are bound by what we have done; it is impossible to set law in motion and not have it produce. What we sow we must also reap, of that there is no doubt; but here is something to think about; the Bible also says that if a man repents his "sins are blotted out, and remembered no more forever." Here we have two statements which at first seem not to agree. The first says that we must suffer from what we have done, and the second that under certain conditions we will not have to suffer. What are those conditions? A changed attitude toward the Law. It means that we must stop thinking and acting in the wrong way. When we do this we are taken out of the old order and established in the new. Someone will say: If that is true what about the law of cause and effect? Is that broken? No, it is this way: The law is not broken, it would still work out if we continued to use it in the wrong way; but when we reverse the cause, that is, think and act in a different way, then we have changed the flow of the Law. It is still the same Law but we have changed its flow, so that, instead of limiting us and punishing us, it frees and blesses. It is still the law but we have changed our attitude toward it. We might throw a ball at the window, and if nothing stopped it, it would break the glass. Here is law in motion. But if someone catches the ball before it reaches the window, the glass will not be broken. Neither the glass nor the law will be broken. The flow of law will be changed, that is all.

## May 8th

Orison Swett Marden

Every time you give way to discouragement, every time you are blue, you are going backward, your destructive thoughts are tearing down what you have been trying to build. One fit of discouragement, visualizing failure or poverty-stricken conditions, will rapidly destroy the result of much triumphant thought building. Your creative forces will harmonize with your thoughts, your emotions and moods; they will create in sympathy with them. Saturate your mind with hope, the expectation of better things, with the belief that your dreams are coming true. Be convinced that you are going to win out; let your mind rest with success thoughts. Don't let the enemies of your success and happiness dominate in your mind or they will bring to you the condition that they represent. Destroy the thoughts, and emotions and convictions which tend to destroy your hope, your ambitions, to tear down the results of your past building. If you don't they will create more failure, more poverty. If you want to realize success, think creative, successful conditions.

## May 9th

Charles F. Haanel

The "I" of you is not the physical body; that is simply an instrument which the "I" uses to carry out its purposes; the "I" cannot be the Mind, for the mind is simply another instrument which the "I" uses with which to think, reason, and plan. The "I" must be something which controls and directs both the body and the mind; something which determines what they shall do and how they shall act. When you come into a realization of the true nature of this "I", you will enjoy a sense of power which you have never before known. Your personality is made up of countless individual characteristics, peculiarities, habits, and traits of character; these are the result of your former method of thinking, but they have nothing to do with the real "I." When you say "I think" the "I" tells the mind what it shall think; when you say "I go" the "I" tells the physical body where it shall go; the real nature of this "I" is spiritual, and is the source of the real power which comes to men and women when they come into a realization of their true nature. The greatest and most marvelous power which this "I" has been given is the power to think, but few people know how to think constructively, or correctly, consequently they achieve only indifferent results. Most people allow their thoughts to dwell on selfish purposes, the inevitable result of an infantile mind. When a mind becomes mature, it understands that the germ of defeat is in every selfish thought. The trained mind knows that every transaction must benefit every person who is in any way connected with the transaction, and any attempt to profit by the weakness, ignorance or necessity of another will inevitably operate to his disadvantage.

## May 10th

### Charles Fillmore

This inexhaustible mind substance is available at all times and in all places to those who have learned to lay hold of it in consciousness. The simplest, shortest, and most direct way of doing this was explained when Jesus said, "Whosoever ... shall not doubt in his heart, but shall believe that what he saith cometh to pass, he shall have it." When we know that certain potent ideas exist in the invisible mind expressions, named by science both "ether" and "space" and that we have been provided with the mind to lay hold of them, it is easy to put the law into action through thought and word and deed. "There is a tide in the affairs of men, Which, taken at the flood, leads on to fortune," said Shakespeare. That flood tide awaits us in the cosmic spaces, the paradise of God. The spiritual substance from which comes all visible wealth is never depleted. It is right with you all the time and responds to your faith in it and your demands on it. It is not affected by our ignorant talk of hard times, though we are affected because our thoughts and words govern our demonstration. The unfailing resource is always ready to give. It has no choice in the matter; it must give, for that is its nature. Pour your living words of faith into the omnipresent substance, and you will be prospered though all the banks in the world close their doors. Turn the great energy of your thinking toward "plenty" ideas, and you will have plenty regardless of what men about you are saying or doing.

### May 11th

Ernest Holmes

Some people visualize everything that they think of and many think that it is impossible to make a demonstration unless they possess the power to visualize. This is not the case. While a certain amount of vision is necessary, on the other hand it must be remembered that we are dealing with a power that is like the soil of the ground, which will produce the plant when we plant seed. It does not matter if we have never before seen a plant like the one that is to be made for us. Our thought is the seed and mind is the soil. We are always planting and harvesting. All that we need to do is to plant only that which we want to harvest. This is not difficult to understand. We cannot think poverty and at the same time demonstrate plenty. If a person wants to visualize let him do so, and if he sees himself in full possession of his desire and knows that he is receiving, he will make his demonstration. If, on the other hand, he does not visualize, then let him simply state what he wants and absolutely believe that he has it and the result will always be the same. Remember that you are always dealing with law and that this is the only way that anything could come into existence. Don't argue over it. That means that you have not as yet become convinced of the truth or you would not argue. Be convinced and rest in peace.

### May 12th

Venice J. Bloodworth

Whenever you find anything bothering you, start some sort of affirmation and hang on to it; do not give worry a chance; resolutely refuse to entertain any kind of negative thought. "The Lord is my Shepherd, I shall not want" helped me to get rid of financial worry and "There shall no evil befall thee, and neither shall any plague come nigh thy tent" was also comforting; read the 91st Psalm as many times as you can —

you could not read it too many times — for in it you find a promise of deliverance from every evil, and even the fears of evil things. When you retire at night always repeat the affirmation, "I AM healthy, strong, young, powerful, loving, harmonious, successful and happy." When you repeat this affirmation, you are impressing your subconscious mind with just those qualities as a basis for the new character you are building, and this character will attract to itself conditions that correspond to it in kind and quality; you remember that the subconscious mind does not argue or prove, but goes to work and brings about conditions that the conscious mind believes to be true. "If you believe it, it is so," and if you fear any condition, fear being a very strong thought, you will be able to say with Job: "The thing I feared has come upon me."

## May 13th

Uriel Buchanan

Each has latent within him the power to determine whether his life shall be eventful or purposeless, whether he shall have bright and beautiful environments and all that the aspiring mind desires, or only the unwholesome, degrading surroundings created by thoughts of fear and despair. The universe is filled with all that is good and beautiful, all that is needful to satisfy man's highest hopes, his fondest dreams and yearnings. Every possible thing that ever was or shall be already exists in potentiality in the great storehouse of the universe, awaiting the magic touch of human thought to bring it forth into the world of form. Every flight of genius, every great attainment in all the varied realms of human endeavor, every grand achievement made through the historic ages, are but prophecies of the more wonderful power concealed in the heart of the race, awaiting the command of a masterful mind to come forth as a living token and proof of man's divinity.

## May 14th

Mrs. Evelyn Lowes Wicker

Habit Mind. If you have a habit of any kind that you wish to destroy, you cannot destroy it easily by thinking about that habit and wishing that you could get rid of it. Wishing is not going to help you very much, except to make you unhappy. Instead of wishing, affirm to yourself the thing that you want to be, and absolutely refuse to voice now and forevermore the fact that you ever had such a habit. Not only is it not wise to admit that you have a bad habit, but it is wisdom to never refer to it, unless you are positively sure that you have completely overcome it by the law of substitution. Mind has the power to command energy to do anything that you desire to have done. The subconscious mental impression always impresses energy with its predominant impression. If that predominant impression is not good, you can change the predominant mental impression by constant affirmation. It is possible to completely rebuild your subconscious mind by daily affirming the thing you want to be. Never at any time use a system of denial. When you deny a thing you bring back the picture by repeating the words. Every word that we speak is a mental picture. If we use destructive words and are trying to get rid of a destructive condition, we are going a long way round in order to bring results. There is a shortcut way. The quickest method is to affirm in constructive words the condition you wish developed.

## May 15th

Ernest Holmes

Now, the reason why so few people get from the metaphysical principle what there is in it is because, and it is a tragedy too, and it is a shame, so few people compared with the number of people there are in the world will take the time to learn to investigate and to understand. Ordinary people are so bound up with their trouble and fears and ignorance, they will not give the time it takes to change their thought. It is only normal and natural from the human standpoint that it should be so. Until your thought is changed your conditions never will be, your body never will be. We are sick because in our consciousness there is an image of disease. We will be sick just as long as that image exists. We are poor because of the same reason. There is not any question about it whatever, not the slightest. We externalize every concept and every consciousness and every state of mind. Now, it depends upon the individuals who are being helped just as much as it does the ones who are helping. For instance, in the infinity of Mind, which is the principle of all metaphysics and of all life, there is nothing but Mind and that which Mind does; That is all there is in the universe. That is all there ever was or ever will be. This Mind is latent. It just waits to be acted upon. And your thought and mind act upon Universal Mind. Your thought and my thought is a law unto ourselves. It is just as much a law unto your life and mine as God's law is in the universe. There is no difference. It is absolute, and moreover all there is in your life and mine is our thought, or our word, or its activity. Nothing can hinder it from manifesting. So receptive, so plastic, so quick to take an impression is this mentality which surrounds us that it receives the impress of our slightest thought.

## May 16th

### Prentice Mulford

All things seen of physical sense have their correspondences of spiritual elements. These (the spiritual) constitute their real power. The sun has its spirit which affects us and our earth. There is a sun unseen of the physical eye and unfelt of physical sense which bears the same relation to the sun we see that our spirit bears to our physical body. The physical sun affects our physical body. But the spiritual sun, or the spirit of the sun affects our spiritual being in proportion as that being is developed to receive of that peculiar power. If you can receive this truth, or even but entertain it, you will receive from the source we speak of a power greater than can come to those whose belief is limited to the idea that the sun or any other thing in the material world has only those elements which are seen and felt of physical sense. Those who can believe only in material things must physically decay, because through such belief they attract to themselves only of material element. There are many more "materialists" than those who profess themselves such as atheists or "infidels." Practical "materialists" often belong to the church, profess religion, live in strict conformity to all religious observance, yet really believe in nothing but the material. This they cannot help. Their material natures master them. Their bodies will decay and die. Their spirits in time will use other bodies. Their former earth life will be a blank to them. They will gain in spiritualization during their next physical life, as they have really gained during all previous physical lives. When through successive reimbodiments that gain is sufficient to have taught them the laws of their spiritual beings they will be freed from all ills now affecting the physical being. Neither fire, nor water, nor disease, nor violence can hurt them. They will not taste of death. The truth will make them free. A few such lives have been recorded in the Bible. There is reason for the belief that there were more. This is the ultimate of all human life as our planet spiritualizes.

## May 17th

### Robert Collier

So let us make use of this dynamo, which is you. What is going to start it working? Your Faith, the faith that is begotten of understanding. Faith is the impulsion of this power within. Faith is the confidence, the assurance, the enforcing truth, the knowing that the right idea of life will bring you into the reality of existence and the manifestation of the All power. All cause is in Mind — and Mind is everywhere. All the knowledge there is, all the power there is, is all about you — no matter where you may be. Your Mind is part of it. You have access to it. If you fail to avail yourself of it, you have no one to blame but yourself. For as the drop of water in the ocean shares in all the properties of the rest of the ocean water, so you share in that all-power, all wisdom of Mind. If you have been sick and ailing, if poverty and hardship have been your lot, don't blame it on "fate." Blame yourself. "Yours is the earth and everything that's in it." But you've got to take it. The Creative Force is there — but you must use it. It h round about you like the air you breathe.

You don't expect others to do your breathing for you. Neither can you expect them to use the Creative Force for you. Universal Intelligence is not only the mind of the Creator of the universe, but it is also the mind of MAN, Your intelligence, your mind. "Let this mind be in you, which was also in Christ Jesus." So start today by knowing that you can do anything you wish to do, have anything you wish to have, be anything you wish to be. The rest will follow. "Ye shall ask what ye will and it shall be done unto you."

## May 18th

### Wallace Wattles

The more clear and definite you make your picture then, and the more you dwell upon it, bringing out all its delightful details, the stronger your desire will be. And the stronger your desire, the easier it will be to hold your mind fixed upon the picture of what you want. Something more is necessary, however, than merely to see the picture clearly. If that is all you do, you are only a dreamer, and will have little or no power for accomplishment. Behind your clear vision must be the purpose to realize it, to bring it out in tangible expression. And behind this purpose must be an invincible and unwavering FAITH that the thing is already yours, that it is "at hand" and you have only to take possession of it. Live in the new house, mentally, until it takes form around you physically. In the mental realm, enter at once into full enjoyment of the things you want. "Whatsoever things ye ask for when ye pray, believe that ye receive them, and ye shall have them," said Jesus. See the things you want as if they were actually around you all the time. See yourself as owning and using them. Make use of them in imagination just as you will use them when they are your tangible possessions. Dwell upon your mental picture until it is clear and distinct, and then take the mental attitude of ownership toward everything in that picture. Take possession of it, in mind, in the full faith that it is actually yours. Hold to this mental ownership. Do not waiver for an instant in the faith that it is real. And remember what was said in a proceeding chapter about gratitude: Be as thankful for it all the time as you expect to be when it has taken form. The person who can sincerely thank God for the things which as yet he owns only in imagination has real faith. He will get rich. He will cause the creation of whatever he wants.

## May 19th

### Ernest Holmes

Since all is Mind and Mind returns to the thinker of thought objectified, what we think, what we hold within ourselves as a mental attitude, becomes the mental equivalent of creative spirit or causation, and the objective life or external result, our environment in the without. Our way of thinking and believing then is the sole medium between causation and its flow through us into manifestation of our affairs. We believe that medium is our thought processes, conscious and unconscious. There are two ways whereby the individual builds up a subjective consciousness. Your subjective consciousness is not a mind separated from you; it is not another mind in you. Subjective consciousness is simply the attraction of thought in the past gathered around you. It is your power of attraction. You can see how that would be. Since there is but one, that which we call subjective mind, which is a reality, and what we are depends largely upon the subjective state of our thinking. Instead of saying objective mind, we should say subjective state of thought. These thoughts which we have created in the past and which still are around us, and the thoughts which we have and still are attracting, this is the medium which we build between Spirit and matter. So what we are and what we shall become depends absolutely upon the state of our subjective thought because that is the power or process within us.

## May 20th

### James Allen

Cease to dwell pessimistically upon the wrongs around you; dwell no more in complaints about, and revolt against, the evil in others, and commence to live free from all wrong and evil yourself. Peace of mind, pure religion, and true reform lie this way. If you would have others true, be true; if you would have the world emancipated from misery and sin, emancipate yourself; if you would have your home and your surroundings happy, be happy. You can transform everything around you if you will transform yourself.

## May 21st

### Joseph Murphy

Whatever thoughts, beliefs, opinions, theories, or dogmas you write, engrave, or impress on your subconscious mind, you shall experience them as the objective manifestation of circumstances, conditions, and events. What you write on the inside, you will experience on the outside. You have two sides to your life, objective and subjective, visible and invisible, thought and its manifestation. Your brain receives your thought, which is the organ of your conscious reasoning mind. When your conscious or objective mind accepts the thought completely, it is sent to the solar plexus, called the brain of your mind, where it becomes flesh and is made manifest in your experience. As previously outlined, your subconscious cannot argue. It acts only from what you write on it. It accepts your verdict or the conclusions of your conscious mind as final. This is why you are always writing on the book of life, because your thoughts become your experiences. The American essayist, Ralph Waldo Emerson said, "Man is what he thinks all day long."

## May 22nd

### Wallace Wattles

When you desire a thing, and your mind and the Mind of things are one, that thing will desire you, and will move toward you. If you desire dollars, and your mind is one with the Mind that pervades dollars and all things else, dollars will be permeated with the desire to come to you, and they will move toward you, impelled by the Eternal Power which makes for more abundant life. To obtain what you want, you only need to establish your own "at-one-ment" with the Mind of things, and they will be drawn toward you. But the primal purpose of the Mind of things is the continuous advancement of ALL into more abundant life; therefore, nothing will be taken away from any man or woman and given to you unless you give to that person more in the way of life than you take away. It will be plainly seen that the Divine Mind cannot be brought into action in the field of purely competitive business. God cannot be divided against Himself. He cannot be made to take from one and give to another. He will not decrease one man's opportunity to advance in life in order to increase another man's opportunity to advance in life. He is no respecter of persons, and has no favorites. He is equally in all, equally for all, and at the service of all alike. To make the "at-one-ment," you must see that your business gives to all who deal with you a full equivalent in life for the money value of what you take from them.

## May 23rd

Ernest Holmes

There is only one fundamental formula, one fundamental proposition, one fundamental principle, and we must always be reiterating the same thing. We do not come to a metaphysical lecture to hear something new. There is nothing new to hear. We get together to discuss the same principle, to see if we can draw something more from it which will enable us to a greater degree to use that principle. That principle itself is simplicity, yet it is infinite. It is Infinite Mind and infinite manifestation of Mind. It is a spiritual universe governing itself through thought, or the word which first becomes law, which law creates the concept of the word into what we call matter. The threefold universe of Spirit, which is the word, the creative power, or the result of the material universe in which we live. Our bodies are included in this material universe. Jesus was a great scientific man; and as Thomas Edison was a man who discerns electrical truth about electricity, so Jesus was a man who discerned the truth about spiritual principles more than any other man who ever lived. He proclaimed the eternal reign of law, understanding, absolute, complete, perfect, and he found that law to be operative through his own thought of consciousness and so through the power of his own word.

You and I must cease looking outside ourselves to any person, any place, or to any thing, and we ultimately must at last realize that whatever truth or power we have must flow through us. And when we begin to interpret our own nature, we shall begin to understand God and law and life and not until. We have discovered this in metaphysics, that we live and move and have our being in what we call an infinite Mind, an infinite creative Mind, an infinite receptive Mind, an all-operative Mind, an omnipotent Mind, an all-knowing Mind. And we have learned that that Mind presses against us on all sides. It flows through us. It becomes operative through our thinking. We have learned that the human race, ignorant of the laws of this Mind, ignorant of the power of our own thought, has misused it through that ignorance. We have abused that creative power of thought, and the human race has brought upon itself the thing which was feared, because all thought is law and all law is Mind in action. The word which you speak today is the law which shall govern your life tomorrow as the word which you speak ignorantly or innocently, consciously or unconsciously yesterday is absolutely governing your life today.

## May 24th

### Robert Collier

When you say "I see — I hear — I smell — I touch," it is your conscious mind that is saying this, for it is the force governing the five physical senses. It is the phase of mind with which you feel and reason — the phase of mind with which everyone is familiar. It is the mind with which you do business. It controls, to a great extent, all your voluntary muscles. It discriminates between right and wrong, wise and foolish. It is the generalissimo, in charge of all your mental forces. It can plan ahead — and get things done as it plans. Or it can drift along haphazardly, a creature of impulse, at the mercy of events — a mere bit of flotsam in the current of life. For it is only through your conscious mind that you can reach the subconscious and the Universal Mind. Your conscious mind is the porter at the door, the watchman at the gate. It is to the conscious mind that the subconscious looks for all its impressions. It is on it that the subconscious mind must depend for the teamwork necessary to get successful results. You wouldn't expect much from an army, no matter how fine its soldiers, whose general never planned ahead, who distrusted his own ability and that of his men, and who spent all his time worrying about the enemy instead of planning how he might conquer them. You wouldn't look for good scores from a ball team whose pitcher was at odds with the catcher. In the same way, you can't expect results from the subconscious when your conscious mind is full of fear or worry, or when it does not know what it wants. The one most important province of your conscious mind is to center your thoughts on the thing you want, and to shut the door on every suggestion of fear or worry or disease.

## May 25th

### Prentice Mulford

If you had been born and bred entirely among people who believed that the earth was a flat surface and did not revolve around the sun, you would in the earlier years of your physical growth believe as they did. Exactly in such fashion do you in your earlier years absorb the thought and belief of those nearest you, who think that the body is all there is of them, and judge of everything by its physical interpretation to them. This makes your material mind. The material mind seeing, what seems to it, depth, dissolution and decay in all human organization, and ignorant of the fact that the real self or intelligence has in such seeming death only cast off a worn-out envelope, thinks that decay and death is the ultimate of all humanity. For such reason it cannot avoid a gloom or sadness coming of such error, which now pervades so much of human life at present. One result or reaction from such gloom born of hopelessness is a reckless spirit for getting every possible gratification and pleasure, regardless of right and justice so long as the present body lasts. This is a great mistake. All pleasure so gained cannot be lasting. It brings besides a hundredfold more misery and disappointment. The spiritual mind teaches that pleasure is the great aim of existence. But it points out ways and means for gaining lasting happiness other than those coming of the teaching of the material mind. The spiritual mind, or mind opened to higher and newer forces of life, teaches that there is a law regulating the exercise of every physical sense. When we learn and follow this law, our gratifications and possessions do not prove sources of greater pain than happiness, as they do to so many. By the spiritual mind is meant a clearer mental sight of things and forces existing both in us and the Universe, and of which the race for the most part has been in total ignorance. We have now but a glimpse of these forces, those of some being relatively a little clearer than those of others. But enough has been shown to convince a few that the real and existing causes for humanity's sickness, sorrow and disappointment have not in the past been seen at all. In other words, the race has been as children, fancying that the miller inside was turning the arms of the windmill, because some person had so told them. So taught they would remain in total ignorance that the wind was the motive power. This illustration is not at all an overdrawn picture of the existing ignorance which rejects the idea that thought is an element all about us as plentiful as air, and that as blindly directed by individuals and masses of individuals in the domain of material mind or ignorance, it is turning the windmill's arms, sometimes in one direction, sometimes in another; sometimes with good and sometimes with evil results.

## May 26th

### Uriel Buchanan

Every idle thought should be banished from the mind. The indwelling magnetic will should have absolute control of the mind and body, and in place of disobedience and confusion there should be established rule and order. You should consciously recognize the divinity of every heart beat; you should feel that every respiration is the inbreathing and outbreathing of the life that pervades the universe; you should feel and know that from the food you eat and the water you drink the wise chemist of the body is appropriating and transmuting the proper elements for the renewing and rebuilding of the physical organism in form and quality corresponding to your highest ideal of symmetry and beauty. The man who can master the magnetic force and learn how to use it, may achieve everything that he desires. In order to do this he must have an indomitable will, must persistently think of and yearn for the object desired, and must project the magnetic suggestions of attraction toward the object or wish. To invoke the power desired and to direct the magnetic currents by the will, it is necessary to establish perfect physical repose, to silence the mind's activity and hold yourself receptive to the impressions that come from within. Clothe the images of your subjective thought with the finest essence of your being, and send them out from the inmost center of consciousness with a living power that nothing can check or hinder. To be able to accomplish this you must have fixedness of purpose. Every thought, aspiration, desire and attachment must be so thoroughly centered on the ideal you wish to attain that nothing external can affect you. No obstacle should discourage, and no experience of the outer man or outer world should have power to swerve you from the ascending path that leads to truth.

## May 27th

Ernest Holmes

It is hard to speak forth and let it go away from you. "I will send forth my word and it shall not return to me void." We have got to learn to trust this unseen power. Until we do, we will get no results. In this Mind there is held and flows the consciousness of the human race. Never forget that! It is one of the things that few people understand, that we are surrounded by a universal consciousness which is creative. And do you remember that I said it is receptive and neutral? It holds within itself all the thoughts of everybody, every thought that has been thought always by the human race, and it holds it and executes it. There has been a thought gone forth into the human race that we are lost. It is perhaps one of the strongest thoughts that has ever been created, that we have fallen. That has become a very great mental suggestion operating on what we might term the universal cosmic plane, operating with terrific power through the consciousness of everybody who believes it. We are not talking about God, we are talking about our creative mind. It is a law, that is all. The very fact that it is not limited intelligence is shown in that it will receive both positive and negative impressions. Never get away from the idea that you are surrounded by such a power. It is the principle of demonstration. It knows everything. As we send forth our thought into it, it does it unto us. But that person who does not know how to deal with the metaphysical principle is bound by the law of human ignorance, absolutely bound hand and foot by conditions.

## May 28th

### Venice J. Bloodworth

If a man is in debt he generally concentrates upon it, and not only ties the debt closer to himself but attracts more debt. Thus we use the Creative Principle constructively or destructively. Think about and concentrate upon what you want, NOT on what you do not want; substitute new constructive ideas in place of those old worn-out beliefs; take the load of worry, criticism, hopelessness off your subconscious mind and let your light shine. It is a poor rule that will not work both ways, and if you have not been successful, healthy and happy in the past — just let that dead past bury its dead — turn your face to the sunrise of truth and forge ahead. Nothing can stop you. Thoughts are causes and conditions are effects; change the conditions to suit yourself, and then you no longer have any cause for fear or worry. There is only one principle, and that principle is good — "God is good and good is all —"; therefore good only can have reality or power.

## May 29th

### Charles Fillmore

Charge your mind with statements that express plenty. No particular affirmation will raise anyone from poverty to affluence, yet all affirmations that carry ideas of abundance will lead one into the consciousness that fulfills the law. Deny that lack has any place or reality in your thought or your affairs and affirm plenty as the only appearance. Praise what you have, be it ever so little, and insist that it is constantly growing larger. Daily concentration of mind on Spirit and its attributes will reveal that the elemental forces that make all material things are here in the ether awaiting our recognition and appropriation. It is not necessary to know all the details of the scientific law in order to demonstrate prosperity. Go into the silence daily at a stated time and concentrate on the substance of Spirit prepared for you from the foundation of the world. This opens up a current of thought that will bring prosperity into your affairs. A good thought to hold in this meditation is this: The invisible substance is plastic to my abundant thought, and I AM rich in mind and in manifestation.

## May 30th

### Charles F. Haanel

All power is from within, and is absolutely under your control; it comes through exact knowledge and by the voluntary exercises of exact principles. It should be plain that when you acquire a thorough understanding of this law, and are able to control your thought processes, you can apply it to any condition; in other words, you will have come into conscious cooperation with Omnipotent law which is the fundamental basis of all things. The Universal Mind is the life principle of every atom which is in existence; every atom is continually striving to manifest more life; all are intelligent, and all are seeking to carry out the purpose for which they were created. A majority of mankind lives in the world without; few have found the world within, and yet it is the world within that makes the world without; it is therefore creative and everything which you find in your world without has been created by you in the world within. This system will bring you into a realization of power which will be yours when you understand this relation between the world without and the world within. The world within is the cause, the world without the effect; to change the effect you must change the cause.

## May 31st

Ernest Holmes

Few people indeed in the day in which we live are well poised. Where do we find the man who can live above his surroundings, who in his own thought can dominate all conditions, and in the midst of the crowd keep his own even way, and his own counsel? When we do meet with such a person we will know him; for we shall find on his face the image of perfect peace. We shall detect in his bearing the ease and independence that comes only to the man who has found himself and who is centered not in the outer but in the inner world. Such a character as this has the power to attract to himself all of the best in the world; he is a center toward which all else must gravitate. The atmosphere which he creates and with which he surrounds himself is one of absolute calm and peace. The world at once sees in this man a master, and gladly sits at his feet. And yet this man who has risen above the thought of the world cares not that other people should sit at his feet. He knows that what he has done all may do, and he well knows that all the teaching in the world will not produce another such as he. He knows that it is not from the teaching but from the being that true greatness springs. So this man does not go around teaching or preaching; he simply IS.

# June

## June 1st

### Orison Swett Marden

Emerson says: "Every soul is not only the inlet but may become the outlet of all that is in God." The consciousness of this great truth is the secret of all power. It is the full realization of our connection with Omnipotence, with Omniscience, with the Source of all there is that enables us to use the vast powers that are within us, always at our command, waiting to accomplish our ends. The Creator puts no limit to our supply. There is no limitation of anything we need except in our own consciousness. That is the door, which, according to its quality, shuts us off from, or admits us to, the great storehouse of infinite supply. The pinched, stingy consciousness never gets in touch with this supply. It is the man who has faith in his own power to meet whatever demands life may make upon him, who spends his last dollar fearlessly, because he knows the law of supply and is in touch with a flow of abundance, that gets on and up in the world. But the one who hoards his last dollar in fear and trembling, afraid to let go of it, even though he must go hungry, who always carries in his mind a vivid picture of the wolf at the door, never conquers poverty, because he never gets the prosperity consciousness.

## June 2nd

### Walter C. Lanyon

Come away from the noisy personality who wants to change the "John Smith" and heal him and make him prosper. You are the Son of the Living God, and when you recognize this you are through with the foolish idea of making demonstrations, and you will see the constant out-pouring of the substance of God through the new idea by the ASSUMPTION of the Son. "One in all and All in One." Be still and serenely assume the God-given qualities, and hide them deep in the cocoon of silence. Then will they burst forth as glorious freed expressions. "Be not afraid; it is I" — the very "I" that is able to ASSUME its God inheritance is at this time speaking to you, "Behold, I stand at the door and knock." It is already there, awaiting recognition. It does not need healing, prosperity, being made happy or joyous. It is already these things. Identify yourself with It. "Acquaint now thyself with HIM and be at peace." — "Know ye not that ye are gods?" Do you know it? If so, when will you ASSUME the God-like qualities and see them into manifestation? Be still — build the secret cocoon about you; presently you shall be transformed by the renewing of your mind.

## June 3rd

### Christian Larson

There is magic in the sunshine of the soul; there is a charmed power in the radiant splendor of a beaming countenance. Such a countenance can dispel anything that may threaten to give disappointment or dismay. So remember to be glad and mean it. It is the greatest remedy in the world, and the greatest protector in the world. It can harm nothing for it turns all wrong into right. It is the sunshine from within that causes all darkness to cease to be. It therefore brings good to everybody, and he who is always glad is always adding to the welfare of every member of the race. When fate seems unkind, do not be unkind to yourself by becoming disheartened or dismayed. Instead, rejoice in the great fact that you are greater and stronger than any fate; that you have the power to master your whole life, and determine your destiny according to your own invincible will. Then resolve that you will begin at once to prove that strength, and cause all the elements of fate to come with you, and work with you, in building for that greater future which you have so often longed for in your visions and dreams. Therefore, whatever your fate may be, just be glad. You can change it all. And as you proceed to exercise this divine right, the darkness of today will become the sunshine of tomorrow, and the disappointments of the present will become the pastures green of the future.

## June 4th

### Ernest Holmes

People will often ask, "What is the best method for demonstration?" There is but one answer to that question; the Word is the only possible method of demonstrating anything; the word really felt and embodied in our thought. Then the word becomes flesh and dwells among us and we behold and experience it. We will ask for no other way when we understand this. The person who does not understand these laws will be likely to say that this is presumptuous; that it is even sacrilegious; but this comes only from a lack of understanding of the fact that all is governed by law, and that all law is impersonal and universal. We have just as much right to use spiritual law as to use so-called physical laws. Strictly speaking there is no such a thing as a physical law, as all things are spiritual and all law is a law of the activity of the Spirit. The greatest use of these laws will always come to that soul who is the most deeply spiritual, as such an one comes the nearest to using law as God uses it. So to the really great soul there must come a very close relationship with the Invisible God; this relationship cannot be expressed in words but only in inner feeling which transcends the power of words to express. God must become the great reality, not simply as the principle of life, but more as the great Mind which knows, and which at all times understands and responds. To say that God does not understand our desires would be to rob the divine mind of all consciousness and place God lower in the scale of being than we ourselves are.

## June 5th

### Emmet Fox

Whatsoever of man soweth that shall he also reap. There is no such thing as luck. Nothing ever happens by chance. Everything, good or bad, that comes into your life is there as the result of unvarying, inescapable Law. And the only operator of that law is none other than yourself. No one else has ever done you any harm of any kind, or ever could do so, however much it may seem that they did. Consciously or unconsciously you have yourself at some time or other produced every condition desirable or undesirable that you find in either your bodily health or your circumstances today. You, and you alone, ordered those goods; and now they are being delivered. And as long as you go on thinking wrongly about yourself and about life, the same sort of difficulties will continue to harass you. For every seed must inevitably bring forth after its own kind, and thought is the seed of destiny. Yet there is a simple way out of trouble. Learn how to think rightly instead of wrongly, and conditions at once begin to improve until sooner or later, all ill-health, poverty, and inharmony must disappear. Such is the Law. Life need not be a battle; it can, and should be a glorious mystical adventure; but living is a science.

## June 6th

### Henry Thomas Hamblin

The cause of all man's weakness, mistakes and failures, has been that he has not realized the Power within; instead, he has thought himself to be separate and friendless, weak and helpless, adrift, without chart or compass upon the sea of life. He has thought himself to be the victim of circumstance, the sport of fate, and the puppet of forces outside himself. He has called himself a worm instead of looking upon himself as a king. He has though, himself to be worthless and insignificant instead of realizing his wonderful interior. POWERS and the grandeur of his being. Instead of being a worm, man is a king. Potentially all the powers of the Infinite Mind are his. Instead of being the victim of circumstances he can control them. Instead of being the puppet of forces outside himself, he has within him the Power to be what he will; to do what he will; to accomplish all that he desires. Now at last the darkness is being pierced and man realizes that he is a mental creature, and that he is MIND as well as matter, that is, as Mind, is one with the Universal or Infinite MIND. That the difference between him and the Infinite or Universal MIND is not one of kind, but of degree. Like a traveler lost in the bush, who, almost dying, at last finds his way to a permanent spring of water, and drinks and drinks again, knowing that he can never exhaust the everlasting supply; so does man after long wanderings, at last realize, that within him is a fountain of never failing Power and Wisdom, and that his subliminal mind is linked up with, and forms a part of, the Infinite Mind of the Universe. This is the greatest discovery in the history of the World; this is the crowning revelation of all the ages; this is the blinding knowledge that dwarfs every other knowledge THAT WITHIN MAN DWELLS THE INFINITE AND UNFATHOMABLE MIND OF THE UNIVERSE.

### June 7th

Charles Wesley Kyle

The "masterhood of matter is no greater achievement than the masterhood of self, for matter is in last analysis but the soul's outward account of itself," and this is but another statement of the truth expressed in the saying: "As a man thinketh in his heart so is he." Not only is man the ruler of his own mind; the divine thinker of his own thoughts, but there is an ultimate and unlimited substance out of 'which he may and does create whatsoever he will, when working with the universal law of life. There is no impulse, impression, thought or suggestion of any nature that comes to man that he is not bound, by the very nature of his being, to regard or to disregard. It is this freedom with which man is endowed to accept or reject the thoughts that come to him that mantles him with the regal power of self-mastery. This ultimate substance, found to exist in the universal ether — which, Science admits — cannot be differentiated from Spirit, Mind, the Absolute, out of which thoughts are formed which become and form the foundation or beginnings of all things appearing in the physical universe. There is no thought without form. Every work of man, building, machine or structure of any nature, first took form in his mind. Everything is a replica of a mental image. The earth, the plants, the birds, the animals and man are all projections of the mental concepts and formations held in the mind of God. All that is perceived by and conceived in the mind, is first formed in and of this immaterial substance. Man was made in the image of God; a replica of Him, which includes everything, potentially. When man shall come to understand this truth he will, by the power of constructive thought, free his mind of doubt and fear, and become so at-one with the great powers of life that disease will vanish and the body become what it was intended to be, a perfect instrument for the expression of health and happiness and peace, and its every energy be devoted to usefulness.

## June 8th

Ernest Holmes

There is something that casts back at us every thought that we think. "Vengeance is mine, I will repay, saith the Lord," is a statement of eternal truth and correspondences against which nothing can stand, and whatever man sets in motion in mind will be returned to him, even as he has conceived within himself and brought forth into manifestation. If we wish to transcend old thoughts we must rise above them and think higher things: We are dealing with the law of cause and effect and it is absolute; it receives the slightest as well as the greatest thought and at once begins to act upon it. And sometimes even when we know this we are surprised at the rapidity with which it works. If we have been misusing this law we need not fail; all that we have to do is to turn from the old way and begin in the new. We will soon work up out of the old law into the new which is being established for us. When we desire only the good the evil slips from us and returns no more.

## June 9th

Eugene Del Mar

Until one is master of the self, until he has secured self-control, one must act physically as well as think mentally, in order that he may attract to him that which he desires; he must think and he must act. The purpose of existence is to spiritualize the body that it may shine forth in spiritual glory. This is accomplished through the greater refinement and grandeur of the mind in its ideals and aspirations, clearer-cut formulations of its ideas giving definite and purposeful activity to the body. Then one's physical environment expands, he relates himself more inclusively to the vast material world, he recognizes the simplicity and harmony of its relationships, and his spiritual realization of Unity renders him a pliant instrument of the Infinite energy. Then man lives the One Life; his spiritual, mental, and physical activities are in concert and accord; and he becomes a creator of conditions, circumstances, situations, and environment. He has become magnetized toward the point of saturation. He is master of the self, and therefore of all else.

## June 10th

### Christian Larson

The average person does not try to be himself, but tries constantly to imitate. He does not try to bring out his own individuality, but tries to fashion his personality and personal life according to some exterior model that is supposed to be the standard in the world's eye. The result is, he misplaces himself; because a person is always misplaced and misdirected when he tries to imitate the life of another; and no misplaced person can master his own fate. Such a mind goes willingly and unconsciously into all sorts of foreign conditions, and then wonders what he has done to bring about such a mixed and undesirable fate. When the individual tries to be himself, he will begin to act wholly in his own world, the only world where he can be his very best. And by trying to be himself, he begins to draw upon the unbounded possibilities that exist within himself, thus making himself a larger and a greater being constantly. The individual that tries to imitate persons or environments does not express himself; therefore, his own hidden powers continue to lie dormant. To express one's own individuality, and to be oneself, the greatest essential is to live real life; the life that is felt in the depth of inner consciousness. To be yourself, be all that you are where you are, and greater spheres of action will constantly open before you. Be satisfied to be what you are, but do not be satisfied to be less than all that you are. When one begins to live in the depth of real life, and begins to draw upon his own inexhaustible self, he will find that he is so much that there is no end to the possibilities that exist in his own life and his own world.

## June 11th

### Orison Swett Marden

All of life and its achievements, its possibilities, depend upon our consciousness, and we can develop any sort of consciousness we wish. The great musician has developed a musical consciousness of which most of us are ignorant, because we are not conscious of this mode of activity. Our musical consciousness has not been developed. The mathematician, the astronomer, the writer, the physician, the artist, the specialist in whatsoever line, has developed a particular consciousness, and he realizes the fruits of that consciousness. He manifests and enjoys a special power just in proportion as he has developed his specialty consciousness. What sort of consciousness do you want to develop? What do you want to get, to do, to become? Make yourself very positive on this point for the first step toward the development of a new consciousness is to get a thorough grip upon your purpose, your desire, your aim; to get a picture of it firmly fixed in your mind; to make it dominant in your thoughts, in your acts, in your life. This is how the successful lawyer at the start develops a law consciousness; the successful physician, a medical consciousness; the successful business man, a business consciousness. It is of the utmost importance to get started right, because whatever the consciousness you develop, your mind will attract that which has an affinity for it, will draw to you the material for your building.

## June 12th

### Ernest Holmes

Creative Mind cannot force itself upon us because we have the power of self-choice. It recognizes us when we recognize it. When we think that we are limited or have not been heard, it must take that thought and bring it into manifestation for us. When we look about us and see nature so beautiful, lavish and so limitless, when we realize that something, some power, is behind all, and sees to it that plenty obtains everywhere, so that in all things manifest there is more than could be used; and when on the other hand we see man so limited, sick, sad and needy, we are disposed to ask this question: "Is God good after all? Does He really care for the people of His creation? Why am I sick? Why am I poor?" Little do we realize that the answer is in our own mouths, in the creative power of our own thought. The average person when told the Truth will still seek some other way.

## June 13th

### Charles Fillmore

Divine Mind is the one and only reality. When we incorporate the ideas that form this Mind into our mind and persevere in those ideas, a mighty strength wells up within us. Then we have a foundation for the spiritual body, the body not made with hands, eternal in the heavens. When the spiritual body is established in consciousness, its strength and power is transmitted to the visible body and to all the things that we touch in the world about us. Spiritual discernment reveals that we are now in the dawn of a new era, that the old methods of supply and support are fast passing away, and that new methods are waiting to be brought forth. In the coming commerce man will not be a slave to money. Humanity's daily needs will be met in ways that are not now thought practical. We shall serve for the joy of serving, and prosperity will flow to us and through us in streams of plenty. The supply and support that love and zeal will set in motion are not as yet largely used by man, but those who have tested their providing power are loud in their praise. The dynamic power of the supermind in man has been sporadically displayed by men and women of every nation. It is usually connected with some religious rite in which mystery and priestly authority prevail. The so-called "common herd" are kept in darkness with respect to the source of the superhuman power of occult adepts and holy men. But we have seen a "great light" in the discovery by physical scientists that the atom conceals electronic energies whose mathematical arrangement determines the character of all the fundamental elements of nature. This discovery has disrupted the science based on the old mechanical atomic theory, but has also given Christian metaphysicians a new understanding of the dynamics back of Spirit.

## June 14th

### Orison Swett Marden

The beginning of every achievement must be in your consciousness. That is the starting point of your creative plan. In proportion to the intensity, the persistence, the vividness, the definiteness of your consciousness of the thing you want, do you begin to create in any line. For instance, consciousness of power reveals power; the consciousness of supremacy is equivalent to supremacy itself; the consciousness of self-confidence is what gives us the assurance that we are equal to the thing we undertake. What we are conscious of, we already possess. But we cannot come into possession of anything we are not conscious of. That is, it cannot be ours until we become conscious of it. If you are not conscious of the ability to succeed, you can't succeed. If you are not conscious of your own superiority, you cannot become superior. But if you hold in your consciousness the picture of masterfulness; if you hold in mind the thought of superiority, you are putting in operation a little law of mastership, a little law of superiority, and you begin to manifest these things in your life. We have unlimited power, boundless resources, in the great within of us, but until we awaken to a consciousness of this hidden power, those invisible resources, we cannot use them.

## June 15th

### Walter C. Lanyon

Every perfect gift cometh down from the Father of Lights, with whom there is no change, neither shadow of turning. Where is the Father? How long will you look for him in some far-off locality? How long will you seek among the husks for the substance of life? Every gift that is to come to you as John Smith will proceed out of the centre of the I AM consciousness within yourself. Behold, I AM he that should come. I AM that I AM has sent me into expression. It is wonderful, it is wonderful. Blessings, blessings, blessings. I AM the Son of the Living God. Claim your rights and press your claim. Son of the Living God, I salute you! Arise! Leave the filth of your human reasoning and go unto your Father within. Let the filthy be filthy still. Let all those who wish to sell the Word of God continue to do so. Let those who want to argue continue their arguments. Let those judges and spiritual busybodies cast their stones. Go thy way; it is well with thee. The new secret has been revealed to you; do you hear? Peace be unto you. It is well. Now and always. "Claim your right and press your claim." It is well with you. Now and always. Son of the Living God, arise and go thy way into Expression. Now is the time. Now is the Day of Salvation. Now are we the Sons of God. Now are millions of blessings yours. Be still. Be still. Be still. It is wonderful, it is wonderful, it is wonderful. Blessings, blessings, blessings.

## June 16th

### Ernest Holmes

"The only possible operation of intelligence is thought, or "The Word." So all things were made by the Word, and "Without the Word was not anything made that hath been made." How simple the process of creation when we understand it. The Spirit speaks — and since there is nothing but the Spirit and it is All-Power, it has only to speak and it is done; "The Word was with God and the Word was God." From the Word, then, comes forth all that appears. Each life, human or divine, each manifestation is a different kind of word coming into expression. The great fact to dwell upon is that Spirit needs nothing to help It; It is self-conscious and has all power and all ability to do whatever It wishes to accomplish. It operates simply by speaking.

## June 17th

### Christian Larson

Would you be a pleasure and a delight to others, then be glad always. And would you add to the measure of your own joy, then give all the joy you can to the largest possible number. This you can do by living more and more in the spirit of that joy that is in itself the essence of real joy. And it is better to become the living incarnation of this spirit than to possess all the wealth in the world. It is better to have attained to perpetual gladness than to have become the crowned monarch of an entire solar system. The reason is simple. The glad heart is the sunshine of all life, a benediction to every man, a perpetual blessing to everything in creation. Inspire every atom in your own being to thrill with the spirit of joy; not the joy of sentiment, but the joy of strength, of triumph, of victory the joy that inwardly feels its power sublime as the soul ascends in masterful mien to the splendor of empyrean heights. It is such a joy that makes life a power, a blessing, an inspiration. And it is such a joy that comes perpetually to him who causes his soul to repeat again and again, that sweet reassuring refrain just be glad. Sing ever the song of triumph, of victory, of freedom the song that declares the supremacy of the spirit over all that may be temporal or wrong. Sing the song of the soul rising above adversity or loss, proclaiming its freedom over all that is or is to be. When the soul continues to sing in this triumphant manner, all the elements of life follow the music of that which is always well; and in such a spirit everything must be always well.

## June 18th

### Henry Thomas Hamblin

Life is not a matter of chance or luck; it is not something out of our control; it is largely the result or effect of our thoughts. Therefore, by controlling our thoughts — and this, thank God, can be done — we can govern and direct our life to an almost unbelievable extent. As conscious thinking beings, created, the Bible says, in God's likeness and image, or in other words, a microcosm of the macrocosm, we possess one of the greatest powers in the universe. and this power is thought. It depends upon how we use this wonderful power what our life shall be. The engine driver sends his engine either backward or forward, but it is the same power that is used in each case. In the same way, thinking man can either build up or destroy himself by the use or misuse of the potent power of thought. It depends upon how he uses this power, either for good or ill, as to whether his life shall be successful, healthy, happy or harmonious, or lacking in definite achievement, true success and happiness. "Whatsoever a man soweth, that shall he also reap."

## June 19th

### Eugene Del Mar

In its physical aspect, individual life could at first recognize only the merest circumference of existence. It had to commence with the most obvious, and it was obliged to develop its thinking capacity and to grow the faculties that could make use of thought as an instrument. This process has proved to be a tedious one, and long-drawn-out — so much so that after æons of time consumed in it, humanity in general still looks upon the circumference as being the centre, the temporary as the permanent, and the actual as the real. Spirit is essentially fluidic, imponderable, and etheric; but in its condensed form as matter Spirit becomes inert, inflexible, and crystallized. It may no longer be recognized as Spirit, any more than ice can be discerned as steam. In essence it is unchanged, but in appearance it is altered completely. Form may be thought of as paralyzed Spirit, as spiritual vibrations that are so reduced in activity as to come within the range of human vision and mental recognition. These slower vibrations are not only capable of being inspired by the faster ones, but that they should be so acted upon is an essential requisite of their very existence. It is in this manner that the Kingdom of Conscious Light is entered. The journey of the Spirit into matter in the lowering of its vibrations is for temporary purposes only. The duration of the journey may be indefinite, but necessarily is of limited duration. Having reached the lowest rung of the ladder of

Spirit, there is nothing else for it to do but to ascend. There is no direction for it to take other than to retrace its steps. The very nature of Spirit compels it to again take up that which previously it had relinquished.

## June 20th

### Ernest Holmes

Consider the life of Jesus. He said about his word, "The word I speak unto you, it is Spirit, it is life" — that word I am saying now. He said, "My word shall never pass away till it fulfills itself; heaven and earth shall pass away but my word shall not." If we had that same conviction, it would be done. The power was and is in the word. It is all intelligence without limitation because it finds its source in a causeless causation. Can you conceive of real causation? There is no limit, since it can image anything that it wants to. The same word we use unconsciously all the time, every time we speak, every time we think, we are using in ignorance and unconsciously. What we have to do is not a strange or peculiar thing. It is to realize this and to begin to use the word constructively the way we want it, speaking the word for what we want and getting what we speak the word for. But can't you see that since the word is first, if you say "My body is wasting away," it will waste away? It cannot help it. The body does not act; it is always acted upon. Conditions do not act. Everything in this universe that you and I see is the result of the activity of intelligence always and the word is the cause, and the law is the medium through which the word operates to produce the effect. And you do not, and I do not care about the law or the effect if we can get the causation. Our word will manifest at the level of our recognition, at the level of our consciousness. My word will be as big as I am conscious of life within myself. If I have a grand, and exalted concept, I have a grand, and exalted, word. Your prosperity is not a thing of condition; your prosperity is not a thing of law over which you have no control. Your prosperity depends upon the grandeur of your thought and nothing else. Your word is the cause of all that is. But few people realize that, even among those who are seeking to realize it, and we are constantly, we are constantly allowing ourselves to come under a condemnation of the race belief and believing in it and accepting that we are controlled by it.

## June 21st

### Christian Larson

To know positively, and feel deeply, that the great power within is working ceaselessly for our expectations and desires, for our visions and ideals — to know this is encouraging, assuring and inspiring. It makes us feel, with growing faith and confidence, that our instructions to the deeper life of the mind are being taken care of absolutely; and, taken care of by a power that is not only there to do what we say, but great enough to do anything we want done. To simply know this will make a vast difference in the outcome as the work develops; and when we learn, in addition, to use the law more extensively and more effectively — going as far in our understanding and application as we possibly can — remarkable results are inevitable. The creative power of the mind, working through the great law, has been responsible, not only for the great deeds and the great achievements of history, but also, for the miracles and wonder works of the ages; for we can well understand that, where an enormous measure of this power has been called forth through a super-faith — believing tremendously — and given definite direction by a master mind, something extraordinary would have to happen. And what has been done before, can be and will be, done again. We all have this power; and we all can learn to use the law.

## June 22nd

### Joseph Murphy

The path to the kingdom is through the inner self and not through any person, including Jesus. He is the WAY means that the inner self is the door. You can only change yourself, not others. We must remember that we create our own world after the image and likeness of our own mental pictures and thought patterns.

## June 23rd

Prentice Mulford

We absorb the thought of those with whom we are most in sympathy and association. We graft their mind on our own. If their mind is inferior to ours and not on the same plane of thought, we, in such absorption, take in and cultivate an inferior and injurious mental graft. If you will keep company with people who are reckless and unaspiring, who have no aim or purpose in life, who have no faith in themselves or anything else, you place yourself in the thought current of failure. Your tendency then will be to failure. Because from such people, your closest associates, you will absorb their thought. If you absorb it, you will think it. You will get into the same mood of mind as theirs. If you think as they do, you will in many things find yourself acting as they do, no matter how great your mental gifts. Your mind surely absorbs the kind of thought it is most with. If you are with the successful you absorb thought which brings success. The unsuccessful are ever sending from them thoughts of lack of order, lack of system, lack of method, or recklessness and discouraged thought. Your mind if much with theirs will certainly absorb these thoughts exactly as a sponge does water. It is better for your art or business that you have no intimate company at all than the company of reckless, careless, slipshod, and slovenly minds. When in your mind you cut yourself off from the unlucky and thriftless, your body will not long remain so near theirs. You get then into another force or current. It will carry you into the lives of more successful people.

## June 24th

Robert Collier

There is one unfailing Law of Increase "Whatever is praised and blessed, MULTIPLIES." Count your blessings and they increase. If you are in need of supply, start in now to praise every small piece of money that come to you, blessing it is a symbol of God's abundance and love. You will be surprised how soon that small piece will increase to many pieces. Take

God into your business. Bless your store, your cash register, every one that works for you, each customer that comes in. If you are working for someone else and want a better job or more pay, start by BLESSING and being THANKFUL for what you have. Bless the work you are doing, be thankful for every opportunity it gives you to acquire greater skill or ability or to serve others. Bless the money you earn, no matter how little it may be. Be so thankful to God for it that you can give a small "Thank offering" from it to someone in greater need than yourself. Suppose the Boss does seem unappreciative and hard. Bless him just the same. Be thankful, for the opportunity to SERVE faithfully, no matter how small the immediate reward may seem to be. Give your best, give it cheerfully, gladly, thankfully, and you will be amazed how quickly the INCREASE will come to you not necessarily from your immediate boss, but from the Big Boss over all.

## June 25th

### Ernest Holmes

Now, for the sake of clearness, I want you to think of yourself as in this Mind. Don't think of this Mind as being in you; rather think of yourself as a center in this Mind. Of course, this mind flows through you, but think of yourself as a center in it. That is your principle. You think and this Mind produces it. Now there is one of the big points in metaphysics and it is one of the reasons why so few people succeed. They do not understand the impersonal nature of Mind. They think, "I've got something tremendous to do, I have to hold the thought." Thinking the thought is what does something. Thought sows the seed in Mind, and without this Mind nothing could be made. You could not be sick without it. It is not your mind, so no human thought has anything to do with it. It is Mind, infinite and changeless, eternal, and all the mind there is. It will give us an entirely different concept of the metaphysical principle if, instead of thinking my mind does so and so, we think Mind does it. Of course, it is your mind; also, it is your principle. That person gets the best results who realizes the impersonality of Mind, the absoluteness of it, and then who can project into it the clearest concept. The reason being that all is a law of cause and effect. We think a thought into Mind and Mind returns it to us manifested as we thought it. First, the impulse to think, then the thought, then the thought is imaged in infinite Mind, and infinite Mind creates and causes it to become an effect. That is always the way it works. Just see how we may relieve ourselves! The responsibility rests in Mind to do the creating, and not in you and not in me. We are not responsible for the slightest thing in this regard.

### June 26th

James Allen

The morally right are the bodily right. To be continually transposing the details of life from passing views and fancies, without reference to fixed principles, is to flounder in confusion; but to discipline details by moral principles is to see, with enlightened vision, all details in their proper place and order. For it is given to moral principle alone, in their personal domain, to perceive the moral order. In them alone resides the insight that penetrates to causes, and with them only is the power to at once command all details to their order and place, as the magnet draws and polarizes the filings of steel. Better even than curing the body is to rise above it; to be its master, and not to be tyrannized over by it; not to abuse it, not to pander to it, never to put its claims before virtue; to discipline and moderate its pleasures, and not to be overcome by its pains — in a word, to live in the poise and strength of the moral powers, this, better than bodily cure, is a yet a safe way to cure, and it is a permanent source of mental vigor and spiritual repose.

### June 27th

Uriel Buchanan

There is no possible source for anything outside of the Infinite Power, for it embraces everything that is. There is no center or place which confines it, yet it is not absent from the minutest point in space. No object or idea can have existence apart from it, for it is omnipresent. It is the only reality of life. It is impossible for the human mind to fathom the mystery of this power, which had no beginning and can have no ending. The more we apprehend of its workings the more evidence we have that its manifestation is governed by immutable laws. Every individuality composing mankind is an inseparable part of this power. The recognition and faith in its reality will enable you to appropriate intelligently and draw upon it as much as you will for your happiness and success. It is a never failing force which you may learn to use in all efforts. It will manifest through you in greater fullness as you keep your mind in the right current of thought. You must cease trying to generate force by a spasmodic effort. Call your wandering thoughts to a peaceful center within the mind, place your reliance on the Supreme Power which you feel flowing to you from the unseen, and use your will only to direct that power as it plays through you, as you would steer a boat that is moved by the wind.

## June 28th

### Joseph Murphy

I knew a man in New York during the financial crisis of 1929, who lost everything he had including his home and all his life's savings. I met him after a lecture which I had given at one of the hotels in the city. This was what he said: "I lost everything. I made a million dollars in four years. I will make it again. All I have lost is a symbol. I can again attract the symbol of wealth in the same way that honey attracts flies." I followed the career of this man for several years to discover the key to his success. The key may seem strange to you; yet it is a very old one. The name he gave the key was, "Change water into wine!" He read this passage in the Bible, and he knew it was the answer to perfect health, happiness, peace of mind, and prosperity. Wine in the Bible always means the realization of your desires, urges, plans, dreams, propositions, etc.; in other words, it is the things you wish to accomplish, achieve, and bring forth. Water in the Bible usually refers to your mind or consciousness. Water takes the shape of any vessel into which it is poured; likewise, whatever you feel and believe as true will become manifest in your world; thus you are always changing water into wine.

## June 29th

### Ernest Holmes

It is a great help to realize mentally that at all times a great stream of thought and power is operating through us; it is constantly going out into Mind, where it is taken up and acted upon. Our business is to keep that stream of thought just where we want it to be: to be ready at any time to act when the impulse comes for action. Our action must never be negative, it must always be affirmative, for we are dealing with something that cannot fail. We may fail to realize, but the power in itself is Infinite and cannot fail. We are setting in motion in the Absolute a stream of thought that will never cease until it accomplishes its purpose. Try to feel this, be filled with a great joy as you feel that it is given to you to use this great and only power. Keep the thought clear and never worry about the way that things seem to be going. Let go of all outer conditions when working in Mind, for there is where things are made; there creation is going on, and it is now making something for us. This must be believed as never believed before; it must be known as the great reality; it must be felt as the only Presence. There is no other way to obtain.

## June 30th

### Joseph Murphy

Quimby, who was a doctor, a wonderful student, and teacher of the mental and spiritual laws of mind, said, "Man acts as he is acted upon." What moves you now? What is it that determines your response to life? The answer is as follows: Your ideas, beliefs, and opinions activate your mind and condition you to the point that you become, as Quimby stated, "An expression of your beliefs." This illustrates the truth of Quimby's statement: "Man is belief expressed."

# July

## July 1st

### Christian Larson

The creative power of the mind will work for that which we vision or imagine; and, with one exception — desire — this power will work more effectively for our visions than for anything else. The reason is, that our visions are, as a rule, very attractive; sometimes brilliant, alluring, fascinating, and even gorgeously attractive. They draw irresistibly upon the mighty power within; and frequently, call that power forth into tremendous action. This explains why we always accomplish the most, and advance the farthest when the vision is high, brilliant and wonderful. And the lesson is clear. We should keep in mind the most brilliant and the most attractive visions that we can possibly create; keep in mind the highest vision conceivable for every purpose, project and ideal. Concerning vision and imagination, there is an amazing statement, to this effect: "Whatsoever a man can imagine, that can he also accomplish." It is a stupendous statement, but absolutely true; and the proof of it can be simply stated. The creative power of the mind is great enough to do anything we want done; and what we vision or imagine — brilliantly — will attract the maximum measure of this power; in many cases, an enormous measure of this power.

## July 2nd

### Prentice Mulford

When a man realizes that his angry mood, or his covetous mood, or his grumbling mood represents so much material put in his body, and that such element will give his body pain and make it sick, he has a good strong reason for having some care as to what his mind runs on, and for making the "inside of the platter clean." Let us remember, so far as we can, that every unpleasant thought is a bad thing literally put in the body. Are some people unpleasant to us? Do their airs or affectations, or their stinginess or dishonesty, or their domineering manners, or their coarseness and vulgarity, offend us? Well, let us try and forget them. Why talk them over for an hour, holding the while all their disagreeable traits in our minds, and think of them, maybe, for hours afterwards, when we know that these unpleasant images which we carry in mind are things which are being literally put in our bodies to affect them injuriously and degenerate them? All such thoughts we must get rid of. Such riddance is the commencement of getting a new body. It is in the way of a literal regeneration. If through long habit we find that we cannot by our own endeavor keep out of these injurious moods, if we find ourselves from time to time drawn into the current of tattle, or greed, or envy, we can cease all endeavor of our own and ask help of the Supreme Power to give us new and better thoughts. That Power, through our demand, will give us a new mind. The new mind will bring the new body.

### July 3rd

Joseph Murphy

Through your capacity to choose, imagine the reality of what you have selected, and through faith and perseverance, you can realize your goal in life. All the riches of heaven are here now within you, waiting to be released. Peace, joy, love, guidance, inspiration, goodwill, and abundance all exist now. All that is necessary in order to express God's riches is for you to leave the present now (your limitation), enter into the mental vision or picture, and in a happy, joyous mood become one with your ideal. Having seen and felt your good in moments of high exaltation, you know that in a little while you shall see your ideal objectively as you walk through time and space. As within, so without. As above, so below. As in heaven so on earth. In other words, you will see your beliefs expressed. Man is belief expressed!

### July 4th

Ernest Holmes

People often ask if the Law will not bring harm as well as good. This question would never be asked if people understood what Universal Law really means. Of course it will bring us what we think. All law will do the same thing. The law of electricity will either light our house or burn it down. We decide what we are to do with the Law. Law is always impersonal. There is no likelihood of using the Law for harmful purposes if we always use it for the more complete expression of life. We must not use it for any purpose that we would not like to experience ourselves. This should answer all questions of that nature. Do I really want the thing I ask for? Am I willing to take for myself what I ask for other people? How can we use the Law for evil if we desire only the good? We cannot and we should not bother about it. We want only the good for ourselves and for the whole world; when we have started causation, at once the Law will set to work carrying out our plans. Never distrust the Law and become afraid lest you misuse it. That is a great mistake, all Law is impersonal and cares not who uses it. It will bring to all just what is already in their thought. No person can long use it in a destructive way, for it will destroy himself if he persists in doing wrong. We have no responsibility for anyone except ourselves. Get over all idea that you must save the world; we have all tried and have all failed. We may, by demonstrating in our own lives, prove that the Law really exists as the great power behind all things. This is all that we can do. Everyone must do the same thing for himself. Let the dead bury their dead, and see that you live. In this you are not selfish but are simply proving that law governs your life. All can do the same when they come to believe, and none until they believe.

## July 5th

### James Allen

All men are, and will continue to be, subject to their own habits, whether they be good or bad — that is, subject to their own reiterated and accumulated thoughts and deeds. Knowing this, the wise man chooses to subject himself to good habits, for such service is joy, bliss, and freedom; while to become subject to bad habits is misery, wretchedness, slavery. This law of habit is beneficent, for while it enables a man to bind himself to the chains of slavish practices, it enables him to become so fixed in good courses as to do them unconsciously, to instinctively do that which is right, without restraint or exertion, and in perfect happiness and freedom. Observing this automatism in life, men have denied the existence of will or freedom on man's part. They speak of him as being "born" good or bad, and regard him as the helpless instrument of blind forces.

## July 6th

### Robert Collier

Like attracts like. Hate brings hate, and all the ills that follow in its wake. Envy and fear and worry attract discord and disease. If you want health, happiness, in your life, it you are seeking riches and success, attune your thoughts to these. BLESS the circumstances that surround you. Bless and praise those who come in contact with you. Bless even the difficulties you meet, for by blessing them, you can change them from discordant conditions to favorable ones, you can speed up their rate of activity to where they will bring you good instead of evil.

## July 7th

### Venice J. Bloodworth

The world without is merely a reflection of what you have acknowledged as true in your world within, so if the state of your health or finances is not all you desire, you must look within yourself for the cause. Regardless of what the condition is, or how it seemed to have come about, its cause had to find place in your consciousness before it came into expression. That a man can change himself, recreate himself, improve himself, control his environment, and master his own destiny is not a theory with the writer but a matter of positive knowledge. There is no such thing as luck or chance; on the contrary our lives are governed by law, by actual, immutable principles that never vary. Law is in operation at all times, in all places; mighty, silent, fixed laws that underlie every human action, that bring to us, with exact precision, the full measure of our thoughts. Laws that favor no individual, and are no respecter of persons. In a sense there is nothing in all the universe but law; every tree that grows, every flower that blooms, every snowflake that falls, testifies to the unceasing operation of this great law.

## July 8th

### Ernest Holmes

When you have a real thing to do, keep it to yourself. Don't talk about it. Just know in your own mind what it is that you want and keep still about it. Often when we think that we will do some big thing we begin to talk about it and the first thing we know all the power seems to be gone. This is what happens. We are all sending out into Mind a constant stream of thought; the clearer it is, the better will it manifest; if it becomes doubtful it will not have so clear a manifestation. If it is confused it will manifest only confusion. All this is according to the Law of Cause and Effect, and we cannot change that Law. Too often, when we tell our friends what we are going to do, they confuse our thought by laughing about it, or by doubting our capacity to do so large a thing. Of course this would not happen if we were always positive, but when we become the least bit negative it will react and we will lose that power of clearness which is absolutely necessary to good creative work. When you want to do a big thing, get the mental pattern, make it perfect, know just what it means, enlarge your thought, keep it to yourself, pass it over to the creative power behind all things, wait and listen, and when the impression comes, follow it with assurance. Don't talk to anyone about it. Never listen to negative talk or pay any attention to it and you will succeed where all others fail.

## July 9th

### Orison Swett Marden

We are the creatures of our convictions. We cannot get beyond what we believe we are; what we believe we have. Hence, if we think that we are never going to be strong or well like other people, or to be successful in our calling, we never will be. If we are convinced that we will always be poor, we will be. You can't get away from poverty when you don't expect to; when you don't believe that you are going to. Many of the people who are living in poverty today never really expect anything else. Their fixed belief that they can never become prosperous keeps them in poverty; that is, it keeps their minds negative, and the mind cannot create, cannot produce, in this condition. It is only the positive mind that can create prosperity; the negative mind is non-creative, nonproductive; it can only tear down, inhibit, prevent the inflow of the good things that we long It is not so much what you do with your hands as what you do with your mind that counts. Everything that has been accomplished by the hand or brain of man had its birth in the mind. The universe itself is the creation of Divine Mind. A hard-working man who longs for prosperity, but is headed in the other direction mentally, who doesn't believe he is going to be prosperous, is neutralizing his hard work by his negative, destructive thought; he is standing on the hose that connects with his supply.

## July 10th

### Henry Thomas Hamblin

Close your eyes, and mentally picture yourself, radiant, strong, successful, happy, full of the joy and zest of life. See yourself treading a path that leads ever upwards. Behind you the air is murky and gloomy, but in front is increasing brightness and loveliness. See yourself progressing, climbing, winning. See yourself trampling old habits and weaknesses under your feet. See yourself meeting difficulties in your path, and see yourself, sustained by a mighty inward power, brushing all obstructions aside, and never faltering in your upward climb. Concentrate with all your powers upon this mental imagery. Persevere until you can see yourself radiant, sublime, shorn of all weaknesses and imperfections, the perfect image of your perfect self. See yourself full of vitality and health, see yourself successful, attracting both people and affluence to you. Make a concrete, sharply defined image in your mind of yourself as you desire to be; see yourself master of circumstances, attracting all good things by the power of your mental forces. Whatever you create, in this manner, in your mental world, will later be manifested in your outward life.

## July 11th

### Joseph Murphy

The subjective mind is always amenable to suggestion; it is controlled by suggestion. We must recognize that the subconscious mind accepts all suggestions; it does not argue with you, but it fulfills your wishes. All things that have happened to you are based on thoughts impressed on the subconscious mind through belief. The subconscious mind will accept your beliefs and your convictions. It is like the soil; it will accept any seed that you deposit in it, whether it is good or bad. Remember: Anything that you accept as true and believe in will be accepted by your subconscious mind, and brought into your life as a condition, experience, or event. Ideas are conveyed to the subconscious mind through feeling.

## July 12th

### Ernest Holmes

The life that has not loved has not lived; it is still dead. Love is the sole impulse for creation; and the man who does not have it as the greatest incentive in his life has never developed the real creative instinct. No one can swing out into the Universal without love, for the whole universe is based upon it. When we find that we are without friends, the thing to do is at once to send our thought out to the whole world, — send it full of love and affection. Know that this thought will meet the desires of some other person who is wanting the same thing, and in some way the two will be drawn together. Get over thinking that people are queer. That kind of thought will only produce misunderstanding and cause us to lose the friends that we now have. Think of the whole world as your friend; but you must also be the friend of the whole world. In this way and with this simple practice you will draw to you so many friends that the time will be too short to enjoy them all. Refuse to see the negative side of anyone. Refuse to let yourself misunderstand or be misunderstood. Do not be morbid. Know that everyone wants you to have the best; affirm this wherever you go and then you will find things just as you wish them to be.

### July 13th

Christian Larson

The creative power of the mind will work for that which you place deeply in the mind, no matter what it is — the worst or the best. This power asks no questions. It is there to do what you say; and everything that is placed deeply in the mind is accepted as "your say." This power does not judge in any matter. It has no opinion, or advice, to offer as to what should, or should not, be done. It is there to act upon your advice, your purpose, your desire. It is there to form, build, produce, develop and create; and whatever you give it to work for — that is what it will produce for you. That is the law. This power can produce illness or health, discord or harmony, weakness or strength, depression or happiness, failure or success — the worst of anything or the best of anything — depending upon what is placed deeply in the mind. It is for each individual, therefore, to decide what he is to place deeply in the mind. He cannot leave this vital situation to chance, suggestion, habit, race belief, nor any other irresponsible agency. He must make this decision himself — the very best he knows — and stand by his decision "though the heavens fall," His whole life depends upon it; his achievements, his attainments, his future — everything.

### July 14th

Prentice Mulford

Let us endeavor, then, with the help of the Supreme Power, to get into the thought current of things that are healthy, natural, strong and beautiful. Let us try to avoid thoughts of disease, of suffering, of deformity, of faultiness. A field of waving grain or the rolling surf is better to contemplate than to pore over the horrors of a railway accident. We do not realize how much we are depressed physically and mentally by the incessant feast of horrors prepared for us by the daily press. We invoke in their perusal a thought current, filled with things and images of horror and suffering. We bring ourselves in this way in connection and one-ness with all other morbid and diseased mind, which lives and revels in this current. it leads not to life, but to disease and death. Neither others nor yourself are one particle aided by your knowing of every fire, explosion, murder, theft or crime which the newspapers chronicle every twenty-four hours. If we read boots written by cynical, sarcastic minds, who are so warped as to be able to see only the faults of others, and at last unable to see good anywhere, we bring on ourselves their unhealthy thought current, and are one with it. The arrow always tipped with ill-nature and sarcasm is deadliest to him who sends it. In other words, the man who is ever inviting and cultivating this thought current, is inviting the unrest, disease and misfortune it will assuredly bring to him, and when we get too much into his mind we invite similar results. You may be neat, careful and methodical in your habits, exact and elaborate in your work, yet if you associate closely with those who are careless and slovenly you may find in yourself a tendency to be also careless and slovenly, and a difficulty in resuming and carrying out your former neat, methodical and orderly methods. Because you have not only absorbed of the careless mind, or the mind lacking patience to do anything reposefully, but the fragment of such mind so absorbed is acting as a magnet in attracting to you its like thought current.

## July 15th

Uriel Buchanan

When matters look dark and uncertain, and you are discouraged and haunted by fear of loss, of sickness and misfortune, if you will look within and invoke the aid of the unseen elements, you will command a silent force which will banish weakness and give renewed strength and cheerfulness. Any great success is gained by the exercise of personal power and the recognition of an unlimited capacity to draw from the unseen currents the inspiration and energy to move things and shape events at will. If you lean on others, their support will be withdrawn. If you play with luck in the game of life, you are sure to lose. If in mind you think it impossible to do what another has done, if you are overawed by the world's pretentiousness, if you behold the display of wealth and feel that these things are beyond you, by your negative, timid thoughts you place the only real barrier to reaching them. If you have sufficient faith in your own ability and in the universal force with which you cooperate, if you feel that the best things the world can give are none too good for you, that you have the knowledge, the talent and the executive ability to move things, to influence people and command attention, if you live in this permanent state of mind, you will draw to you the material counterpart of every thought demand. Put your mind in harmony with the Infinite Source and in line of correspondence with the things you seek, then you will receive impressions in regard to the steps to be taken to reach the goal desired. The less you depend upon others and the more you trust your enlightened reason, the clearer you will see and the more strength you will have to stand alone. You will realize that as an inseparable part of the infinite power of good, you may command the qualities needed to accomplish wonderful results. You will receive an impulse and inspiration that will be finer and more effective. You will advance to higher planes of usefulness and grow in knowledge and understanding.

## July 16th

### Ernest Holmes

Prosperity is in our own hands to do with as we will, but we will never reach it until we learn to control our thought. We must see only what we want and never allow the other things to enter. If we wish activity we must be active in our thought, we must see activity and speak it into everything that we do. The spoken word shall bring it to pass. We speak the word, it is brought to pass of the Power that we speak it into. We can only speak the word that we understand, the activity will correspond to our inner concepts. If they are large the results will be large. The thing to do is to unify ourselves with all the biggest ideas that we can compass; and realizing that our ideas govern our power of attraction, we should be constantly enlarging within ourselves. We must realize our at-one-ment with All Power and know that our word will bring it to pass. We speak the word, it is brought to pass. As consciousness grows it will manifest in enlarged opportunities and a greater field of action. Most people think in the terms of universal powers. Feel that you are surrounded by all the power that there is when you speak and never doubt but that what you say will spring into being.

## July 17th

Charles F. Haanel

All agree that there is but one Principle or Consciousness pervading the entire Universe, occupying all space, and being essentially the same in kind at every point of its presence. It is all powerful, all wisdom and always present. All thoughts and things are within Itself. It is all in all. There is but one consciousness in the universe able to think; and when it thinks, its thoughts become objective things to it. As this Consciousness is omnipresent, it must be present within every individual; each individual must be a manifestation of that Omnipotent, Omniscient and Omnipresent Consciousness. As there is only one Consciousness in the Universe that is able to think it necessarily follows that your consciousness is identical with the Universal Consciousness, or, in other words, all mind is one mind. There is no dodging this conclusion. The consciousness that focuses in your brain cells is the same consciousness which focuses in the brain cells of every other individual. Each individual is but the individualization of the Universal, the Cosmic Mind. The Universal Mind is static or potential energy; it simply is; it can manifest only through the individual, and the individual can manifest only through the Universal. They are one. The ability of the individual to think is his ability to act on the Universal and bring it into manifestation. Human consciousness consists only in the ability of man to think. Mind in itself is believed to be a subtle form of static energy, from which arises the activities called 'thought,' which is the dynamic phase of mind. Mind is static energy, thought is dynamic energy — the two phases of the same thing.

Thought is therefore the vibratory force formed by converting static mind into dynamic mind.

### July 18th

Robert Collier

"To Him That Hath" — Take as an example the science of numbers. Suppose all numbers were of metal — that it was against the law to write figures for ourselves. Every time you wanted to do a sum in arithmetic you'd have to provide yourself with a supply of numbers, arrange them in their proper order, work out your problems with them. If your problems were too abstruse you might run out of numbers, have to borrow some from your neighbor or from the bank. "How ridiculous," you say. "Figures are not things; they are mere ideas, and we can add them or divide them or multiply them or subtract them as often as we like. Anybody can have all the figures he wants." To be sure he can. And when you get to look upon money in the same way, you will have all the money you want. "To him that hath shall be given, and from him that hath not shall be taken away even that which he hath." To him that hath the right idea everything shall be given, and from him who hath not that right idea shall be taken away everything he hath.

### July 19th

Eugene Del Mar

If not directed or controlled, the subconscious tendencies will prevail, and one will be bound fast by tradition, convention, and conservatism — habit-bound, thought-bound, sectarian, and superstitious. Yes; and be proud of his servitude! Instead of living Life, he will have permitted Life to live him, frozen and crystallized at a low average of human attainment! Control of the subconscious involves thinking for oneself, which seems to most people to be the most unusual and tiresome thing there is. Why go to this trouble and exertion, when the priests, doctors, lawyers, politicians, and all the many other pillars of society are willing to do it for us, at the usual rate? It is much easier to leave one's thinking to others. It has been left to them, speaking generally, and a sorry mess they have made of it. What has been the result? The result has been a world bound by tradition and convention, by habits and customs, all inherited readymade, and cut on such a pattern that no amount of mere patching will make it fit the thought-form of humanity of the present day. The result has been that the individual has become the slave of his environment, when he might command and control it. He has become thought-blind, quoting the dead wisdom of others, when he might be alive with the wisdom of his own.

## July 20th

### Christian Larson

When calamities or catastrophies have overtaken your life, do not think that fate or Providence has ordered it so. Do not think that it has to be. Instead, forget the sorrow and the loss, and congratulate yourself over the fact that you now have the privilege to build for greater things than you ever knew before. Do not weep over loss; but rejoice to think that now you are called upon to prove the greater wisdom and power within you. You have been taken out into a new world. Before you lie vast fields of undeveloped and unexplored opportunities fields that you would not have known had not this seeming misfortune come upon you. So count it all joy. All things are working together for a greater good. Now it is for you to come forward in joy and accept the greater good. A richer life and a greater future are in store. Therefore, rejoice and be glad, and give strength to your rejoicing. Let your soul repeat again and again that sweet reassuring refrain just be glad. In that refrain there is comfort and peace; it lifts the burdens, removes the clouds, dispels the gloom; it takes away the sadness and the loss, and all is well again. And naturally so, for all things respond to the call of rejoicing; all things gather where life is a song.

## July 21st

### Ernest Holmes

The word spoken once from the mind that knows is immediately taken up by the Mind in which we live, and this Mind begins to create around the word, which is the seed, the thing thought of. We must speak that word with authority. There can be no wondering if it is going to work. When we plant a seed in the ground and water and care for it, we never doubt but a plant will spring into being. So it is with the word. It is acted upon by some power which we do not see, but that the power is there, there is no doubt, since all who go about it get results. As Thomas Edison says of electricity, "It Is; use it;" so we say of mind, "It Is; use it."

## July 22nd

### James Allen

No matter how apparently helpless a man has become under the tyranny of a bad habit, or a bad characteristic — and both are essentially the same — he can, so long as sanity remains, break away from it and become free, replacing it by its opposite good habit; and when the good possesses him as the bad formerly did, there will be neither wish nor need to break from that, for its dominance will be perennial happiness, and not perpetual misery.

## July 23rd

### Joseph Murphy

Trust the subconscious mind to heal you. It made your body, and it knows all of its processes and functions. It knows much more than your conscious mind about healing and restoring you to perfect balance. The subconscious mind, sometimes called the deep-self, knows more about your body than all of the wisest men in the world. Never try to coerce or force the mind. We do not infer that some people who say, "I AM whole, pure, and perfect," do not get results; of course they do, because they succeed in convincing themselves of it.

Blind belief and faith will bring results due to the subjective faith of the individual.

## July 24th

### Wallace Wattles

Thinking is the hardest and most exhausting of all labor; and hence many people shrink from it. God has so formed us that we are continuously impelled to thought; we must either think or engage in some activity to escape thought. The headlong, continuous chase for pleasure in which most people spend all their leisure time is only an effort to escape thought. If they are alone, or if they have nothing amusing to take their attention, as a novel to read or a show to see, they must think; and to escape from thinking they resort to novels, shows, and all the endless devices of the purveyors of amusement. Most people spend the greater part of their leisure time running away from thought, hence they are where they are. We never move forward until we begin to think. Read less and think more. Read about great things and think about great questions and issues. Thinking, not mere knowledge or information, makes personality. Thinking is growth; you cannot think without growing. Every thought engenders another thought. Write one idea and others will follow until you have written a page. You cannot fathom your own mind; it has neither bottom nor boundaries. Your first thoughts may be crude; but as you go on thinking you will use more and more of yourself; you will quicken new brain cells into activity and you will develop new faculties. Heredity, environment, circumstances — all things must give way before you if you practice sustained and continuous thought. But, on the other hand, if you neglect to think for yourself and only use other people's thought, you will never know what you are capable of; and you will end by being incapable of anything. There can be no real greatness without original thought. All that a man does outwardly is the expression and completion of his inward thinking. No action is possible without thought, and no great action is possible until a great thought has preceded it. Action is the second form of thought, and personality is the materialization of thought. Environment is the result of thought; things group themselves or arrange themselves around you according to your thought. There is, as Emerson says, some central idea or conception of yourself by which all the facts of your life are arranged and classified. Change this central idea and you change the arrangement or classification of all the facts and circumstances of your life. You are what you are because you think as you do; you are where you are because you think as you do.

### July 25th

Ernest Holmes

We cannot make affirmations for fifteen minutes a day and spend the rest of our time denying the thing which we have affirmed, and affirming the thing which we have denied, and obtain the results which we seek. We send out the word and it sets the power in motion; then we think the opposite thing which neutralizes the first word, and zero is the result. We cannot demonstrate one iota beyond our mental ability to conceive and steadfastly to embody. Infinite as Creative Power is, receptive and quick as it is, it can only become to us what we first think into it. God can do for us only what He can do through us.

### July 26th

Prentice Mulford

A thought, be it good or bad, is a thing or construction of unseen element as real as a tree, a flower, a clock. It is already made before you think or receive it, as your mind through its mood, frame, or attitude attracts it. As you think it, you put it out again to act, move, or influence others. But your thought spoken or whispered in the privacy of your room is put out with more force so to act on others than if you merely "think it." And if two or more persons talk together without wrangle or disagreement on a common purpose in any business, they send out a proportionately greater volume of force to work on other minds relative to such business. If your company so putting out thought-element or force do not agree, if they are angry and wrangle with each other, the force so sent from them is injurious to that business. If they talk peacefully, and will set aside individual preferences or prejudices in order to work out the common purpose in view, the thought or force they generate is constructive, and acts favorably on other minds far and near to advance that business.

## July 27th

Christian Larson

There is a power in the mind — in the deeper life of the mind — that is creative; and it works through all the energies, activities, processes, faculties, thoughts, ideas and concepts of the mind. It works so deeply and so thoroughly, in every aspect of mind and consciousness, that it causes the whole of the mind to become creative. We may say, then, that the mind is creative — forming, producing and creating continuously — and in myriads of ways. The mind works, in all of its creative activities, according to a certain law; and to understand this law, and know how to give it definite direction, is to take the creative power of the mind into our own hands completely. Thus we may determine, in every mode and manner, what this power is to form, produce or create, in us; and for us. A gigantic achievement; for the individual who can do this, becomes a creator in his own domain. He may decide absolutely what this power is to produce in his own mind, in his own life, in his own world. The creative power of the mind is constantly in action—producing and creating — whether we give it specific direction or not. It is there at work — working according to a certain law; and all that we now are, or have, is the result of what this power has been doing for us — deep in the mind all these years. It is not a power that we have to place in action; it always is in action — producing, producing continuously. What we seek to know is how it works, and the law through which it works, so that we may direct this power to produce for us what we want — and only what we want. We specify only in small measure, as a rule, what we want this power to produce for us; and we do this indirectly most of the time — having little or no knowledge of the law. We permit this power, in nearly all of its activities, to be directed by suggestions and impressions from without, by inherited tendencies and impulses from the unconscious; and by any dominant emotion, thought or desire. That is why this power produces so much that is useless or detrimental; why it produces so much that we do not want; and why only a fraction of its activities, in the average mind, is devoted to the creation of the worthwhile.

## July 28th

### Robert Collier

For the world without is but a reflection of that world within. Your thought creates the conditions your mind images. Keep before your mind's eye the image of all you want to be and you will see it reflected in the world without. Think abundance, feel abundance, BELIEVE abundance, and you will find that as you think and feel and believe, abundance will manifest itself in your daily life. But let fear and worry be your mental companions, thoughts of poverty and limitation dwell in your mind, and worry and fear, limitation and poverty will be your constant companions day and night. Your mental concept is all that matters. Its relation to matter is that of idea and form. There has got to be an idea before it can take form.

## July 29th

### Ernest Holmes

All are alike; there is no difference between one person and another. Come to see all as a divine idea; stop all negative thought; think only about what you want, and never about what you do not want, as that would cause a false creation. Too much cannot be said about the fact that all are dealing with only one power, making and unmaking for man through the creative power of his own thought. If there is something in your life that you do not want there, stop fighting it — forget it!

## July 30th

Genevieve Behrend

The power within you which enables you to form a thought-picture is the starting point of all there is. In its original state it is the undifferentiated formless substance of life. Your thought-picture makes the model, so to say, into which this formless substance takes shape. Visualizing, or mentally seeing things and conditions as you wish them to be, is the condensing, the specializing power in you which might be illustrated by comparison with the lens of a magic lantern, which is one of the best symbols of the imaging faculty. It illustrates the idea of the working of the Creative Spirit on the plane of initiative and selection — or in its concentrated, specializing form — in a remarkably clear manner. The picture slide illustrates your own mental picture — invisible in the lantern of your mind until you turn on the light of your will. That is to say, you light up your desire with absolute faith that the Creative Spirit of Life, in you, is doing the work. By the steady flow of the light of the Will on the Spirit, your desired picture is projected upon the screen of the physical world — an exact reproduction of the pictured slide in your mind.

## July 31st

James Allen

A man's mind may be likened to a garden, which may be intelligently cultivated or allowed to run wild; but whether cultivated or neglected, it must, and will, bring forth. If no useful seeds are put into it, then an abundance of useless weed seeds will fall therein, and will continue to produce their kind. Just as a gardener cultivates his plot, keeping it free from weeds, and growing the flowers and fruits which he requires, so may a man tend the garden of his mind, weeding out all the wrong, useless, and impure thoughts, and cultivating toward perfection the flowers and fruits of right, useful, and pure thoughts, By pursuing this process, a man sooner or later discovers that he is the master gardener of his soul, the director of his life. He also reveals, within himself, the laws of thought, and understands with ever-increasing accuracy, how the thought forces and mind elements operate in the shaping of his character, circumstances, and destiny.

# August

## August 1st

Prentice Mulford

One secret of the kings of finance is that they know when to rid themselves of possessions on seeing how those possessions can be of no farther use to them. In so doing they work by a spiritual method. Far-sighted men are at this moment "unloading" themselves of properties which they see have no immediate money in them, and near-sighted men are at this moment buying those properties, which will for years lay on their hands a care without recompense, and an encumbrance and obstacle to more immediate gain. The real cost of keeping things is the amount of thought you put in their keeping. If you will keep an old bedstead or bureau, or anything else you never have any use for, and pack it about with you at every house-moving, and put study and calculation as to the place it shall occupy, and worry then because it takes room which you need for everyday purposes, you are putting from time to time force enough on a (to you) useless article which, if properly directed, would buy a hundred new bureaus. In this way does this, the blind desire of mere keeping and hoarding, keep many people poor, and even makes paupers. Mere hoarding is not business. If everyone put away money as they gained it, and lived on as little as possible, and continually decreased their expenses, the world's business would soon stop, not so much from lack of money lying useless in chests and old stockings, but because there would soon be little left for people to do to gain money. It is large outlays, expensive and luxurious styles of living, the making of the costliest articles, the erection of magnificent buildings, and not hovels, the demand for the very best of everything, that keeps the laborer, the mechanic, the artist in any department, at work, and keeps the stream of wages pouring into their pockets. Mere hoarding brings nothing in the end to him who hoards but pain and trouble.

## August 2nd

Ernest Holmes

In practice the emancipated soul must always realize that he is in union with the Father; what the Father does, he can do in his own life; what God is, he can become. His word must be spoken with absolute authority; he must know; there should be no uncertainty. The word is the only power; everything must come from it, and nothing can stand against it; it is the great weapon which he is to use against all evil and for all good. It is his shield against all adversity and his sure defense against all seeming limitation.

## August 3rd

Joseph Murphy

The feeling of wealth produces wealth; the feeling of being successful produces success; keep this in mind at all times. The subconscious mind is like a bank — a sort of universal bank; it magnifies whatever you deposit or impress upon it, whether it is good or evil. You sign blank checks when you make such statements as: "There is not enough to go around;" or "There is a shortage;" maybe, "I will lose the mortgage;" etc. If you are full of fear about the future, you are also writing a blank check, and attracting negative conditions to you. The subconscious mind takes your fear and belief as your requests, proceeding in its own way to bring obstacles, delays, lack, and limitation into your life. To him that hath the feeling of wealth, more wealth shall be added; to him that hath the feeling of lack, more lack shall be added. The subconscious mind gives you compound interest also. Every morning as you awaken deposit thoughts of prosperity, success, wealth, and peace; dwell upon these concepts; busy your mind with them as often as possible. These positive thoughts will find their way as deposits in your subconscious mind, and bring forth abundance and prosperity.

## August 4th

Robert Collier

Why is it that so many millions of men and women go through life in poverty and misery, in sickness and despair? Why? Primarily because they make a reality of poverty through their fear of it. They visualize poverty, misery and disease, and thus bring them into being. And secondly, they cannot demonstrate the law of supply for the same reason that so many millions cannot solve the first problem in algebra. The solution is simple — but they have never been shown the method. They do not understand the law. The essence of this law is that you must think abundance, see abundance, feel abundance, believe abundance. Let no thought of limitation enter your mind. There is no lawful desire of yours for which, as far as mind is concerned, there is not abundant satisfaction. And if you can visualize it in mind, you can realize it in your daily world. "Blessed is the man whose delight is in the law of the Lord: And he shall be like a tree planted by the rivers of water, that bringeth forth his fruit in his season: his leaf also shall not wither; and whatsoever he doeth shall prosper."

## August 5th

Christian Larson

When we concentrate absolutely upon the greater things we expect to attain or achieve, we gradually train all the forces of the mind and all the powers of thought to work for those greater things. We shall thereby begin in earnest to build for ourselves a greater destiny; and sooner or later we shall find ourselves gaining ground in many directions. Later on, if we proceed, we shall begin to move more rapidly, and if we pay no attention to the various troubles that may be brewing in our environment, those troubles will never affect us nor disturb us in the least. The mental law involved in the process of scientific thinking may be stated as follows: The more you think of what is right, the more you tend to make every action in your mind right. The more you think of the goal you have in view, the more life and power you will call into action in working for that goal. The more you think of your ambition, the more power you will give to those faculties that can make your ambitions come true. The more you think of harmony, of health, of success, of happiness, of things that are desirable, of things that are beautiful, of things that have true worth, the more the mind will tend to build all those things in yourself, provided, of course, that all such thinking is subjective.

## August 6th

### Ernest Holmes

Nearly all people are controlled by outer suggestions, and not by inner realizations. Ordinarily man thinks only what he sees others do, and hears others say. We must all learn so to control the inner life that outside things do not make an impression upon our mentalities. As we are thinking beings, and cannot help thinking, we cannot avoid making things happen to us, and what we need to do is so to control our thought processes that our thinking will not depart from the realization of that which is perfect. Man is governed by a mind which casts back to him every thought he thinks; he cannot escape from this and need not try; it would be useless. The laws of mind are simple and easy to understand. The trouble with us has been that we have laid down great obstructions, and then have tried to overcome them. Stop trying, stop struggling, begin to be calm, to trust in the higher laws of life, even though you do not see them; they are still there.

## August 7th

### Orison Swett Marden

If you would attract success, keep your mind saturated with the success, idea. Develop an attitude of mind that will attract success. When you think success, when you act it, when you live it, when you talk it, when it is in your bearing, then you are attracting it. When we once get this law of attraction thoroughly fixed in our minds we will be careful about attracting our enemies, contacting with them through our mind, thinking about them, worrying about them, fearing, and dreading them. We will hold the sort of thoughts that will attract the things we long for and are seeking, not the things we dread, and despise, and are trying to avoid. It is just as easy to attract what you want as to attract what you don't want. It is just a question of holding the right thought, and making the right effort. There is no exception to the law of attraction, any more than there is to the law of gravitation, or the laws of mathematics.

## August 8th

### Christian Larson

Whether we believe that life was made for happiness or that happiness was made for life, matters not. The fact remains that he alone can live the most and enjoy the best who takes for his motto just be glad. Whatever comes, or whatever may fail to come, this one thing he will always remember just be glad. Though every mind in the world may give darkness, his will continue to give light; and though all may be lost, so there seems nothing more to give, he will not forget to give happiness. The one great thing to do under every circumstance and in the midst of every event is this just be glad. Wherever you may be, add sunshine. Whatever your position may be, be also a human sunbeam. What a difference when the sunbeam comes in; then why should the sunbeam remain without? There is a sunbeam in every heart. Why hide it at any time? Does not the world need your smiles? Is not everybody made happier and better when in the presence of a radiant countenance? Do. we ever forget the face that shines as the sun? And does not such a memory continue to give us strength and inspiration all through the turnings and complexities of life? We are not here to give sadness, but joy. We were not made to hide our souls in a dark thunder cloud, but to let the spirit shine in all its splendor and beauty. We are made to make life an endless song, and the sweet refrain of that beautiful song is just be glad.

## August 9th

### Joseph Murphy

If you believe that wealth or money is dependent on your job or more hours of work, you have a limited concept; you are bound by your own beliefs. This is a world of cause and effect. If you worry and fret about money, this mood of lack will produce a greater lack of money. Your mental attitude is the cause; less money is the effect. There is one emotion which is the cause of financial lack in the lives of many. Most people learn this fact the hard way. It is envy. For example, if you see a competitor depositing large sums of money in the bank, and you have only a meager amount to deposit, does it make you envious? The way to overcome this emotion is to say to yourself, "Isn't it wonderful! I rejoice in that man's prosperity. I wish for him greater and greater wealth." Do you know what you are doing? You are actually impressing the subconscious mind with the idea of wealth! To entertain envious thoughts is devastating, because it places you in a very negative position; therefore, wealth flows from you, instead of to you. If you are ever annoyed or irritated by the prosperity or great wealth of another, claim immediately that you truly wish for him greater prosperity in every possible way. This will neutralize the negative thoughts in your mind, and cause a greater measure of wealth to flow to you by the law of your own subconscious mind.

## August 10th

### Ernest Holmes

For the sake of clearness, think of yourself as in this Mind, think of yourself as a center in it. That is your principle. You think, and Mind produces the thing. One of the big points to remember is that we do not have to create; all that we have to do is to think. Mind, the only Mind that there is, creates. Few people seem to understand the nature of the law and so think that they have got to do something, even if it is only holding a thought; thinking or knowing is what does the thing. It will make it much easier for us when we realize that we do not have to make anything, just to know; that there is something back of the knowing which does the work for us. That person gets the best results who realizes that he can use this divine principle; he who can get the clearest concept of his idea, and who can rely on mind to do for him, keeping everything out of his thought that would contradict the supremacy of Spirit or Mind. By simply holding a thought we could not make anything but by knowing in mind what cannot we do?

## August 11th

### Prentice Mulford

What we call the drawing power of mind is not that of longing for things. Longing implies impatience, because they do not come so soon as we desire. The impatient state of mind will either drive what you desire from you or delay its advance. When your thought takes this form, " I want the thing desired now — right now; I'm tired of waiting; I can't stand waiting any longer; I'm sick and tired of waiting," you are in the wrong mood. You are then using your force in scolding or grieving or finding fault, because what you desire does not come. When you scold or complain or grieve, because the things you desire do not come, your force is set upon that scolding or grieving, and is not working to bring them to you. It is analogous to the man who, in a fit of rage, should tear his wagon to pieces, because it is stuck in a mire. The force he used to tear it to pieces might have drawn it out. The force of mind you need to put out to draw good things to you lies in that mood, which says, continually and calmly: " I must have these things; I am going to have them, provided that a Wisdom greater than mine sees that it will not work me injury to have them." It must be a mental state of serenity and determination decided and positive, but never angered or impatient, or anxious or worrying. So that you keep your mind in the proper drawing mood, you need not have in mind continually the thing you desire. It is the state of mind that draws money, and things desirable, and not the constant recollection of the special thing desired.

## August 12th

James Allen

The natural grades in human society — what are they but spheres of thought, and modes of conduct manifesting those spheres? The proletariat may rail against these divisions, but he will not alter or affect them. There is no artificial remedy for equalizing states of thought having no natural affinity, and separated by the fundamental principles of life. The lawless and the law-abiding are eternally apart, nor is it hatred nor pride that separates them, but states of intelligence and modes of conduct which in the moral principles of things stand mutually unrelated. The rude and ill-mannered are shut out from the circle of the gentle and refined by the impassable wall of their own mentality which, though they may remove by patient self-improvement, they can never scale by a vulgar intrusion. The kingdom of heaven is not taken by violence, but he who conforms to its principles receives the password. The ruffian moves in a society of ruffians; the saint is one of an elect brethren whose communion is divine music. All men are mirrors reflecting according to their own surface. All men, looking at the world of men and things, are looking into a mirror which gives back their own reflection.

## August 13th

Uriel Buchanan

Every thought of yours is a force which is building for the future. If at the present you are obliged to live amid discordant environments, to associate with uncongenial people, do not feel that you will be forced to continue such relationship. You are there now because the associations are kindred to past thoughts and desires. The mood of mind you are most in now will determine your future for good or ill. If you cultivate cheerfulness, are full of hope and ambition, and are living in imagination in better surroundings, among superior people, you will develop forces which will carry you forward to higher truth and possibility. You absorb the thought and take on the characteristics of those with whom you are most associated. If their mind is on a lower plane of thought, if they are coarse and materialistic, they fetter your aspiration and deaden the finer sensibilities. You have latent in you some special capacity different from that possessed by any other person. To discover your talents and set diligently to work to develop them, to allow no influence to check you, no barrier to discourage, you will grow into ever increasing possibilities of strength and usefulness. It is your rightful heritage to be permanently freed from all disease, all weakness and the slavery of fear, and to live in close relationship with the Infinite Mind, from which you may draw life, strength and inspiration sufficient for all demands.

### August 14th

Ernest Holmes

So long as the Word exists the thing will exist, for since the Word is All-Power there is nothing beside It. "I AM that I AM, and beside me there is none other." This "I AM" is Spirit, God, All. There is no physical explanation for anything in the universe; all causation is Spirit and all effect spiritual. We are not living in a physical world but in a spiritual world peopled with spiritual ideas. We are now living in Spirit. God, or Spirit, governs the universe through great mental laws that work out the divine will and purpose, always operating from Intelligence. This Intelligence is so vast, and the power so great that our human minds cannot even grasp it; all that we can hope to do is to learn something of the way in which it works, and by harmonizing ourselves with it, to so align ourselves with Spirit that our lives may be controlled by the great harmony that obtains in all the higher laws of nature, but has been very imperfectly manifested in man.

### August 15th

Venice J. Bloodworth

Man is the highest expression of individual life, because he thinks. We sometimes blame God for our misfortune, but the fact remains that we are entirely responsible for our success or failure, happiness or misery. Man makes himself, creates his own personality, character and circumstances. Destiny is fixed by subconscious action; you are not the slave of circumstance, but the creator of your own destiny. We attract to ourselves only that which corresponds to our subconscious impressions, and you can always make a new start and create new conditions by changing your subconscious impressions. If you have thought failure, think success; replace sick thoughts with thoughts of health. If there is any reason for unhappiness, resolutely put it out of your mind, for LIKE ATTRACTS LIKE, and the more you think of discordant conditions, the more such conditions will manifest for you. CONCENTRATE ON WHAT YOU WANT. When you do think you are impressing that desire on your subconscious mind; NEVER let your thoughts dwell on what you DO NOT WANT.

## August 16th

Christian Larson

The whole mind, conscious and subconscious, does possess the power to solve any problem that may come up, or provide the necessary ways and means through which we can carry out or finish anything we have undertaken. Here, as elsewhere, practice makes perfect. The more you train the subconscious to work with you, the easier it becomes to get the subconscious to respond to your directions, and therefore the subconscious mind should be called into action, no matter what comes up; in other words make it a practice to use your whole mind, conscious and subconscious, at all times, not only in large matters, but in all matters. Begin by recognizing the subconscious in all thought and in all action. Think that it can do what you have been told it can do, and eliminate doubt absolutely. Take several moments every day and suggest to the subconscious what you want to have done. Be thoroughly sincere in this matter; be determined; have unbounded faith, and you can expect results; but do not permit the mind to become wrought up when giving directions. Always be calm and deeply poised when thinking out or suggesting to the subconscious, and it is especially important that you be deeply calm before you go to sleep. Do not permit any idea, suggestion or expectation to enter the subconscious unless it is something that you actually want developed or worked out, and here we should remember that every idea, desire or state of mind that is deeply felt will enter the subconscious. When there are no results, do not lose faith. You know that the cause of the failure was the failure of the conscious to properly touch the subconscious at the time the directions were given, so therefore try again, giving your thought a deeper life and a more persistent desire. Always be prepared to give these methods sufficient time. Some have remarkable results at once, while others secure no results for months; but whether you secure results as soon as you wish or not, continue to give your directions every day, fully expecting results. Be determined in every effort you may make in this direction, but do not be over-anxious.

## August 17th

### Henry Thomas Hamblin

To other creatures, life and the visible world are fixed quantities. To man, life and the world are reflexes of inward mental states. Thus, can he make life what he will; thus can he live in a world of his own creating. Man alone has the power to realize and recognize the inward Power of the Infinite, and to consciously bring It into objectivity. The inward powers of the mind are potentially illimitable, but they lie dormant and unexpressed, until they are recognized, and aroused into action, by the individual. This is why the majority of people are so worried and distressed. Why they either fail to make life worth living or achieve only partial success, and that with great difficulty. They try to achieve without the power to achieve. They marvel at their own weakness, not realizing that within them lie immeasurable powers which are patiently waiting to find expression. Until man calls these powers into activity they can never act. Within him is that which is connected with the Power-House of the Universe, yet he never feels its power. Within him is Infinite Wisdom, Knowledge, Inspiration, Creative Power and driving Force, yet he slumbers on, unconscious of their existence. But to those who realize their own interior Powers, what a mine of inexhaustible treasure do they find, what force and energy for all accomplishment.

## August 18th

Ernest Holmes

We find, then, that the Word, which is the inner activity of thought, comes first in the creative series, and all else comes from the effect of the Word operating upon a universal substance. If the Word precedes all else, then the Word is what we are looking for, and when we get it we shall have what the world has sought from time immemorial. We must, if we wish to prove the power of the Spirit in our lives, look not to outside things or effects, but to the Word alone. The human eye sees and the human hand touches only that which is an effect. Unseen law controls everything; but this Law also is an effect; Law did not make itself; the Law is not intelligence or causation. Before there can be a Law there must be something that acts, and the Law is the way it acts; it is intelligence. "In the beginning was the Word." This Word or the activity of the Spirit, is the cause of the law, and the law in its place is the cause of the thing, and the thing is always an effect; that is, it did not make itself; it is a result. The Word always comes first in the creative series; "The Word was with God and the Word was God" and the Word still is God. When we realize that man is like God (and he could not be otherwise, being made out of God), we will realize that his word also has power. If there is but One Mind then it follows that our word, our thought is the activity of that One Mind in our consciousness; the power that holds the planets in their place is the same power that flows through man. We must place the Word where it belongs, whether it is the word of God in the Universe or the word of man in the individual; it is always first, before all else, in the beginning. The real sequence is this: Cause, Spirit, Intelligence, God; the Word, the activity of Intelligence; the effect, or the visible thing, whether it is a planet or a peanut. All are made out of the same thing. What we need to do is to learn how to use the word so that all will come to see that they are creative centers within themselves.

## August 19th

Robert Collier

Back of everything is the immutable law of the Universe — that what you are is but the effect. Your thoughts are the causes. The only way you can change the effect is by first changing the cause. People live in poverty and want because they are so wrapped up in their sufferings that they give out thoughts only of lack and sorrow. They expect want. They open the door of their mind only to hardship and sickness and poverty. True — they hope for something better — but their hopes are so drowned by their fears that they never have a chance. You cannot receive good while expecting evil. You cannot demonstrate plenty while looking for poverty. "Blessed is he that expecteth much, for verily his soul shall be filled." Solomon outlined the law when he said:

"There is that scattereth, and increaseth yet more;
And there is that withholdeth more than is meet,
but it tendeth only to want.
The liberal soul shall be made fat;
And he that watereth shall be watered also himself.

## August 20th

Joseph Murphy

As you go to sleep tonight, practice the many techniques which we occasionally refer to. Repeat the word, "Wealth," quietly, easily, and feelingly. Do this over and over again as a lullaby. Lull yourself to sleep with the one word, "Wealth." You should be amazed at the results. Wealth should flow to you in avalanches of abundance; this is another example of The Miracles of The Subconscious Mind.

## August 21st

Charles F. Haanel

We are related to the world without by the objective mind. The brain is the organ of this mind and the cerebro-spinal system of nerves puts us in conscious communication with every part of the body. This system of nerves responds to every sensation of light, heat, odor, sound and taste. When this mind thinks correctly, when it understands the truth, when the thoughts sent through the cerebro-spinal nervous system to the body are constructive, these sensations are pleasant, harmonious. The result is that we build strength, vitality and all constructive forces into our body, but it is through this same objective mind that all distress, sickness, lack, limitation and every form of discord and inharmony is admitted to our lives. It is therefore through the objective mind, by wrong thinking, that we are related to all destructive forces. We are related to the world within by the subconscious mind. The solar plexus is the organ of this mind; the sympathetic system of nerves presides over all subjective sensations, such as joy, fear, love, emotion, respiration, imagination and all other subconscious phenomena. It is through the subconscious that we are connected with the Universal Mind and brought into relation with the Infinite constructive forces of the Universe. It is the coordination of these two centers of our being, and the understanding of their functions, which is the great secret of life. With this knowledge we can bring the objective and subjective minds into conscious cooperation and thus coordinate the finite and the infinite. Our future is entirely within our own control. It is not at the mercy of any capricious or uncertain external power.

## August 22nd

### Ernest Holmes

Your life is governed by more than a sentiment; it is governed by law, something that cannot be broken, something that picks up every mental attitude and does something with it. This fundamental proposition of the law should then work out into our conditions. Always remember that it does just as we think. It does not argue, it simply does the thing as we think it. Now how are we thinking? Never ask a patient how he is feeling; ask, how are you thinking today? This is the only thing that matters. How are we thinking about life and our conditions? Are we receiving the race suggestion; are we saying that there is not enough to go around? If we are saying this, it is our belief, and there is something that will see that it becomes a part of our expression. Most people, through ignorance of the higher laws of their being, are suffering from the thoughts imposed upon them from a negative and doubtful world. We who are claiming the use of the greater law must emancipate ourselves from all sense of limitation. We are not to be governed by the outer confusion but by the inner realization. We are to judge life not from the way that things in the past have been done, but from the way that the Spirit does things.

## August 23rd

### Wallace Wattles

You must form a clear and definite mental picture of what you want. You cannot transmit an idea unless you have it yourself. You must have it before you can give it, and many people fail to impress thinking substance because they have themselves only a vague and misty concept of the things they want to do, to have, or to become. It is not enough that you should have a general desire for wealth "to do good with." Everybody has that desire. It is not enough that you should have a wish to travel, see things, live more, etc. Everybody has those desires also. If you were going to send a wireless message to a friend, you would not send the letters of the alphabet in their order and let him construct the message for himself, nor would you take words at random from the dictionary. You would send a coherent sentence, one which meant something. When you try to impress your wants upon the thinking substance, remember that it must be done by a coherent statement. You must know what you want and be specific and definite. You can never get rich or start the creative power into action by sending out unformed longings and vague desires.

## August 24th

Christian Larson

To train the objective mind to act directly upon the subjective, consciousness should be more thoroughly developed in the realms of the finer feelings and the finer elements of life. Efforts should be made to come in touch with the higher vibrations in the system, because whenever we act in the higher vibrations, we act upon the subjective. Whatever we desire the subjective to do while we act in the finer feeling of the higher vibrations that the subjective will proceed to do. To act consciously and directly upon the subjective will also deepen the realization of life, which is extremely important; because the deepest life gives the strongest power, and in the creation of a greater destiny we need all the power we can secure. When this deepening of life is continued in the serene attitude, mind is kept constantly in touch with the source of unbounded power, and thus receives as much power each day as may be required. This brings us to one of the greatest essentials in the mastery of fate living; because there is nothing that contributes so much to the supremacy of man as a real, full life. To bring out the best that is within him, man must not merely exist; he must live. When man actually lives he is what he is, and is all that he is. He does not try to be something else, or someone else. He does not imitate, but continues to be himself. And this is one of the secrets in the creation of a greater destiny.

## August 25th

Eugene Del Mar

It is true that theory must precede method, and thought be prior to action; but it is not every theory that will work out in practice, nor every thought that will induce the expected result. The theory must be put to work through use before it can be accepted as practical. It would be folly completely to cast aside theories, ideas, and speculations, these being the approaches to higher truths, but it were well to test them through use before accepting them finally as truly representative of what they claim to be. Practical ideals are those which produce the exterior conditions that they represent interiorly. It is practical use alone that converts an ideal into a fact and a theory into a demonstration. The theory may be old or new, tried or untried, but it becomes practical only when use justifies its pretensions. For ideals to be of acknowledged value in this busy world they must be proven to be workable, and the conversion of theories into facts is at the very heart of all progress. be workable, and the conversion of theories into facts is at the very heart of all progress. It would be a great mistake to assume a particular ideal to be impractical because it had not already been worked out successfully in practice. There are ideals that have been heralded throughout the ages, and continuously rejected as impractical, which are today being accepted as practical by hardheaded business men. An ideal remains impractical until it is discovered how to use it rightly, or until one's understanding of it enables him to make right use of it. In fact, the practicality of an ideal depends, not upon itself, but upon its user.

## August 26th

Ernest Holmes

When fifty-one percent of your thinking is health and life and power, that day the fifty-one percent will swallow up, erase, kill out the rest. The day you, as an individual, through fifty-one percent of your thought, pass beyond the perception of limitation, you will draw out of the universe everything you desire; poverty will desert you and you will be emancipated forever. The day you think fifty-one percent of happiness, misery shall depart and never return. Is it not then worth your time and your effort, and should it not be the greatest purpose in the life of any awakened soul so to depict this principle as to emancipate himself?

## August 27th

Prentice Mulford

Every thought of yours is literally building for you something for the future of good or ill. What then is your mind dwelling on now in any matter? The dark or the bright side? Is it toward others ugly or kind? This is precisely the same as asking "what kind of life and results are you making for yourself in the future?" If now you are obliged to live in a tenement house or sit at a very inferior table, or live among the coarse and vulgar, do not say to yourself that you must always so live. Live in mind or imagination in the better house. Sit in imagination at better served tables and among superior people. When you cultivate this state of mind your forces are carrying you to the better. Be rich in spirit, in mind, in imagination, and you will in time be rich in material things. It is the mood of mind you are most in, whether that be groveling or aspiring, that is actually making physical conditions of life in advance for you. The same law applies to the building-up of the body. In imagination live in a strong, agile body, though yours is now a weak one. Do not put any limits to your future possibilities. Do not say: " I must stop here. I must always rank below this or that great man or woman. My body must weaken, decay and perish, because in the past so many people's bodies have weakened and perished." Do not say: "My powers and talents are only of the common order and as an ordinary person. I shall live and die as millions have done before me." When you think this, as many do unconsciously, you imprison yourself in an untruth. You bring then to yourself the evil and painful results of an untruth. You bar and fetter your aspiration to grow to powers and possibilities beyond the world's present knowledge. You cut from you the higher truth and possibility. You have latent in you, some power, some capacity, some shading of talent different from that ever possessed by any human being. No two minds are precisely alike, for the Infinite Force creates infinite variety in its every expression, whether such expression be a sunset or a mind. Demand at times to be permanently freed from all fear. Every second of such thought does its little to free you forever from the slavery of fear. The Infinite Mind knows no fear, and it is your eternal heritage to grow nearer and nearer to the Infinite Mind. We absorb the thought of those with whom we are most in sympathy and association. We graft their mind on our own. If their mind is inferior to ours and not on the same plane of thought, we, in such absorption, take in and cultivate an inferior and injurious mental graft. If you will keep company with people who are reckless and unaspiring, who have no aim or purpose in life, who have no faith in themselves or anything else, you place yourself in the thought current of failure. Your tendency then will he to failure. Because from such people, your closest associates, you will absorb their thought. If you absorb it, you will think it. You will get in the same mood of mind as theirs. If you think as they do, you will in many things find yourself acting as they do, no matter how great your mental gifts. Your mind surely absorbs the kind of thought it is most with. If you are with the successful you absorb thought which brings success. The unsuccessful are ever sending from them thoughts of lack of order, lack of system, lack of method, or recklessness and discouraged thought. Your mind if much with theirs will certainly absorb these thoughts exactly as a sponge does water. It is better for your art or business that you have no intimate company at all than the company of reckless, careless, slipshod and slovenly minds. When in your mind you cut from the unlucky and thriftless, your body will not long remain so near theirs. You get then into another force or current. It will carry you into the lives of more successful people.

### August 28th

Joseph Murphy

The captain is the master of his ship, and his decrees are carried out. Likewise, your conscious mind is the captain and the master of your ship, which represents your body, environment, and all your affairs. Your subconscious mind takes the orders you give it based upon what your conscious mind believes and accepts as true. When you repeatedly say to people, "I can't afford it," then your subconscious mind takes you at your word and sees to it that you will not be in a position to purchase what you want. As long as you persist in saying, "I can't afford that car, that trip to Europe, that home, that fur coat or ermine wrap," you can rest assured that your subconscious mind will follow your orders, and you will go through life experiencing the lack of all these things.

## August 29th

### James Allen

There is no physician like cheerful thought for dissipating the ills of the body; there is no comforter to compare with good will for dispersing the shadows of grief and sorrow. To live continually in thoughts of ill will, cynicism, suspicion, and envy, is to be confined in a self-made prison hole. But to think well of all, to be cheerful with all, to patiently learn to find the good in all such unselfish thoughts are the very portals of heaven; and to dwell day to day in thoughts of peace toward every creature will bring abounding peace to their possessor.

## August 30th

### Robert Collier

"Prove me now herewith, saith the Lord of Hosts," cried the Prophet Malachi, "if I will not open you the windows of heaven and pour you out a blessing that there shall not be room enough to receive it... And all nations shall call you blessed, for ye shall be a delightsome land." Your mind is part of Universal Mind. And Universal Mind has all supply. You are entitled to, and you can have, just as much of that supply as you are able to appropriate. To expect less is to get less, for it dwarfs your power of receiving. It doesn't matter what your longings may be, provided they are right longings. If your little son has his heart set on a train and you feel perfectly able to get him a train, you are not going to hand him a picture book instead. It may be that the picture book would have greater educational value, but the love you have for your son is going to make you try to satisfy his longings as long as those longings are not harmful ones. In the same way, Universal Mind will satisfy your longings, no matter how trivial they may seem, as long as they are not harmful ones. "Delight thyself also in the Lord, and He shall give thee the desires of thine heart." If we would only try to realize that God is not some far-off Deity, not some stern Judge, but the beneficent force that we recognize as Nature — the life Principle that makes the flowers bud, and the plants grow, that spreads abundance about us with lavish hand. If we could realize that He is the Universal Mind that holds all supply, that will give us the toy of our childhood or the needs of maturity, that all we need to obtain from Him our Heart's Desire is a right understanding of His availability — then we would lose all our fears, all our worries, all our sense of limitation. For Universal Mind is an infinite, unlimited source of good. Not only the source of general good, but the specific good things you desire of life. To It there is no big or little problem. The removal of mountains is no more difficult than the feeding of a sparrow.

## August 31st

### Ernest Holmes

We are all immersed in an aura of our own thinking. This aura is the direct result of all that we have ever said, thought or done; it decides what is to take place in our life; it attracts what is like itself and repels what is unlike itself. We are drawn towards those things that we mentally embody. Most of the inner processes of thought have been unconscious; but when we understand the law all that we have to do is to embody consciously what we wish, and think of that only, and then we shall be drawn silently toward it. We have this law in our hands to do with as we will. We can draw what we want only as we let go of the old order and take up the new; and this we must do to the exclusion of all else. This is no weak man's job but an undertaking for a strong, self-reliant soul; and the end is worth the effort. The person who can hold his thought one-pointed is the one who will obtain the best results.

# September

## September 1st

### Christian Larson

A great many new ideas of extreme value have recently appeared in current thought, but one of the most valuable is the idea that "he can who thinks he can;" and in the mastery of fate it will not only be necessary to keep this idea constantly in mind, but also to make the fullest possible use of the law upon which this idea is based. To accomplish anything, ability is required; and it has been demonstrated that when man thinks he can do a certain thing, he increases the power and the capacity of that faculty which is required in doing what he thinks he can do. To illustrate: When you think that you can succeed in business, you cause your business ability to develop, because by thinking that you can succeed in business you draw all the creative energies of the system into the business faculties, and consequently those faculties will be developed; and as those faculties are being developed, you gain that ability which positively can produce success in business. You develop the power to do certain things by constantly thinking that you can do those things, because the law is that wherever in mind we concentrate attention, there development will take place; and we naturally concentrate upon that faculty that is required in the doing of that which we think we can do.

## September 2nd

### Robert Collier

All power is from within and is therefore under our own control. When you can direct your thought processes, you can consciously apply them to any condition, for all that comes to us from the world without is what we've already imaged in the world within. Do you want more money? Sit you down now quietly and realize that money is merely an idea. That your mind is possessed of unlimited ideas. That being part of Universal Mind, there is no such thing as limitation or lack. That somewhere, somehow, the ideas that shall bring you all the money you need for any right purpose are available for you. That you have but to put it up to your subconscious mind to find these ideas. Realize that — believe it — and your need will be met. "What things soever ye desire, when ye pray, believe that ye receive it and ye shall have it." Don't forget that "believe that ye receive it." This it is that images the thing you want on your subconscious mind. And this it is that brings it to you. Once you can image the belief clearly on your subconscious mind, "whatsoever it is that ye ask for...ye shall have it." For the source of all good, of everything you wish for, is the Universal Mind, and you can reach it only through the subconscious.

## September 3rd

Prentice Mulford

Your spirit, or thought, acts and works on others while your body sleeps. It may do this with those whose bodies are also asleep. If you are angry or discouraged on going to sleep, your invisible self on leaving its body will probably be attracted to some other angry or discouraged nature. The better mood you are in on quitting your body at night, and entering on your other existence, the better the thought or person you will meet in that existence to further your purpose. If you have no purpose, you will then probably meet with another purposeless nature. To have no special purpose in life, to simply drift, is to have nothing on which to focus or concentrate your thought-power. If it is not so concentrated, but scattered, fastening on one thing today, and another tomorrow, you will be restless, moping, and unhappy in mind. If unhappy in mind, you can never be healthy in body.

## September 4th

Ernest Holmes

Man is created an individual and as such he has the power of choice. Many people seem to think that man should not choose, that since he has asked the Spirit to lead him, he need no longer act, or choose. This is taught by many teachers but is not consistent with our individuality. Unless we had this privilege, this power of choice, we would not be individuals. What we do need to learn is that the Spirit can choose through us. But when this happens it is an act on our part. Even though we say, "I will not choose," we are still choosing; because we are choosing not to choose. We cannot escape the fact that we are made in such a way that at every step life is a constant choice. What we do need to do is to select what we feel to be right and know that the universe will never deny us anything. We choose and Mind creates. We should endeavor to choose that which will express always a greater life and we must remember that the Spirit is always seeking to express love and beauty through us. If we are attuned to these, and are working in harmony with the great creative power, we need have no doubt about its willingness to work for us. We must know exactly what it is that we wish and get the perfect mental picture of it. We must believe absolutely that we now have it and never do or say anything that denies it.

## September 5th

Uriel Buchanan

It is the universal law that man should live in harmony, gratitude and unselfishness; and whoever departs from this law must suffer the penalty of the transgression. Sorrow and pain are not the result of an evil power, but come as ripening experiences to force mankind into truer conditions. The further you progress, the more closely will you come into relationship with the law which will protect you from all harm. You will control your thought so that you will rise superior to adverse environment. You will control your feelings so that the heart will obey the dictates of reason, leading no more to harmful entanglements. You will have that happiness and serenity which will make your presence magnetic, drawing others within the charmed circle where all is contentment. The time will come, if it has not already come, when you will know the cause of your seeming failures. You will know why your efforts were futile. You will know why the events were shaped by influences beyond your control. You have had visions of things which you cried out for in the darkness; you have caught glimpses of what you are, but had not the strength to reach out and claim them. You thought then that it was a cruel, inexorable fatality which had implanted yearnings without the possibility of their attainment. But all the past struggles have been the result of the evolutionary impulse — the incarnated ray of divinity — consuming the dross and preparing the mind for its awakening.

## September 6th

Eugene Del Mar

The road to the Kingdom of Conscious Light lies along the avenues of recognition and realization. One must recognize that the mental controls the physical, and that the spiritual dominates the mental. Without this understanding he will be unable to place the appropriate emphasis on the various aspects of life, or relate them rightly. One must comprehend that the life that is expressing through his mentality and manifesting through his physical form is the One Life; and that continually it will function more perfectly as he directs the activities of his life in accord with its inherent harmonies, and without the introduction of the inharmonies of false beliefs. The purpose of existence seems to be that each and every aspect of life shall attain to its fullest realization of the Light that is inherent in the Universal Life itself. This is acquired through gradual mental development and its corresponding physical growth, each higher form of life assuming the texture and refinement enabling it consciously to express more nearly the Perfection that is of its very essence. If each and every aspect of the Infinite had always possessed the consciousness that inheres in the Infinite as an entity, manifestly there would have been no reason or necessity for individual existence. But to this end it was evidently essential that the consciousness should develop through experience with matter, that appearance should appeal to the senses, and that the mind should traverse its maze of delusions and illusions. As this seems to have been the method ordained, apparently there was no other way whereby the individual should gradually acquire that realization which the Universal always possessed.

## September 7th

Venice J. Bloodworth

Our difficulties are due to ignorance of the truth; we have accepted any sort of doctrine or creed without very much consideration, but because the world has been taught for so long to think that some must be rich, and some poor, that trials and tribulations are a sort of predestined lot, that this world is necessarily a vale of tears — is no reason for us to keep on accepting any such ridiculous creeds. Look at Nature. How profoundly abundant she is in everything. Can you suppose that the Mind that imaged such profusion as we see on every hand, ever intended you to be limited or to have to scrimp and save and count pennies? No! You don't believe it; after you stop to think it over you must realize there has been a mistake somewhere. We just have not understood that everything is first an IDEA. So let us reform our ideas. All reforms must begin at cause. Cause is mind, and mind does all its creative work in the Silence. Elijah found God, not in the whirlwind, the earthquake, nor the fire, but in the still small voice. Let us follow Paul's advice, "Be ye transformed by the renewal of your mind."

## September 8th

Joseph Murphy

The great law is, "As you would that men should think about you, think you about them in the same manner. As you would that men should feel about you, feel you also about them in like manner." Say from your heart, "I wish for every man who walks the earth, what I wish for myself. The sincere wish of my heart is, therefore, peace, love, joy, abundance, and God's blessings to all men everywhere." Rejoice and be glad in the progression, advancement, and prosperity of all men. Whatever you claim as true for yourself, claim it for all men everywhere. If you pray for happiness and peace of mind, let your claim be peace and happiness for all. Do not ever try to deprive another of any joy. If you do, you deprive yourself. When the ship comes in for your friend, it comes in for you also. If someone is promoted in your organization, be glad and happy. Congratulate him, rejoice in his advancement and recognition. If you are angry or resentful, you are demoting yourself. Do not try to withhold from another his God-given birthright to happiness, success, achievement, abundance, and all good things.

**September 9th**

Ernest Holmes

Daily we must train our thought to see that only which we wish to experience, and since we are growing into what we are mentally dwelling upon, we should put all small and insignificant thoughts and ideals out of our thinking and see things in a larger way. We must cultivate the habit of an enlarged mental horizon, daily seeing farther and farther ahead, and so experiencing larger and greater things in our daily life. A good practice for the enlargement of thought is daily to see ourselves in a little bigger place, filled with more of activity, surrounded with increased influence and power; feel more and more that things are coming to us; see that much more is just ahead, and so far as possible, know that we now have all that we see and all that we feel. Affirm that you are that larger thing; that you are now entered into that larger life; feel that something within is drawing more to you; live with the idea and let the concept grow, expecting only the biggest and the best to happen. Never let small thoughts come into your mind, and you will soon find that a larger and greater experience has come into your life.

**September 10th**

James Allen

The soul attracts that which it secretly harbors; that which it loves, and also that which it fears. It reaches the height of its cherished aspirations. It falls to the level of its unchastened desires and circumstances are the means by which the soul receives its own. Every thought seed sown or allowed to fall into the mind, and to take root there, produces its own, blossoming sooner or later into act, and bearing its own fruitage of opportunity and circumstance. Good thoughts bear good fruit, bad thoughts bad fruit.

## September 11th

Prentice Mulford

There is a certain fascination in watching the working of a powerful steam-engine, — in seeing tons of iron, that a hundred men could with their hands barely lift, rise and fall with the elasticity of a rubber-ball, or in watching the never-ceasing pour of the waters of a Niagara. That is because it is in human nature to love force. Our spirits, in so contemplating such exhibitions of force, connect themselves closer with the element of force and draw then and add eternally to themselves more of this element; and this fascination and admiration of power is, at the same time, your prayer or desire for power, which is immediately answered. And there is great profit in watching for an hour the heave and roll and wash of the ocean-billows against the rocks. And that certain repose and quiet and dreaminess you may feel when in the ocean's company, is because you are then actually absorbing of its element of force; you are then taking in a spiritual quality — force; and when you go away, you have gained more force to use in any way you choose, — in business, in some form of art, or the management of a family. And when at night, if but for a moment, you lift your eyes toward the countless stars, and try to realize that these are all suns with other earths wheeling around them; and that all the combined force of all the rivers, Niagaras, and oceans on our own little earth is, as compared with the force going on in what we see above us, but as the feeble might of a fly's wing, — then you have spent another profitable moment in the actual absorption of that much-needed element — force. That is one way of getting force. You are then praying for force; for all intense admiration is true worship, and all true worship is prayer or demand for the quality admired in that which is worshipped.

## September 12th

Christian Larson

When man ceases to believe that he is controlled by environment, he departs from a belief that is detrimental; and when he begins to realize that he has the power to completely control himself, he enters a conviction that is favorable to the highest degree. While he is in the attitude of self-submission, he is controlled by environment, and the belief that he is thus controlled, is true to him. But when he enters the attitude of self-supremacy, he is not controlled by environment; therefore, the belief that he is controlled by environment is no longer true to him. While we are in the dark, we can truthfully say that we are in darkness; but when we enter the light, we cannot say, truthfully, that we are in darkness. There is such a thing as being influenced by conditions that exist in our surroundings; but when we transcend that influence we are in it no more; therefore, to say that we are in it when we are out of it, is to contradict ourselves. And we equally contradict ourselves when we state that we are controlled by environment after we are convinced that we are inherently masters of everything in the personal life. What is not true to us now, we should not admit now, even though it had been true to us for all previous time. To state that you are controlled by environment, and to permit that belief to possess your mind, is to submit yourself almost completely to the control of environment. To recognize the principle of your being, and to realize that within that principle the power of complete supremacy does exist; to establish yourself absolutely upon that principle, and to state that you are not controlled by environment, is to depart from the control of environment.

## September 13th

Robert Collier

Your ability to think is your connecting link with Universal Mind, that enables you to draw upon It for inspiration, for energy, for power. Mind is the energy in static form. Thought is the energy in dynamic form. And because life is dynamic

— not static; because it is ever moving forward — not standing still; your success or failure depends entirely upon the quality of your thought. For thought is creative energy. It brings into being the things that you think. Think the things you would see manifested, see them, believe them, and you can leave it to your subconscious mind to bring them into being. Your mind is a marvelous storage battery of power on which you can draw for whatever things you need to make your life what you would have it be. It has within it all power, all resource, all energy — but YOU are the one that must use it. All that power is static unless you make it dynamic. In the moment of creative thinking your conscious mind becomes a Creator — it partakes of the power of Universal Mind. And there is nothing static about one who shares that All-power. The resistless Life Energy within him pushes him on to new growth, new aspirations. Just as the sap flowing through the branches of the trees pushes off the old dead leaves to make way for the new life, just so you must push away the old dead thoughts of poverty and lack and disease, before you can bring on the new life of health and happiness and unlimited supply.

### September 14th

Ernest Holmes

In metaphysics, as in everything else, we are dealing with a proposition which is the substance of things which are not seen by the physical eye. The human eye sees only that which is effect; the human hand touches only that which is effect; and we are very apt to say these effects are controlled by law. That is true; everything must be governed by law. Law controls everything, absolutely. But we are not as apt to realize that the law itself is an effect. Did you ever stop to think that not only is this planet an effect, that is, this planet did not make itself, it is an effect? When you do, you will see it is governed by law and made by law, but that law which governs this planet is also an effect. The law did not make itself. The law is not intelligence, as causation, it is the result of intelligence as causation, and that brings us back, and we say then, what is the cause? As metaphysicians we claim that the word is the cause, the word is the cause of the law, and the law is the cause of the thing and the thing is the effect of the law and the law is the effect of the word. It means this in practice: that the law is written into our own hearts and that we speak the word and the word creates the law and the law governs the thing. The word was with God and the word was God, and the word still is God. Our word, our thought, is the activity of that one Mind in our consciousness; the thing that holds the planet in its place; the thing that causes your blood to circulate and your food to digest, the thing that causes your business to succeed, the thing that makes the tide come in and go out, the thing that holds the planets in space is all the same thing.

### September 15th

Orison Swett Marden

A wonderful uplift and courage comes to the man who follows the aspiring tendency in his nature that bids him trust and look up, no matter how dark the outlook. Faith in the Power that orders all things well tells him that there is a silver lining to the black cloud which temporarily shuts out the light, and he goes serenely on, feeling confident that his plans will succeed, that his demands will be met. His is the consciousness that assures him, no matter what happens, that "God's in his Heaven; all's right with the world." If you keep this one thing in mind, that we are always creating, always manifesting in our lives the conditions we hold in our consciousness, you will not make the mistake millions are making today, manifesting the things they don't want instead of the things they want. When we realize that our enjoyment, our happiness, our satisfaction, our achievement, our power, our personality, all depend on the nature of our consciousness, the aim and direction in which it is unfolding, we will not deliberately build up a consciousness of the very opposite of all that we are struggling to attain. On the contrary, we will hold constantly in mind the consciousness of our ambition, whatever it is, the consciousness of our heart's longings, our soul's desires; we will hold the truth consciousness, the God consciousness, the harmony consciousness, the opulent consciousness, and then we shall really begin to live. Then life will mean something more to all of us than it now does to most of us — a mere struggle for existence.

## September 16th

### Joseph Murphy

True prayer is a mental marriage feast, and it teaches us all how to resolve the mental conflict. In prayer, you "write" what you believe in your own mind. Emerson said, "A man is what he thinks all day long." By your habitual thinking you make your own mental laws of belief. By repeating a certain train of thought you establish definite opinions and beliefs in the deeper mind called the subconscious; then such mental acceptances, beliefs, and opinions direct and control all the outer actions. To understand this and begin to apply it is the first step in changing "water into wine," or changing lack and limitation into abundance and opulence. The man who is unaware of his own inner spiritual powers is, therefore, subject to race beliefs, lack, and limitation.

## September 17th

### Henry Thomas Hamblin

By thought man either blesses or curses himself. By it he brings into his life either success or failure, health or disease, happiness or unhappiness, poverty or prosperity. It is all in his mind and the character of his thought. Whatever there is in your life or mine, of disharmony, lack, sickness or unhappiness, is the result of our disharmonious thought. We live in an orderly Universe, but we do not react harmoniously to our environment, we are not in correspondence with the hidden law and order around us. It is not necessary for the universe to be altered; what is needed is that we ourselves should be changed. Within ourselves is the cause of the disorder in our own individual world — for we each live in a little world of our own creation — therefore, the disorder and trouble that afflicts us, or the lack that restricts our life, can never be overcome, save by a change of mind, habit of thought, and mental attitude.

## September 18th

Venice J. Bloodworth

You must realize also that any inharmonious condition is apparent only. It was generated by thought and can be erased by thought. We are individualized spirit and we create our conditions with exact mathematical precision according to our character and belief. The one who has strength, faith, self-respect and love for his fellow man draws all good to himself; while the man who draws the sword of anger or criticism on his brother simply throws a boomerang for himself. The man who is healthy, happy and prosperous is the man who believes in himself, in his fellows, and the goodness of God.

## September 19th

Ernest Holmes

Never let go of the mental image until it becomes manifested. Daily bring up the clear picture of what is wanted and impress it on the mind as an accomplished fact. This impressing on our own minds the thought of what we wish to realize will cause our own minds to impress the same thought on Universal Mind. In this way we shall be praying without ceasing. We do not have to hold continually the thought of something we want in order to get it, but the thought that we may inwardly become the thing we want. Fifteen minutes, twice each day, is time enough to spend in order to demonstrate anything, but the rest of the time ought also to be spent constructively. That is, we must stop all negative thinking and give over all wrong thought, holding fast to the realization that it is now done unto us. We must know that we are dealing with the only power there is in the Universe; that there is none other beside it, and that we are in it partaking of its nature and its laws. Always, behind the word that we send forth, must be the calm confidence in our ability to speak into the power, and the willingness of Mind to execute for us. We must gradually grow in confidence and in trust in the unseen world of spiritual activity. This is not hard, if we but remember that the Spirit makes things out of

Itself by simply becoming the thing that it makes, and since there is no other power to oppose it, it will always work. The Spirit will never fail us if we never fail to believe in its goodness and its responsiveness.

### September 20th

James Allen

Man is always the master, even in his weakest and most abandoned state; but in his weakness and degradation he is the foolish master who misgoverns his "household." When he begins to reflect upon his condition, and to search diligently for the Law upon which his being is established, he then becomes the wise master, directing his energies with intelligence, and fashioning his thoughts to fruitful issues. Such is the conscious master, and man can only thus become by discovering within himself the laws of thought; which discovery is totally a matter of application, self-analysis, and experience.

### September 21st

Prentice Mulford

Success in any business or undertaking comes through the working of a law. It never comes by chance: in the operations of nature's laws, there is no such thing as chance or accident. The so called accidental tumbling of the stone from the mountain-side is the result of forces which have been acting in that stone through countless ages. You and your fortunes are no more the things of chance than is the tree from its earliest growth. You are the product of the elements, and that product through the working of a law. You can, as you find out the law, make of yourself whatever you please. Your thought, or spirit, and not your body, is your real self. Your thought is an invisible substance, as real as air, water, or metal. It acts apart from your body; it goes from you to others, far and near; it acts on them, moves and influences them. It does this whether your body be sleeping or waking. This is your real power. As you learn how this power really acts; as you learn how to hold, use, and control it, — you will do more profitable business, and accomplish more in an hour than now you may do in a week. You will continually increase this power by exercise. This, and only this, was the basis of the miracles, the magic or occult power of ancient times.

## September 22nd

### Uriel Buchanan

Be earnest and purposeful in all you do. Perfect harmonic mental action, straightforward thought and strong will power will charge your being with a superabundance of life, and you will diffuse about you a glow of deep and abiding sincerity which others will recognize and emulate. As you gain control over the thoughts and feelings of your own mind and heart you will gain strength to influence other minds and to inspire those you meet in daily life with a confidence which will cause them to trust you implicitly in all you do and say. Banish from your life all that is disagreeable or demoralizing. Encourage your mind to dwell on thoughts that are hopeful and helpful. Recall every noble deed you have witnessed, and every pleasant experience that has come to you. To do this repeatedly will cause your feelings to change. Your mind will open to finer impressions. Your faith in humanity will grow. The inner consciousness of advancement will prompt you to greater effort. You will be fearless in regard to the opinion of others. You will be impervious to reproach and insensible to flattery. If there are times when you become depressed and discouraged, search for the cause and you will find that the enemy has entered by way of uncontrolled thought or foolish fancies. Having discovered the cause, sum up your possibilities and invoke the aid of the hidden forces at your command; then press on with renewed determination, supported by the thought that thousands of hearts are beating in unison with your own, that thousands of purposeful minds are pressing on against the same opposing influences which are met by you, and every victory you achieve will influence others who will become the stronger for your endeavor.

### September 23rd

Ernest Holmes

By thinking, you set in motion a power that creates. It will be exactly as you think. You throw out into mind an idea, and mind creates it for you and sets it on the path of your life. Think of it, then, as your greatest friend. It is always with you wherever you may be. It never deserts you. You are never alone. There is no doubt, no fear, no wondering; you know. You are going to use the only power that there is in the universe. You are going to use it for a definite purpose. You have already fixed this purpose in your thought; now you are going to speak it forth. You are speaking it for your own good. You desire only the good and you know that only the good can come to you. You have made your unity with life, and now life is going to help you in your affairs.

### September 24th

Joseph Murphy

The scripture says, "God is love, God is all, over all, through all, all in all" Love, therefore, is resident in all men and in all things; so let us seek it in all. "Seek and ye shall find." Yes, if you truly look for the God-Love in the other, it will shine forth in all of its pristine glory. The first thing we do when we see another is to look for that Divine Love to radiate through his thoughts, words, and deeds. If we truly recognize It as being within him, he must radiate this Love. "As within, so without." "As above, so below." "As in heaven (consciousness), so on earth (manifestation)."

### September 25th

Christian Larson

When we transcend the world of things and begin to live on the borderland of the splendor and immensity of the cosmic world, we discover that the vision of the soul was true. Those lofty realms that we have dreamed of so often and so long are dreams no more; we find those realms to be real, the prophetic visions of our sublime moments are fulfilled, and our joy is great beyond measure. The soul no longer dwells in the limitations of personal form, but is awakened to the glory and magnificence of its own divine existence. The mind is illumined by the light of the great eternal sun, and the body becomes the consecrated temple of the spirit. The ills of life take flight, the imperfect passes away, and we find ourselves in a new heaven and a new earth.

## September 26th

Wallace Wattles

The desire for riches is simply the capacity for larger life seeking fulfillment. Every desire is the effort of an unexpressed possibility to come into action. It is power seeking to manifest which causes desire. That which makes you want more money is the same as that which makes the plant grow; it is life seeking fuller expression. The one living substance must be subject to this inherent law of all life. It is permeated with the desire to live more, and that is why it is under the necessity of creating things. The one substance desires to live more in and through you. Therefore it wants you to have all the things you can use. It is the desire of God that you should get rich. He wants you to get rich because he can express himself better through you if you have plenty of things to use in giving him expression. He can live more in you if you have unlimited command of the means of life. The universe desires you to have everything you want to have. Nature is friendly to your plans. Everything is naturally for you. Make up your mind that this is true. It is essential, however, that your purpose should harmonize with the purpose that is in all. You must want real life, not mere pleasure or sensual gratification. Life is the performance of function, and the individual really lives only when he performs every function — physical, mental, and spiritual — of which he is capable, without excess in any.

## September 27th

Orison Swett Marden

When you limit yourself in your thought, you are limiting yourself outwardly in a way which corresponds with your mental attitude, because you are obeying a law which is unchangeable. You will notice that the man who puts a nickel in the contribution box, is not only stingy, close, and mean in all his money matters, but his face, his whole person, has a cramped, worried, pinched look. He is forever saving pennies, watching out for little things and never doing big things. No matter how much natural ability he has, his narrow, limited, poverty thought dwarfs him and cuts off his stream of supply. He cannot do big things because he never thinks big things. His warped mind will admit only a pinched supply instead of the big flow that is literally at his command. It is because we have not learned how to use our thought forces that most of us go about like paupers, never glimpsing the marvelous inheritance left us by the All-supply, the All-good. Our parsimonious thought pinches our supply.

## September 28th

Ernest Holmes

Again let us say that the Spirit creates by becoming the thing that it thinks. There is no other possible way in which it could work. Since it is all and there is no other, the thought of opposing forces never enters into its mental working; when we are judging from the outer we are not working in line with the power that we should be using. We must come to see that there is only One Power and that we are touching it at all points, for there is not a power of poverty and a power of prosperity. There is the one becoming the many; it makes and it unmakes that a higher form may appear to express through it. All that is not in line with its forward movement will soon pass away, for it recognizes no opposite. As far as we are concerned what we are and what we are to become depends only upon what we are thinking, for this is the way that we are using creative power.

## September 29th

### Christian Larson

To properly direct and impress the subconscious, the first essential is to realize that the subconscious mind is a finer mentality that permeates every fiber of the entire personality. Though the subconscious can be impressed most directly through the brain-center, the volume of subconscious expression will increase in proportion to our conscious realization of subconscious life in every part of mind and body. To concentrate attention frequently upon the subconscious side of the entire personality will steadily awaken the great within; this will cause one to feel that a new and superior being is beginning to unfold, and with that feeling comes the conviction that unbounded power does exist in the deeper life of man. When the awakening of the subconscious is felt in every part of mind and body, one knows that anything may be attained and achieved; doubts disappear absolutely, because to feel the limitless is to believe in the limitless. While impressing the subconscious, attention should be directed upon the inside of mind, and this is readily done while one thinks that the subconscious mentality permeates the personality, as water permeates a sponge. Think of the interior essence that permeates the exterior substance, and cause all mental actions to move toward the finer mental life that lives and moves and has its being within the interior mind. This will cause the conscious action to impress itself directly upon the subconscious, and a corresponding reaction or expression will invariably follow.

## September 30th

### Prentice Mulford

All of us do really "pray without ceasing." We do not mean by prayer any set formality or form of words. A person who sets his or her mind on the dark side of life, who lives over and over the misfortunes and disappointments of the past, prays for similar misfortunes and disappointments in the future. If you will see nothing but ill luck in the future, you are praying for such ill luck and will surely get it. You carry into company not only your body, but what is of far more importance, your thought or mood of mind, and this thought or mood, though you say little or nothing, will create with others an impression for or against you, and as it acts on other minds will bring you results favorable or unfavorable according to its character. What you think is of far more importance than what you say or do. Because your thought never for a moment ceases its action on others or whatever it is placed upon. Whatever you do has been done because of a previous, long held mood or state of mind before such doing.

# October

## October 1st

Robert Collier

As David V. Bush says in "Applied Psychology and Scientific Living" — "Thoughts are things; thoughts are energy; thoughts are magnets which attract to us the very things which we think. Therefore, if a man is in debt, he will, by continually thinking about debt, bring more debts to him. For thoughts are causes, and he fastens more debts on to himself and actually creates more obligations by thinking about debts. "Concentrate and think upon things that you want; not on things which you ought not to have. Think of abundance, of opulence, of plenty, of position, harmony and growth, and if you do not see them manifested today, they will be realized tomorrow. If you must pass through straits of life where you do not outwardly see abundance, know that you have it within, and that in time it will manifest itself. "I say, if you concentrate on debt, debt is what you will have; if you think about poverty, poverty is what you will receive. It is just as easy, when once the mind becomes trained, to think prosperity and abundance and plenty, as it is to think lack, limitation and poverty." Prosperity is not limited to time or to place. It manifests when and where there is consciousness to establish it. It is attracted to the consciousness that is free from worry, strain, and tension. So never allow yourself to worry about poverty. Be careful, take ordinary business precautions — of course. But don't center your thought on your troubles. The more you think of them, the more tightly you fasten them upon yourself. Think of the results you are after — not of the difficulties in the way. Mind will find the way. It is merely up to you to choose the goal, then keep your thought steadfast until that goal is won.

## October 2nd

Christian Larson

When things go wrong, just be glad. It is sunshine that brings forth the flowers from the cold and soggy earth. It is lightheartedness that puts to flight the burdens of life. It is the smile of human sweetness that dispels the chilly night of isolation and brings friendship and love to the bosom of the yearning soul. Then why be sad when gladness can do so much? Why be sad for a single moment when the smile of a single moment has the power even to change the course of human destiny. We all remember how soon a smile of God can change the world. Why not always live in that magical smile and just be glad? Then we should remember that all things respond to the song of rejoicing; all things gather where life is a song. Do you think that life is too difficult for smiles, and that you have too much to pass through to ever have happiness? Then remember that the glad heart knows no difficulty. The sunbeam even smiles at darkness, and converts the blackness of the storm into a brilliant rainbow. Just be glad, and your tears shall also become a bow of promise; yes, and more, for in that promise you shall discern the unmistakable signs of a brighter day upon the coming morn. Do not think that happiness must keep its distance so long as you have so much to pass through. The more you have to pass through, the more you need happiness. It is the shining countenance that never turns back; it is the glad heart that finds strength to go on; it is the mind with the most sunshine that can see the most clearly where to go and how to act that the goal in view may be gained. Just be glad, and half the burden is gone. Just be glad, and your work becomes mostly pleasure. Just be glad, and you take the keenest delight in meeting even the greatest of obstacles and the most difficult of problems.

## October 3rd

### Ernest Holmes

Expect the best to happen. Don't sit around waiting for trouble; have absolutely nothing to do with it. It is no part of the divine plan. It is an illusion of the material sense. One who has learned to trust will not be surprised even when he finds things coming from the most unexpected sources. All things are man's to use and then let go of. What more can we ask? We want nothing that we have to keep; things are to use not to hold. Expect that everything is to come your way. Be content and cheerful if you wish to attract from out the store of the infinite. Open up your whole consciousness to the greater possibilities of life. Line up with the big things. When you speak the word expect it to happen. Know that it must be as you say. This will not be fooling yourself, it will simply be using the law as it is meant to be used.

### October 4th

### Joseph Murphy

A technique of impressing the subconscious mind is as follows: This consists essentially in inducing the subconscious mind to take over your request as handed it by the conscious mind. This "passing over" is best accomplished in the reverie-like state. Know that in your deeper mind is infinite intelligence and infinite power. Just calmly think over what you want; see it coming into fuller fruition from this moment forward. Be like the little girl who had a very bad cough and sore throat. She declared firmly and repeatedly, "It is passing away now. It is passing away now." It passed away in about an hour. Use this technique with complete simplicity and naiveté. In using the subconscious mind you infer no opponent; you use no will power. You use imagination, not will power. You imagine the end and the freedom state. You will find your intellect trying to get in the way, but persist in maintaining a simple, child-like, miracle-making faith. Picture yourself without the ailment or problem. Imagine the emotional accompaniments of the freedom-state you crave. Cut out all red tape from the process. The simple way is always the best.

### October 5th

### James Allen

Men do not attract that which they want, but that which they are. Their whims, fancies, and ambitions are thwarted at every step, but their inmost thoughts and desires are fed with their own food, be it foul or clean. The "divinity that shapes our ends" is in ourselves; it is our very self. Man is manacled only by himself. Thought and action are the jailers of Fate — they imprison, being base. They are also the angels of Freedom — they liberate, being noble. Not what he wishes and prays for does a man get, but what he justly earns. His wishes and prayers are only gratified and answered when they harmonize with his thoughts and actions.

## October 6th

### Christian Larson

Man is inherently master over everything in his own life, because the principle of his being contains the possibility of complete mastership; and the realization of this principle produces the attitude of self-supremacy. While mind is in this attitude, only those impressions are formed that are consciously selected; consequently, only those thoughts are created that conform to the purpose that may predominate in mind at the time. To remain constantly in the attitude of self-supremacy, is therefore the secret of original thinking; and since the mastery of fate comes directly from original thinking, everything that interferes with the attitude of self-supremacy must be eliminated completely. The most serious obstacle to this attitude is the belief that man is, for the greater part, the product of his environment; and that man cannot change to any extent until a change is first produced in his environment. The result of this belief is the attitude of self-submission; and the more deeply this belief is felt, the more completely does man submit himself to the influence of his surroundings. While mind is in this attitude, it has only a partial control over the process of thinking; it accepts willingly every impression that may enter through the senses, and permits the creation of thought in the likeness of those impressions without the slightest discrimination. To remove the attitude of self-submission, man must cease to believe that he is controlled by environment, and must establish all his thinking upon the conviction that he is inherently master over his entire domain. This, however, may appear to be not only impossible, but absurd, when considered in the presence of the fact that man is controlled by environment. To tell a man to cease to believe as true that which he knows to be true, may not, at first sight seem to contain any reason; but at second sight it proves itself to mean the same as to tell a man to leave the darkness and enter the light.

## October 7th

Ernest Holmes

Remember that in the Divine plan no mistakes are made and that if God could have done it in a better way he would have done it differently. No souls are lost, for all "Live and move and have their being in Him" and "God is not a God of the dead but of the living, for in His sight all are alive." Too long have we believed in the negative simply because we have allowed ourselves to become hypnotized by a few strong-minded people, and by those who have imposed upon the race a mass of false philosophy.

## October 8th

Orison Swett Marden

In my youth one of the hardest things in the Bible for me to understand was the statement, "To him that, hath shall be given." I couldn't reconcile this with the Bible. It seemed positively unjust. But now I know that it illustrates a law. "To him that hath shall be given," because in getting what he has a man has made his mind a magnet to attract more. On the other hand, "To him that hath little, that which he hath shall be taken away," because he is headed in the wrong direction mentally. He is closing the avenues of supply by his little thoughts, his doubts and fears. He is in no mental condition to get more, to attract more. If you want to demonstrate prosperity, you must think prosperity; you must hold your mind everlastingly toward prosperity; you must saturate your mind with it, just as a law student must saturate his mind with law, must think it, must read it, must talk it, must keep with lawyers and in a law atmosphere as much as possible, to be successful as a lawyer. It was intended that we should have an abundance of the good things of the universe. None of them are withheld from us except by our poverty-stricken mental attitude. There is no more possible lack for a human being of all that the heart can wish for than there is lack of water or food supply for the fish in the great ocean. The fish swims in the ocean of supply, as we swim in the great cosmic ocean of supply that is all around us. All we have to do is to open our minds, our faith, our confidence, to its reality, and use our intelligent effort to get all the good there is in it, — that is everything we need and desire.

### October 9th

Joseph Murphy

Here is a simple technique for you to increase your consciousness of wealth; use these statements several times a day: "I like money; I love it; I use it wisely, constructively, and judiciously. Money is constantly circulating in my life. I release it with joy, and it returns to me multiplied in a wonderful way. It is good and very good." This will help you get the right attitude toward money. Never criticize money by saying, "It is filthy lucre; it is bad; it is tainted." You cannot attract what you criticize. When you begin to think things through, you will realize that real wealth depends on the circulation of wonderful ideas in your mind which well up from the subconscious levels.

### October 10th

Uriel Buchanan

The five pointed star is a good emblem of the mind. It should be drawn on a cardboard about twelve inches square, and at the five points should be written the following words, one of the words being placed opposite each point: Virtue, Wisdom, Power, Riches, Glory. Hang the cardboard in a prominent place, and when looking at the star think of the different words and their meaning. Virtue is the first principle. Without virtue it is impossible to achieve anything great or glorious. It is the underlying principle which governs the attainment of every exalted position. See that the thoughts are kept pure and the heart clean. Let the emotions outgrow passion, and shun every temptation. The second principle is wisdom. Let its light always direct you. Say to yourself mentally: I can do nothing that is not good and true. I am guided by Infinite Wisdom. I turn from all error. I will rise above every appearance of evil. I will transmute the memory of past experiences into the pure gold of knowledge and wisdom, and will walk in the way of truth and goodness. The third principle is power. You should affirm mentally. I have planted my feet on the rock of virtue and wisdom. On this rock I will stand. No matter how fierce the storms, no matter how great the conflict, I AM fearless, confident and free. I will remain steadfast. I will unfold into the divine likeness. I AM conscious of unlimited power. My faith and loyalty to truth shall not be shaken. I have dominion over all things. I have realized the perfect ideal. The fourth principle is riches. Affirm mentally: In my individual supremacy as the expression of Infinite Power, I command all the resources that are needful. The treasures of the earth are my rightful possessions. Every demand I make shall compel response. Every effort shall receive its reward. I rise to higher power, to wider planes and greater riches. The fifth principle is glory. Affirm: I rejoice because my words and my works follow me. I have caused blessings to spring up in the lives of many. Because of my life, art is more beautiful and nature fairer. Because of my thoughts, humanity lives nearer the ideal. My mind and body are in tune with divine peace.

## October 11th

### Prentice Mulford

"Dreamers" do far more than the world realizes. The "daydream" of a person who may sit for an hour almost unconscious of what is going on directly around him, is a force working out results in the unseen and mighty kingdom of thought, concerning which we know so little. Only at present, he or she whose thought is so disengaged from the body as to make them for the time quite unconscious of its existence, having no knowledge of the power they are using, no belief that it is doing something, have consequently no faith in it; and without faith, most of the result must be lost to them. If you know nothing of gold-mining, or of the formations in which gold is found, or the methods for extracting it from the soil, you may dig in rich gold bearing earth for months, and cart it off to fill in sunken lots. With no knowledge of the treasure in your soil, you have no faith in it. We are, as regards our mental or spiritual powers, in an analogous condition. Yet every imagining is an unseen reality; and the longer and more firmly it is held to, the more of a reality does it make itself in things which can be seen, felt, and touched by the physical senses. Dream, then, so much as you can by day of health and vigor. The more you so dream of it by day, the more likely is your thought to enter the same vigorous domain at night, and so recuperate you all the quicker. But if you dream by day of sickness or weakness, your thought at night will be the more apt to connect itself with the current of sick, weak, diseased thought, and you are, on waking, the worse for it. Ignorantly you may store gunpowder in your cellar, thinking it some harmless material. A spark may then destroy your house and your body. In an analogous manner mankind are now constantly bringing pain and evil on themselves through an unwise or ignorant use of their mental forces. As we most think, imagine, or dream, can we store up gold or gunpowder. A daydream, or reverie, is an outflow of force working results. The more abstracted the reverie, the greater is the force working separate and apart from the instrument, the body. When for a time you can forget, or lose consciousness of, your physical self and immediate surroundings, you are working your spiritual or thought power possibly a hundred or a thousand miles away. All occult power, so called, all the miracle power of biblical record, was wrought by this method. If thought can be concentrated in sufficient volume on an image in mind, it can produce instantly that image in visible substance. This is the only secret of magic. Magic infers the instantaneous production of the visible by such concentration.

## October 12th

### Ernest Holmes

There is only One power, but we use it in two ways, either to destroy or to save. The blessing and the curse are one and the same thing; the power of mind used either affirmatively or negatively; the word used in fear and doubt or in faith and assurance. You do not have to understand material philosophy or be learned in the books of the human race. All these things may be good in their place, but to one who understands the greater laws of life they are as simple babblings.

### October 13th

Christian Larson

Be glad, and smile with the smile that is sincere, the smile that shines just as sweetly and as naturally as the sunbeam. It is such a smile that is a smile indeed; it is such a smile that comes from the soul from the soul that is ever singing just be glad. And how soon such a smile can change the world. Meet adversity with such a smile; charm away tribulation with such a smile bursting forth into song; and let the music of the soul restore peace, love and harmony where these might have been absent. Then be stronger than adversity; rise superior to tribulation, and know that you are infinitely greater than all that is unfortunate or wrong. In the midst of adversity combine strength with rejoicing, and fate must change. Before that music of the soul that is so high and so strong that it stirs the depth of every soul, all the world pays homage on a bended knee. And wisely, because such a power can change anything, transform anything, elevate anything, emancipate anything. Go forth therefore into life with strength in your soul and music in your soul, and the future shall steadily and surely shape itself to comply with your dearest wishes and your highest aspirations. Array yourself in the strength of truth, conviction, courage, faith, resolution, victory and triumph; and add to these another raiment — the music of gladness — and yours will be a life filled with glory, power and light.

### October 14th

Henry Thomas Hamblin

It must not be forgotten that true success is based on service. It is only by our cooperative help of the world that we can ever find happiness, and this is in itself true success. Money and fame are useless if they fail to bring happiness and satisfaction. Service and cooperative helpfulness bring the truest and most lasting success. Combined with efficiency they make us indispensable in our particular branch or calling. Sooner or later quality of character tells its own story. Those who rise rapidly, laughing at such things as service, integrity, etc., generally go down later in ruin and dishonor. Therefore, our thoughts should be not merely of success and achievement, but of service and helpfulness. We should not think so much of "what shall I get out of it", as "how helpful can I be", for all solid success is based upon the extent of our helpfulness to the community. The more helpful we are, the more indispensable we become, therefore, the greater the reward, as a rule. Apart from all this, the fact remains that thinking in terms of success and achievement, at the same time maintaining a consciousness of abundance and prosperity, tends to attract these things to us. The mind is creative to a degree undreamed of by most people, and our thoughts attract things to us after their kind — opportunities for achievement and more abundant circumstances on the one hand, or failure and lack on the other.

## October 15th

Venice J. Bloodworth

The Magic Secret of attainment is one INTENSIVE DESIRE. Fix one goal at a time, concentrate on just one desire. If you wanted to climb a mountain, you would not start up one path and every little while come down and select a new trail. If you did, you would never reach the top. It is the same way with your desires. You have got to concentrate on one idea at a time. Hold in mind the thing you desire most. Declare it to be an existing fact, understand that it is YOURS, for the very moment you desire anything it is GIVEN you, but you must hold it steady and want it with all your heart so that the law of growth can take effect. If you planted seed in your garden and dug them up every little while to see if they were sprouted or THREW THEM AWAY TO PLANT OTHER SEED, nothing would ever grow for you, and as the same law governs growth of any description, you can readily see that you must plant your thought seed and tend them with confident desire and expectation, all of which means that you must realize that you HAVE received a thing even before it comes forth in tangible expression.

## October 16th

Ernest Holmes

How limited we are, how little our thought! How the human race rises in the morning, plods off to the day's work, plods home at night, sore and tired, eats and sleeps, works and dies. As has been said of man, "Man works hard to get money to buy food to get strength to work hard to get money to buy food to get strength to work hard to get money, etc." This was never intended; it is the curse imposed on the man who believed in two powers, one of good and one of evil. To us there has come a greater vision, and to those who believe and act as though it were true it is proving itself.

## October 17th

Eugene Del Mar

One's perceptions are his ideals. He possesses them, but he never lives up to his ideals. His horizon is always at a distance. But he always thinks and acts in accord with his realizations, for these are so identified with him that they possess him. He manifests his realizations always, for he cannot be or do other than what he is. The difference between individual methods denotes the extent to which each approximates his ideals or higher perceptions in daily life. As one is faithful to his higher perceptions, he lives a life of principle, and more and more converts perceptions into realizations. A life of principle does not lack in warmth of feeling, of sympathy or love — quite the contrary. A life of principle is the very embodiment of feeling, sympathy and love. While it is deeply emotional, the emotions are controlled, they are not permitted to interfere with one's exercise of justice and love. The Universe is governed by law, and is exact and invariable in all its activities. Mathematical accuracy does not preclude love; on the contrary, it is love's highest expression; it is the guarantee of justice without which there is no expression of love. There is neither coldness nor lovelessness in infinite justice. And the more nearly just one is, the more nearly Godlike is he.

## October 18th

Robert Collier

There was once a prince who had a crooked back. He could never stand straight up like even the lowest of his subjects. Because he was a very proud prince his crooked back caused him a great deal of mental suffering. One day he called before him the most skilful sculptor in his kingdom and said to him: 'Make me a noble statue of myself, true to my likeness in every detail with this exception — make this statue with a straight back. I wish to see myself as I might have been. For long months the sculptor worked hewing the marble carefully into the likeness of the prince, and at last the work was done, and the sculptor went before the prince and said: 'The statue is finished; where shall I set it up?' One of the courtiers called out: 'Set it before the castle gate where all can see it,' but the prince smiled sadly, and shook his head. 'Rather,' said he, 'place it in a secret nook in the palace garden where only I shall see it.' The statue was placed as the prince ordered, and promptly forgotten by the world, but every morning, and every noon, and every evening the prince stole quietly away to where it stood and looked long upon it, noting the straight back and the uplifted head, and the noble brow. And each time he gazed, something seemed to go out of the statue and into him, tingling in his blood and throbbing in his heart. The days passed into months and the months into years; then strange rumors began to spread throughout the land. Said one: 'The prince's back is no longer crooked or my eyes deceive me.' Said another: 'The prince is more noble-looking or my eyes deceive me.' Said another: 'Our prince has the high look of a mighty man,' and these rumors came to the prince, and he listened with a queer smile. Then went he out into the garden to where the statue stood and, behold, it was just as the people said, his back had become as straight as the statue's, his head had the same noble bearing; he was, in fact, the noble man his statue proclaimed him to be. A novel idea? Not at all! 2,500 years ago, in the Golden Age of Athens, when its culture led the world, Grecian mothers surrounded themselves with beautiful statues that they might bring forth perfect children and that the children in turn might develop into perfect men and women. Eleven months from now you will have an entirely new body, inside and out. Not a single cell, not a single bit of tissue that is now in you will be there then. What changes do you want made in that new body? What improvements? Get your new model clearly in your mind's eye. Picture it. VISUALIZE it! Look FORWARD daily to a better physique, to greater mental power. Give that model to your Subconscious Mind to build upon — and before eleven months are out, that model WILL BE YOU!

## October 19th

### Wallace Wattles

There is a science of getting rich, and it is an exact science, like algebra or arithmetic. There are certain laws which govern the process of acquiring riches, and once these laws are learned and obeyed by anyone, that person will get rich with mathematical certainty. The ownership of money and property comes as a result of doing things in a certain way, and those who do things in this certain way — whether on purpose or accidentally — get rich, while those who do not do things in this certain way — no matter how hard they work or how able they are — remain poor. It is a natural law that like causes always produce like effects, and, therefore, any man or woman who learns to do things in this certain way will infallibly get rich.

## October 20th

### Joseph Murphy

Your subconscious mind is principle and works according to the law of belief. You must know what belief is, why it works, and how it works. Your Bible says in a simple, clear, and beautiful way: Whosoever shall say unto this mountain, Be thou removed, and be thou cast into the sea; and shall not doubt in his heart, but shall believe that those things which he saith shall come to pass; he shall have whatsoever he saith. MARK 11:23. The law of your mind is the law of belief. This means to believe in the way your mind works, to believe in belief itself. The belief of your mind is the thought of your mind — that is simple — just that and nothing else. All your experiences, events, conditions, and acts are the reactions of your subconscious mind to your thoughts. Remember, it is not the thing believed in, but the belief in your own mind, which brings about the result. Cease believing in the false beliefs, opinions, superstitions, and fears of mankind. Begin to believe in the eternal verities and truths of life, which never change.

### October 21st

Ernest Holmes

If you believe absolutely that you can do a certain thing, the way will always be opened for you to do it; if also you believe that time will have to elapse, then you are making that a law, and time will have to elapse. If on the other hand you believe that mind knows just how and never makes mistakes, but lets it be done unto you, then it will be done. Confusion brings more confusion; peace begets more peace; we cannot imagine the Great Spirit hurrying or worrying, fretting or trying to make anything happen. The only reason we worry and fret is because we have thought there was some other power which could bring confusion. Such is not the case. There is but one, and we are always using that one but using it according to our belief. This is our divine birthright, nothing hinders but ourselves. Remember that since all is mind, you cannot demonstrate beyond your ability to comprehend mentally, that is, beyond your ability to know about a certain thing.

### October 22nd

Genevieve Behrend

Every living thing has faith in something or somebody. Faith is that quality of Power which gives the Creative Energy a corresponding vitality, and the vitality in the word of Faith you use causes it to take corresponding physical form. Even intense fear is alive with faith. You fear smallpox because you believe it possible for you to contract it. You fear poverty and loneliness because you believe them possible for you. It is the Faith which understands that every creation had its birth in the womb of thought-words, that gives you dominion over all things, your lesser self included, and this feeling of faith is increased and intensified through observing what it does. Your constant observation should be of your state of consciousness when you did; not when you hoped you might, but feared it was too good to be true. How did you feel that time when you simply had to bring yourself into a better frame of mind and did, or you had to have a certain thing and got it? Live these experiences over again and again — mentally — until you really feel in touch with the self which knows and does, and then the best there is, is yours.

### October 23rd

### Prentice Mulford

So whenever you think, you are affecting your fortunes for good or ill; and whenever you talk to others, you are making a force still greater to make or lose for you health, friends, and money. Every thought of yours, silent or spoken, has a literal value. If you receive (that is, think) the thought that you cannot succeed in any undertaking, that thought also goes out, meets and attracts other discouraged, despondent " I can't" thought, brings you nearer and nearer the hopeless, fretting peopled bodies it is in advance of, injures your health and all pushing business ability, and brings you at last in personal contact with people who only help to ruin each other. You are working then your thought-power for nonsuccess. You can use this power to bring you good or ill results, as you can use the locomotive to carry your body on a journey, or to crush your body by throwing yourself before it. Whatever plan or scheme of business you fix your mind persistently upon in the determination to succeed, it commences then as a thought-construction of unseen element to draw aiding forces to you. By "aiding forces" is meant first, ever growing fertility of mind to breed new plans for pushing your business; secondly, drawing to you the best people to aid you in your plans.

## October 24th

Joseph Murphy

From infancy on the majority of us have been given many negative suggestions. Not knowing how to thwart them, we unconsciously accepted them. Here are some of the negative suggestions: "You can't." "You'll never amount to anything." "You mustn't." "You'll fail." "You haven't got a chance." "You're all wrong." "It's no use." "It's not what you know, but who you know." "The world is going to the dogs." "What's the use, nobody cares." "It's no use trying so hard." "You're too old now." "Things are getting worse and worse." "Life is an endless grind." "Love is for the birds." "You just can't win." "Pretty soon you'll be bankrupt." "Watch out, you'll get the virus." "You can't trust a soul," etc Unless, as an adult, you use constructive autosuggestion, which is a reconditioning therapy, the impressions made on you in the past can cause behavior patterns that cause failure in your personal and social life. Autosuggestion is a means releasing you from the mass of negative verbal conditioning that might otherwise distort your life pattern, making the development of good habits difficult.

## October 25th

Ernest Holmes

This Universe is the reason, first of an Infinite Intelligence which speaks or thinks, and as this thought becomes active within itself, it creates from itself, at the power of its own word, the visible Universe. We are living in a Universal activity of mental law, we are surrounded by a Mind which receives every impression of our thought and returns to us just what we think. Every man, then, is living in a world made for him from the activity of his thought. It is a self-evident proposition that Mind must create out of Itself; and this Self being Limitless, it follows that its creative power is without limit.

## October 26th

Orison Swett Marden

During his lecture tour in the United States, the great scientist, Sir Oliver Lodge, speaking on "The Reality of the Unseen," said: "Our senses are no criterion of existence. They were evolved for earthly reasons, not for purposes of philosophy, and if we refuse to go beyond the direct evidence of our senses we shall narrow our outlook on the universe to a hopeless and almost imbecile extent." It is the most difficult thing in the world to convince people of the reality of anything they cannot perceive through the senses. Yet the realest things we know anything about are invisible; have never been seen by mortal eyes. And right here lies the great difficulty for most people in changing undesirable conditions; in getting away from poverty and the things that are holding them back. They can't see beyond the present; they haven't learned to visualize the future, to see beyond the material things about them into the unseen world, packed with all creative energies, where the mind starts the creative processes. They do not realize that everything in the visible world that man has produced began in a mental vision; that the power of mind picturing, of visualizing the things we want to come into our lives, is God's priceless gift to man, to enable him to bring into visibility out of the invisible world whatever he wills.

## October 27th

Christian Larson

The mastery of fate implies the constant improvement of everything in one's world physical or mental; and since the improvement of one's exterior environment requires financial increase, the problem of recompense and reward must be solved. There are vast numbers who claim they are not being remunerated according to their worth, and this claim is keeping the industrial world in constant turmoil. The result is detrimental to everybody, whether they are directly connected with industrial activity or not. Therefore, to find a solution for the problem would be one of the greatest discoveries that could possibly be made. That a great deal of injustice exists in the world, is true; and that many who are strong are taking advantage of multitudes that are weak, is also true; but there is a peaceful way for every individual to secure his own. And it remains wholly with the individual. There is no remedy in sight that the whole world can adopt, through which industrial justice can be established by law; but each individual can so relate himself to the world that his recompense will correspond exactly with his worth. To do this he must neither undervalue nor overvalue his work; and he must not compare his legitimate efforts with the efforts of those who employ questionable means. There are a great many who think they are worth more than they really are, because they compare themselves with the unscrupulous. When a certain person gains great wealth through illegitimate means, many imagine that they ought to gain as much; they are just as good and just as able as he, and work equally as hard. But in the mastery of fate all kinds of unjust methods must be eliminated completely, because in the creation of one's future there must be no flaws, or the entire structure may have to be discarded. There is no wisdom in making any comparison between oneself and the man who is gaining wealth by undermining his own future welfare. We do not care for the destiny of such a personage, and there is only loss in store for those who imitate his ways.

## October 28th

### Charles Fillmore

It is an easy matter to give thanks for what we have already received. It is not so easy to give thanks for what we hope to receive. Giving thanks in advance brings to pass a present expectation. Pray believing that you have received, and you shall receive. Praising and giving thanks liberate the finer essence of soul and body when we center our attention upon Spirit. Spirit is the dynamic force that releases the pent-up energies within man. The energies have been imprisoned in the cells and when released are again restored to action in the body by the chemistry of creative Mind. The perfection of this restoration is in proportion to the understanding and industry of the individual. Every thought we loose in our mind carries with it a certain substance, life, and intelligence. Whenever praise is bestowed it is carried to every part of the body and through a large area of our soul aura, and our whole consciousness and everything about us is tinctured with praise. Praise and thanksgiving divinely directed tap the mighty reservoirs of infinite Mind.

## October 29th

### Ernest Holmes

Spirit creates through law. The law is always mind in action. Mind cannot act unless intelligence sets it in motion. In the great universal mind man is a center of intelligence, and every time he thinks he sets mind into action. What is the activity of this mind in relation to man's thought? It has to be one of mental correspondence; that is, mind has to reflect whatever thought it casts into it. Wonderful as Universal Mind is, it has no choice but to create whatever thought is given it; if it could contradict that thought, it would not be a unit, since this would be recognizing something outside itself. This is a point in Truth which should not be overlooked. The ONE MIND knows only its own ability to make whatever is given It; It sees no other power and never analyzes or dissects; It simply KNOWS, and the reason why people do not understand this is that they have not realized what mind is. The ordinary individual thinks of mind only from the limitation of his own environment. The concept he has of mind is the concept of his own thinking, which is very limited.

## October 30th

### Uriel Buchanan

Recognizing your vital relationship with the Infinite Mind and all nature, you will know there is nothing to fear. Then you will step out into the sunshine of your true life. Strengthened and renewed mentally and physically, you will no longer cling to the outgrown past, but will strike out boldly into new and untried realms of activity, knowing that you will never be left guideless in the dark or unsupported by the Infinite Power.

You will keep in the current and let it bear you on to the realization of health, happiness and freedom. You will grow tired of laboring for that which gives so little return, of the business cares pressing upon you, of the misunderstanding and opposition, of your happiness all crossed with strife and pain; you will follow the monitions of the higher self, and you will find the way out of bewilderment into serene regions where all the problems that have vexed you will disappear. Then you will threaten to pass by all that has held you, and to ignore what once seemed essential to happiness. You will gain the strength of unwavering perseverance and will walk in the light of high ideals, reaching up after all that is true and good.

## October 31st

Robert Collier

Don't worry. Don't doubt. Don't dig up the seeds of prosperity and success to see whether they have sprouted. Have faith! Nourish your seeds with renewed desire. Keep before your mind's eye the picture of the thing you want. BELIEVE IN IT! No matter if you seem to be in the clutch of misfortune, no matter if the future looks black and dreary — FORGET YOUR FEARS! Realize that the future is of your own making. There is no power that can keep you down but yourself. Set your goal. Forget the obstacles between. Forget the difficulties in the way. Keep only the goal before your mind's eye — and you'll win it!

# November

## November 1st

### Joseph Murphy

The effectiveness of an affirmation is determined largely by your understanding of the truth and the meaning back of the words, "In praying use not vain repetition." Therefore, the power of your affirmation lies in the intelligent application of definite and specific positives. For example, a boy adds three and three and puts down seven on the blackboard. The teacher affirms with mathematical certainty that three and three are six; therefore, the boy changes his figures accordingly. The teacher's statement did not make three and three equal six because the latter was already a mathematical truth. The mathematical truth caused the boy to rearrange the figures on the blackboard. It is abnormal to be sick; it is normal to be healthy. Health is the truth of your being. When you affirm health, harmony, and peace for yourself or another, and when you realize these are universal principles of your own being, you will rearrange the negative patterns of your subconscious mind based on your faith and understanding of that which you affirm.

## November 2nd

### Christian Larson

When man is in a state of self-supremacy, he is in a state where no, influence from without exists; he is in a world where the power of self-mastery is the only controlling power; therefore, he cannot truthfully recognize any other. While in the attitude of self-submission, your mind is open to all kinds of impressions from without; and consequently, your thinking will be suggested to you by your environment. The result is that you will become like your environment, and will think, act and live as your environment may suggest. If your environment be inferior, you will think inferior thoughts, live an inferior life, and commit deeds that are low or perverse, so long as you are in the attitude of self-submission. But if you should submit yourself to a better environment, your life, thoughts, and deeds would naturally become better. In each case you would be the representation of the impressions that enter through the senses. However, the very moment you pass from a superior environment to one that is inferior, you will begin to change for the worse, unless you have in the meantime attained a degree of self-supremacy. To enter a superior environment will not of itself develop self-supremacy, nor the art of original thinking; because so long as you permit yourself to be influenced by environment, you prevent your mind from gaining consciousness of the principle of self-supremacy. A change of environment, therefore, will not give man the power to master his fate. This power comes only through a change of thought. While in the attitude of self-supremacy your mind is not open to impressions from any source; but you can place your mind, at will, in the responsive attitude, so that it may receive impressions from any source that you may select. By proper selection, consciousness can, in this way, be trained to express itself only through those mental channels that reach the superior side of things, and thereby come in contact with the unlimited possibilities of things.

### November 3rd

Ernest Holmes

Everything depends upon our mental concepts. "As a man thinketh in his heart, so is he"; the Bible reiterates this statement telling us many times of the creative power of thought; Jesus taught nothing else; He said "the words which I speak unto you, they are Spirit and they are life." The Centurion coming to Jesus recognized the power of the word spoken by the latter. He said, "I also am one in authority"; but his authority was on the physical plane, and he saw that Jesus had authority on a Spiritual plane, for he said, "Speak the word only." The Bible also tells us that the word is not afar off but in our own mouth. It is neither here nor there; it is within every living soul. We must take the responsibility for our own lives. All must awake to the facts that they have absolute control over their lives, and that nothing can happen by chance. Then they will have a broader concept of God, a greater tolerance for their neighbor, and a greater realization of their own divine nature. What a relief from strenuous labor; no more struggle or strife. "Be still and know that I AM God, and beside me there is none other." The Spirit being all there is, we cannot conceive of anything that can hinder its working. When the Spirit has spoken, the Word becomes Law, for before the Law is the Word; It precedes all else. First is Absolute Intelligence, All-Power, All-Presence, All-Causation; then the movement upon itself through the power of the Word; then the Word becoming Law; the Law producing the thing and holding it in place.

## November 4th

### Robert Collier

Just as the first law of gain is desire, so the formula of success is belief. Believe that you have it — see it as an existent fact — and anything you can rightly wish for is yours. Belief is the substance of things hoped for, the evidence of things not seen. It is your BELIEF in yourself that counts. It is the consciousness of dominant power within you that makes all things attainable. You can do anything you think you can. This knowledge is literally the gift of the gods, for through it you can solve every human problem. It is the open door to all good that you desire. But do not let doubts or fears creep in. Remember the admonition of St. James: "He that wavereth is like a wave of the sea driven with the wind and tossed. Let not that man think that he shall receive anything of the Lord." Baudouin said the same in different words: "To be ambitious for wealth and yet always expecting to be poor; to be always doubting your ability to get what you long for, is like trying to reach east by traveling west. There is no philosophy which will help a man to succeed when he is always doubting his ability to do so, and thus attracting failure. "You will go in the direction in which you face. There is a saying that every time the sheep bleats, it loses a mouthful of hay. Every time you allow yourself to complain of your lot, to say 'I am poor; I can never do what others do; I shall never be rich; I have not the ability that others have;' you are laying up so much trouble for yourself. "No matter how hard you may work for success, if your thought is saturated with the fear of failure, it will kill your efforts, neutralize your endeavors, and make success impossible." Learn to control your thought. Learn to image upon your mind only the things you want to see reflected in your outer circumstances. Your achievements of today are but the sum of your thoughts and beliefs of yesterday. Your chances of success in any undertaking can always be measured by your belief in yourself.

## November 5th

Prentice Mulford

It cannot be told too often, that all material things are the outgrowth or product of spiritual or unseen forces. Whatever you think of is made at once in unseen substance. So soon as made, it commences at once to attract its like order of substance to itself: so, no matter how weak you are, when in mind you see your body active, strong, and vigorous, you have really made the spiritual body so. That spiritual body is drawing, then, the elements of health and strength to itself. Always in mind see yourself well when your body is sick. This is a simple process, but it involves a wonderful and wonder-working law. When in mind you see yourself diseased, though your body may be so, you are working this law the wrong way. The imagining of a fresh, sound, vigorous body, is in actual substance, though unseen, a fresh, sound, healthy, and vigorous body. It is a spiritual reality. The material body must grow to be like the spiritual reality. If your body is weak, do not see it in your mind's eye as weak. See yourself full of life and playful vigor. Don't see yourself as an invalid propped up in a chair, or confined to the house, though for the time being your body is in such conditions. You are healing yourself when you see yourself running foot-races. You are keeping yourself an invalid when you see yourself ever as one. Don't expect or fear sickness or pain for tomorrow, no matter what sickness or pain you have today. Expect nothing but health and strength. In other words, let health, strength, and vigor be your daydream. The desirable condition of mind is better expressed by the word "dream" than by the terms" hoping " or " expecting."

## November 6th

Christian Larson

The upward look of mind, devoid of restless yearning, but fully serene and responsive, is the true attitude. Expect to receive the desired information from the superior wisdom of your higher mentality, and know that there positively is such a wisdom. While expecting this superior wisdom to unfold what you desire to know, be positive to your environment and to everything in the without. Do not permit the senses to suggest anything on the subject. But be responsive to your interior life; that is, feel in the within that your mind is open to the real wisdom from the within. Never doubt the existence of the superior wisdom within. This will close the mind to that wisdom. You know that there is such a wisdom; you have evidence to prove it every day; and the more faith you have in its reality, the more perfectly will your mind respond to its unfoldment. Another essential to the full expression of interior insight is to refine the physical brain so that the finer mental actions may produce perceptible impressions. This is accomplished by awakening the finer forces of the system, and directing those forces through a deep, serene concentration, upon every part of the brain. This exercise should be taken for a few minutes, several times a day; and the more highly refined you feel throughout the system at the time, the greater the results. In the use of interior insight, reason and objective understanding should not be ignored, because the best results are secured when the exterior and interior aspects of judgment are developed simultaneously and used together at all times. In this way the mind acquires the power to discern the internal causes on the one hand, and on the other, understands how to adapt the present movements of those causes to present exterior conditions. This brings the ideal and the practical into united action at every turn, which is absolutely necessary.

## November 7th

Ernest Holmes

The man who has arrived will realize that he has done so in the midst of an outer confusion; he will be the one who has gone into the silence for strength, and has come out into the world equipped with power from on high; but that light which he has received must be kept burning. Not alone in the silence but in the busy throng must all of us find the way of life. Our every thought creates. For the majority of us these thoughts come in every-day affairs, some of which are very trivial, but these too will be demonstrated. We have missed the whole point, unless we have learned so to control our thought that time and place make no difference.

## November 8th

Henry Thomas Hamblin

We cannot become adepts in right thinking and thought-control all at once. We all have to grow from small beginnings, gradually increasing in strength and stature. In other words, we all have to make a start in an apparently small and humble way. I say "apparently" advisedly, for although it may seem to be a small thing deliberately to think thoughts opposite in character to those which our feelings and natural or lower nature prompt us to think, yet it is really a big undertaking and, if we are successful, a high achievement. It may seem to be a small thing deliberately to think thoughts of goodwill about one who has wronged us, or upset us, but it is really a tremendous thing of eternal importance. If we merely give way to the promptings of our earth nature we remain on par with the beasts, allying ourselves with mortality, death and decay. But if we deliberately think thoughts of goodwill we step out in the path of liberation and freedom, which has no end, reaching up to the stars. It may appear to be a small thing to think deliberately thoughts of things pure and noble in place of thoughts of sensuality; yet, in reality it is a great achievement, for thoughts of the latter kind form the very taproot of man's unhappiness, weakness and woe. It may appear to be but a small thing to think thoughts of steadfastness and overcoming, in the face of apparent defeat and failure, yet it is not such a small thing after all, for upon it the success of our life largely depends. It may seem to be a small thing to think deliberately of God and things eternal in place of thoughts of mortality and things temporal; yet to do so is of importance for it is only thus that we can enter into eternal life, through becoming at one with that which knows no decay. It may seem to be a small thing to think deliberately of one's unity and one-ness with the Source of all Light and Life, instead of as separate and alone, but this also is a matter of importance, for through this we enter into a realization of the Truth. It may seem to be a small thing to think deliberately of health, wholeness and the joy of living, instead of brooding over disease, sickness and death; but the results of such thinking are far reaching, for upon it our health largely depends, and without health it is very little we can accomplish.

### November 9th

James Allen

Intellectual achievements are the result of thought consecrated to the search for knowledge, or for the beautiful and true in life and nature. Such achievements may be sometimes connected with vanity and ambition but they are not the outcome of those characteristics. They are the natural outgrowth of long an arduous effort, and of pure and unselfish thoughts. Spiritual achievements are the consummation of holy aspirations. He who lives constantly in the conception of noble and lofty thoughts, who dwells upon all that is pure and unselfish, will, as surely as the sun reaches its zenith and the moon its full, become wise and noble in character, and rise into a position of influence and blessedness. Achievement, of whatever kind, is the crown of effort, the diadem of thought. By the aid of self-control, resolution, purity, righteousness, and well-directed thought a man ascends. By the aid of animality, indolence, impurity, corruption, and confusion of thought a man descends. A man may rise to high success in the world, and even to lofty altitudes in the spiritual realm, and again descend into weakness and wretchedness by allowing arrogant, selfish, and corrupt thoughts to take possession of him. Victories attained by right thought can only be maintained by watchfulness. Many give way when success is assured, and rapidly fall back into failure.

## November 10th

Christian Larson

Love the true side of life; love the soul side of persons; and love the greater possibilities that are latent in circumstances, conditions and things. And love these things with a passion that thrills every atom in your being. The result will be simply remarkable. Where the heart is, there we concentrate; and where we concentrate we give our life, our thought, our ability and our power. Therefore, if we wish to build up the superior, we must deeply love the high, the true and the worthy, wherever these may be found. When difficulties are met, they should be met in the attitude of joy; and we should look upon the experience as a privilege through which greater power may be brought into evidence. To count everything joy is not a mere sentiment, but the application of a great scientific principle. The mind that meets everything in joy, conquers every time, because the attitude of joy is an ascending attitude; it transcends, and goes above that with which it comes in contact. Therefore, whatever we meet in the attitude of joy, we rise above; and whatever we rise above, that we overcome in every instance. The feeling of joy is also expansive, enlarging and constructive, and is a developing power of extreme value. To count everything joy may at first seem difficult; but when we realize that the attitude of real joy rises above everything, and overcomes everything by taking life to a higher level, we shall soon find it easier and more natural to meet everything in joy than otherwise.

## November 11th

Ernest Holmes

We must not deny that which we affirm. We must reason only from that cause which is spiritual and mental and weed out all thought that would deny its power in our lives. There seems to be something in the race thought that says man is poor; man is limited; that there is a lack of opportunity; that times are hard; that prices are high; that nobody wants what I have to offer. No person succeeds who speaks these ideas. When we express ourselves in this way we are using a destructive power. All such thoughts must go, and we must all realize that we are an active center in the only power there is.

## November 12th

Wallace Wattles

Riches secured on the competitive plane are never satisfactory and permanent. They are yours today and another's tomorrow. Remember, if you are to become rich in a scientific and certain way, you must rise entirely out of competitive thought. You must never think for a moment that the supply is limited. Just as soon as you begin to think that all the money is being "cornered" and controlled by others, and that you must exert yourself to get laws passed to stop this process, and so on — in that moment you drop into the competitive mind and your power to cause creation is gone for the time being. And what is worse, you will probably arrest the creative movements you have already begun. KNOW that there are countless millions of dollars' worth of gold in the mountains of the earth, not yet brought to light. And know that if there were not, more would be created from thinking substance to supply your needs. KNOW that the money you need will come, even if it is necessary for a thousand men to be led to the discovery of new gold mines tomorrow. Never look at the visible supply. Look always at the limitless riches in formless substance, and KNOW that they are coming to you as fast as you can receive and use them. Nobody, by cornering the visible supply, can prevent you from getting what is yours.

### **November 13th**

Robert Collier

Thought externalizes itself, through the Creative Force working through us. What we are depends entirely upon the images we hold before our mind's eye. Every time we think, we start a chain of causes which will create conditions similar to the thoughts which originated it. Every thought we hold in our consciousness for any length of time becomes impressed upon our subconscious mind and creates a pattern which the Creative Force weaves into our life or environment. All power is from within and is therefore under our own control. When you can direct your thought processes, you can consciously apply them to any condition, for all that comes to us in the world without is what we've already imaged in the world within. The source of all good, of everything you wish for, is Mind, and you can reach it best through your subconscious. Mind will be to you whatever you believe it to be — the kind and loving Father whom Jesus pictured, always looking out for the well-being of his children — or the dread Judge that so many dogmatists would have us think.

### **November 14th**

Joseph Murphy

Infinite riches are all around you if you will open your mental eyes and behold the treasure house of infinity within you. There is a gold mine within you from which you can extract everything you need to live life gloriously, joyously, and abundantly. Many are sound asleep because they do not know about this gold mine of infinite intelligence and boundless love within themselves. Whatever you want, you can draw forth. A magnetized piece of steel will lift about twelve times its own weight, and if you demagnetize this same piece of steel, it will not even lift a feather. Similarly, there are two types of men. There is the magnetized man who is full of confidence and faith. He knows that he is born to win and to succeed. Then, there is the type of man who is demagnetized. He is full of fears and doubts. Opportunities come, and he says, "I might fail; I might lose my money; people will laugh at me." This type of man will not get very far in life because, if he is afraid to go forward, he will simply stay where he is. Become a magnetized man and discover the master secret of the ages.

### November 15th

Ernest Holmes

Practically the whole human race is hypnotized, thinking whatever it is told to think. We get our concepts from our physical environment, we say, "See sin, sickness and death, misery, unhappiness and calamity." And this concept we are giving to the creative, impersonal Mind, and so we are making a law for ourselves that will produce what we believe in. Do we really know what law means? It means that which will exact the utmost farthing from our thought. Like produces like, attracts like, creates like. If we could see our thought and take a picture of it and of our conditions we would see no difference between the two, for they are really but the inside and the outside of the same thing.

### November 16th

Uriel Buchanan

Back of all that we see — back of the vast universe of countless forms — is the self existent principle which is eternally building and destroying through the agency of immutable laws. Invisible influences, sustained by the energies of nature, are ever working in man to awaken a deeper consciousness and nobler ideal. And he who faithfully responds to the evolutionary forces which spring up in the heart as an everlasting fountain will find the true source of goodness and peace, and his mind will be illumined by the unfading light of wisdom and love. There is a faculty of the mind which has power to arouse and direct the latent energies and stamp with the character of purpose every thought and act. By the focalization of the will the brain is made plastic and capable of receiving suggestions from the super conscious mind. The magnetic influence sent out from the inmost center of consciousness is transmitted from the brain to the different nerve centers of the body until the whole organism is thrilled by the fire of internal energy. When the conscious and subconscious faculties of the mind are attuned with one accord and dominated by a singleness of purpose, a battery is formed which is invincible, brooking no interference and heeding no obstacles. Will power is intensified by the deep desire of the subliminal self reaching out through the avenues of the senses in search of things desired. By the nature and intensity of desire, which governs the use of the will, man relates himself either to the kingdom of light or to the realm of darkness.

## November 17th

Christian Larson

When we examine the nature of the subconscious, we find that it responds to almost anything the conscious mind may desire or direct, though it is usually necessary for the conscious mind to express its desire upon the subconscious for some time before the desired response is secured. The subconscious is a most willing servant, and is so competent that thus far we have failed to find a single thing along mental lines that it will not or cannot do. It submits readily to almost any kind of training, and will do practically anything that it is directed to do, whether the thing is to our advantage or not. In this connection, it is interesting to learn that there are a number of things in the human system usually looked upon as natural, and inevitable, that are simply the results of misdirected subconscious training in the past. We frequently speak of human weaknesses as natural, but weakness is never natural. Although it may appear, it is invariably the result of imperfect subconscious training. It is never natural to go wrong, but it is natural to go right, and the reason why is simple. Every right action is in harmony with natural law, while every wrong action is a violation of natural law. It has also been stated that the aging process is natural, but modern science has demonstrated that it is not natural for a person to age at sixty, seventy, or eighty years. The fact that the average person does manifest nearly all the conditions of old age at those periods of time, or earlier, simply proves that the subconscious mind has been trained through many generations to produce old age at sixty, seventy, eighty or ninety, as the case may be, and the subconscious always does what it has been trained to do. It can just as readily be trained, however, to produce greater physical strength and greater mental capacity at ninety than we possess at thirty or forty. It can also be trained to possess the same virile youth at one hundred as the healthiest man or woman of twenty may possess.

### November 18th

James Allen

The world of things is the other half of the world of thoughts. The inner informs the outer. The greater embraces the lesser. Matter is the counterpart of mind. Events are streams of thought. Circumstances are combinations of thought, and the outer conditions and actions of others in which each man is involved are intimately related to his own mental needs and development. Man is a part of his surroundings. He is not separate from his fellows, but is bound closely to them by the peculiar intimacy and interaction of deeds, and by those fundamental laws of thought which are the roots of human society.

### November 19th

Ernest Holmes

We can so fill ourselves with the drawing power of attraction that it will become irresistible. Nothing can hinder things from coming to the man who knows that he is dealing with the same power that creates all from itself, moves all within itself, and yet holds all things in their places. I AM one with the Infinite Mind. Let this ring through you many times each day until you rise to that height that, looking, sees. In order to be sure that we are creating the right kind of a mental atmosphere and so attracting what we want, we must at first watch our thinking, lest we create that which we should not like to see manifest. In other words, we must think only what we wish to experience. All is mind, and mind casts back at the thinker that only which he thinks. Nothing ever happens by chance. Law governs all life, and all people come under that law. But that law, so far as we are concerned, we ourselves set in motion, and we do this through the power of our thought.

## November 20th

### Orison Swett Marden

When man realizes the tremendous significance of the reality of the unseen; when he grasps the truth of his unity with his Maker, the unity of life, the oneness of the source of all things in the universe, and that all is a manifestation of Divine Mind, he will come into possession of the illimitable power the Creator has implanted in every one of us. When Christ emphasized the fact that the kingdom of heaven is within us, he meant that this kingdom within is identical with the Divine Mind, and that it is there man taps the source of all power, of all supply. The kingdom within is the kingdom of power, where all man's creative work is started. It is there he connects with the universal substance, the great creative energy; and thought is the invisible tool with which he fashions his creations. Acting upon the hidden, mysterious substance from which everything in the universe is evolved, the thought tool directs, controls, creates according to his desires. It finds its material in the unseen world, and in proportion as the mind grasps the reality of the unseen, the power and the possibilities are there. It is in the unseen world that man, animated and inspired by the consciousness of his partnership with Divinity, is beginning to find some of the secrets of the universe — lifting the race from animalism and drudgery, changing the face of the world, pushing civilization up to new and more glorious heights.

## November 21st

Venice J. Bloodworth

The law of attraction is the law of your being. It is neither good nor evil, neither moral nor immoral. It is simply a blind law that cooperates always in perfect accord with individual demand. It is the one source of perfect justice, and by its action you reap what you have sown and that which you measure unto others is measured back to you. There is no way to escape this law. You may use it consciously or unconsciously but use it you must; it is the law of Life and controls the universe with absolute undeviating precision and justice. The benefit man receives by the operation of this law is represented by the forms of supply that add to his comfort, his human needs, and happiness AS DETERMINED BY HIM INDIVIDUALLY. Food, clothes, money, houses, automobiles, etc., are all symbols of this law of attraction and are all related to man through this law as cause and effect, desire and response, demand and supply. It is the operation of this law that produces such varied conditions and circumstances: riches, poverty, sickness, health, joy, sorrow. With such a conglomeration of conditions as we see manifested on every hand, you can understand how people came to believe in evil, poverty, disease, and discord as being necessary somehow to human nature. But when you realize fully that all these conditions have no power within themselves and are simply the results of individual thought, you will have found the birthright of every human being. You must first know that such a law exists and then LIVE IN ACCORD WITH IT.

## November 22nd

Prentice Mulford

When you read with interest in your morning's paper of murders, burglaries, scandals and dreadful accidents on sea and land, you are attracting to you unseen things of the same character. You connect yourself with this a lower order of spiritual realities, and being then in this current as you so read with interest, day after day, you are the more likely to bring some form of these horrors and miseries to you. These of the unseen form a current of real element in the unseen world of realities. You connect your spirit with this current when you keep these ghastly things so much in mind. That current then acts on you. You are borne along and carried by it. It will then all the quicker bring to you the elements of crime or evil. If you love to read of the acts of burglars and thieves, you are the more likely to have burglars and thieves about you and in your house. You and they will be brought together, because you and they are in the same current of thought. Neither you nor the thief is aware of the power which brings you together. But no power is so irresistible as one of whose action upon us and of whose very existence we are entirely ignorant. If you think but for ten seconds of something ghastly or horrible, something which causes pain of body or distress of mind to another, then you set in motion a force to draw some form of this trouble to you. If you think ten seconds of something pleasant, cheerful or beautiful — something which can give pleasure to another, leaving no sting behind — then you set in motion a force to bring some of this pleasure to you.

## November 23rd

### Joseph Murphy

Money is simply a subconscious conviction on the part of the individual. You will not become a millionaire by saying, "I AM a millionaire. I AM a millionaire." You will grow into a wealth consciousness by building into your mentality the ideas of wealth and success. One of our students who was formerly a seventy-five dollar a week salesman is now a sales manager at a salary of twelve thousand yearly. It all happened within a period of a month. Every morning as this person shaved, he would look into the mirror, and say to himself, "You are wealthy; you are a big success;" this went on for weeks. In about eight weeks he was suddenly promoted over the heads of eighty other salesmen. While shaving, you are relaxed. As previously outlined, you can convey an idea to the subconscious mind by repeating it again and again at intervals with faith and a joyous expectancy.

## November 24th

Ernest Holmes

Always when we pray we must believe. Our idea of prayer is not so much asking God for things as it is believing that we already have the things that we need. As we have said before, this already-believing is necessary because all is mind, and until we have provided that full acceptance we have not made a mold into which mind could pour itself and through which it could manifest. This positive belief is absolutely essential to real creative work; and if we do not at present have it, then we must develop it. All is law, and cause and effect obtain through all life. Mind is cause, and what we term matter, or the visible, is effect. As water will freeze into the form that it is poured, so mind will solidify only into the forms that our thought takes. Thought is form. The individual provides the form; he never creates or even manifests, — that is, of himself; there is something that does all this for him. His sole activity is the use of this power. This power is always at hand ready to be spoken into and at once ready to form the words into visible expression. But the mold that most of us provide is a very poor one, and we change it so quickly that it is more like a motion picture than anything else. Already we have the power; it is the gift of the Most High in its Finite Expression. But our ignorance of its use has caused us to create the wrong form, which in its turn has caused mind to produce the form which we have thought into it.

## November 25th

Robert Collier

The Universal Mind expresses itself largely through the individual. It is continually seeking an outlet. It is like a vast reservoir of water, constantly replenished by mountain sp rings. Cut a channel to it and the water will flow in ever-increasing volume. In the same way, if you once open up a channel of service by which the Universal Mind can express itself through you, its gifts will flow in ever-increasing volume and YOU will be enriched in the process. This is the idea through which great bankers are made. A foreign country needs millions for development. Its people are hard-working, but lack the necessary implements to make their work productive. How are they to find the money? They go to a banker — put their problem up to him. He has not the money himself, but he knows how and where to raise it. He sells the promise to pay of the foreign country (their bonds, in other words) to people who have money to invest. His is merely a service. But it is such an invaluable service that both sides are glad to pay him liberally for it. In the same way, by opening up a channel between universal supply and human needs — by doing your neighbors or your friends or your customers service — you are bound to profit yourself. And the wider you open your channel the greater service you give or the better values you offer — the more things are bound to flow through your channel, the more you are going to profit thereby. But you've got to use your talent if you want to profit from it. It matters not how small your service — using it will make it greater. You don't have to retire to a cell and pray. That is a selfish method — selfish concern for your own soul to the exclusion of all others. Mere self-denial or asceticism as such does no one good. You've got to DO something, to USE the talents God has given you to make the world better for your having been in it. Remember the parable of the talents. You know what happened to the man who went off and hid his talent, whereas those who made use of theirs were given charge over many things. That parable, it has always seemed to me, expresses the whole law of life. The only right is to use all the forces of good. The only wrong is to neglect or to abuse them.

### November 26th

### Christian Larson

Always remember that whatever is impressed on the subconscious will after a while be expressed from the subconscious into the personality; and where the physical conditions that you wish to remove are only slight, enough subconscious power can be aroused to restore immediate order, harmony and wholeness. When the condition you wish to remove has continued for some time, however, repeated efforts may be required to cause the subconscious to act in the matter. But one thing is certain, that if you continue to direct the subconscious to remove that condition, it positively will be removed. The subconscious does not simply posses the power to remove undesirable conditions from the physical or mental state. It can also produce those better conditions that we may want, and develop further those desirable conditions that we already possess. To apply the law for this purpose, deeply desire those conditions that you do want, and have a very clear idea in your mind as to what you want those conditions to be. In giving the subconscious directions for anything desired in our physical or mental makeup, we should always have improvement in mind, as the subconscious always does the best work when we are thoroughly filled with the desire to do better. If we want health, we should direct the subconscious to produce more and more health. If we want power, we should direct the subconscious not simply to give us a great deal or a certain amount of power, but to give us more and more power. In this manner, we shall secure results from the very beginning.

### November 27th

Robert Collier

Through every man there flows this Creative Force, with infinite power to draw to itself whatever is necessary to its expression. It doesn't matter who you are, what your environment or education or advantages, the Creative Force in you has the same power for good or evil. Mind you, that Force never brings forth evil. Its life is good. But just as you can graft onto the trunk of the finest fruit tree a branch of the upas tree, and thereupon bring forth deadly fruit, so can you engraft upon the pure energy of your Creative Force any manner of fruit you desire. But if the fruit be bad, it is you who are to blame, not the perfect Force that flows through you.

## November 28th

Ernest Holmes

We can only hope to bring to ourselves that which we draw through the avenue of love. We must watch our thinking and if we have aught against any soul, get rid of it as soon as possible. This is the only safe and sure way. Did not Jesus at the supreme moment of sacrifice ask that the Father forgive all the wrong that was being done to Him? Shall we suppose that 'we can do it in a better way? If we do not at the present time love all people, then we must learn how to do it, and the way will become easier, when all condemnation is gone forever and we behold only good. God is good and God is Love; more than this we cannot ask nor conceive.

## November 29th

Joseph Murphy

Man is here to discover the joy of living. He must awaken from his dream of limitation to claim his Sonship. He can use the law of life two ways. "I form the light, and create darkness: I make peace, and create evil: I the Lord do all these things." When he gets tired of using the law of life negatively, — in other words, when he is tired of being pushed around, — he begins to ask questions: Why? where? whence? and whither? His dissatisfaction leads to satisfaction; he deduces a law from all of his experiences. The thrill is in discovery.

## November 30th

Christian Larson

Anyone who wishes to change his fate can do so by imaging upon mind a different fate, and by keeping that image so constantly before mind that every thought becomes the likeness of the new fate. The law is that the external world of man changes when his mental world changes; and through the constructive use of the imagination the mental world can be changed in any way that we may desire. When failure seems near, we should image success, refusing absolutely to think of the dark side. By imaging success, we impress upon mind the idea of success; thoughts will be created containing the elements of success, and from these thoughts we shall receive the power that can produce success. Any threatening failure can be overcome and entirely averted by this simple process, providing we live and work as we think. By training the imagination to serve the system of ideals that we may have adopted, we shall soon gain full control of the process that forms impressions upon mind; and when this is accomplished every high ideal, every great purpose and every superior quality that we have in mind will be so well impressed upon the mental creative process that perpetual growth into every desirable condition must positively take place. But to promote this advancement, we must learn to let go completely of everything that has served its purpose, or that in any way interferes with the steady progress of the whole man.

# December

## December 1st

James Allen

Men are anxious to improve their circumstances, but are unwilling to improve themselves. They therefore remain bound. The man who does not shrink from self-crucifixion can never fail to accomplish the object upon which his heart is set. This is as true of earthly as of heavenly things. Even the man whose sole object is to acquire wealth must be prepared to make great personal sacrifices before he can accomplish his object; and how much more so he who would realize a strong and well-poised life?

## December 2nd

Uriel Buchanan

Aspiration, demand, desire, when concentrated in the right direction, for the most enduring good, will lift the mind above all morbid fancies, all hatred, apprehension and fear, will free the body from physical ills, and give support, confidence and courage. If it is your desire to live in harmony and peace with the world, to be just and kind, to be progressive, prosperous and happy, keep yourself in sympathetic touch with the Infinite Power. Its hidden light will make your pathway clear to the realization of all that is true and good. Can you not realize the wonderful possibilities at your command, patiently awaiting recognition? Within your being are sympathetic chords which should vibrate in response to all the symphonies of nature. If there are visions of beauty to which you are blind, and joyous harmonies you have not heard, and depths of feeling you have not fathomed, know this for a certainty, that as you open your mind and heart to the higher and purer influences and place yourself in a child like attitude to receive, you will draw nearer to the bright and beautiful unseen world, and the finer forces of the world will draw nearer to you.

## December 3rd

Ernest Holmes

The metaphysical principle can be demonstrated; there is not any question about that. It is not any good unless it can be. It can. You can draw from an invisible principle which receives your thought and acts upon it just what you believe you will get. Now, there is not any question about that. I want to say again that what that principle is further than that it must be mind, of its real nature I am profoundly ignorant and so is everybody else, and it is useless to make any claims that we cannot substantiate. There is not any living soul knows what God is. We say God is the life essence of all that there is. That is true, but it can be said of electricity that no living soul knows what electricity is, but electricity is; we may as well use it. Mind is and we may as well use that. It is productive of wonderful results when we contact it in the right way. There is no longer any question but what we are surrounded by something and we call it mind which receives every impress of our thought and which acts upon every impress of our thought and tends to bring it out into outer manifestation; so that if you and I want to entertain a mental concept long enough, it would be created for us. There is no question about that. You and I do constantly entertain mental concepts; indeed, we cannot help it. We are thinking beings and we cannot help thinking. It depends then upon what we think what we shall become, and the sooner individuals who are seeking to operate this principle will realize that it depends only upon what they think, and depends upon nothing else, and the sooner they learn to depend upon nothing else, the sooner they will demonstrate that principle. To any thinking person there must come a time when there is a realization that everything which is seen comes from that which is not seen; that, since that which is not seen is the cause of everything, it is also the effect of everything — that is, it is the cause behind it, that it is the effect in manifestation and that the whole process of creation takes place on an invisible plane, absolutely. We are learning that this creative process is the result of some activity of thought in Mind, whether it is God's thought or your thought or my thought. When we think, our thought, we will say goes forth, is immediately surrounded by this Mind that immediately begins to act upon it, just like the creative power in the soil acts upon the seed.

## December 4th

Christian Larson

To explain further the nature of scientific thinking, as well as unscientific thinking, it is well to take several well-known illustrations from real life. When things go wrong, people usually say, "That's always the way"; and though this may seem to be a harmless expression, nevertheless, the more you use that expression the more deeply you convince your mind that things naturally go wrong most of the time. When you train your mind to think that it is usual for things to go wrong, the forces of your mind will follow that trend of thinking, and will also go wrong; and for that reason it is perfectly natural that things in your life should go wrong more and more, because as the forces of your mind are going wrong, you will go wrong, and when you go wrong, those things that pertain to your life cannot possibly go right. A great many people are constantly looking for the worst. They usually expect the worst to happen; though they may be cheerful on the surface, deep down in their heart they are constantly looking for trouble. The result is that their deeper mental currents will tend to produce trouble. If you are always looking for the worst, the forces of your mind will be turned in that direction, and therefore will become destructive. Those forces will tend to produce the very thing that you expect. At first they will simply confuse your mind and produce troubled conditions in your mental world; but this will in turn confuse your faculties, your reason and your judgment, so that you will make many mistakes; and he who is constantly making mistakes will certainly find the worst on many or all occasions. When things go wrong, do not expect the wrong to appear again. Look upon it as an exception. Call it past and forget it. To be scientific under these circumstances, always look for the best. By constantly expecting the best, you will turn the different forces of your mind and thought to work for the best. Every power that is in you will have a higher and finer ideal upon which to turn its attention, and accordingly, results will be better, which is perfectly natural when your whole system is moving towards the better.

### December 5th

Prentice Mulford

Of anything which annoys you, make up your mind that it shall not annoy you. This decision will increase the drawing power of your mind. But if in mind you give way to annoyances, and do not resist them, you increase their power to annoy you. You bring on also by this mental condition more and more annoyances. You lessen also your force for drawing things to you. Or in other words you use that same force to draw annoying things to you. Resist the devil and he will flee from you. A disagreeable habit in another person, and impertinence or rudeness in another, a creaking door, anything in the working of the physical world about us, if we do not set our minds against its annoying us, will grow more and more upon us. It will master us. All these things represent the devil to be resisted. When we allow ourselves to be annoyed by any person we are ruled by that person. For if we cannot abide their presence in a room, then that person drives us from that room. If we cannot be agreeable to others with that person in our presence, then that person governs our speech and makes us silent and sulky. But when this resisting power is used, and we endeavor to turn our mind from the annoyance, we shall be carried at last beyond the reach of all annoying things. That is the real power for driving from us whatever annoys us.

### December 6th

Joseph Murphy

Love is the fulfilling of the law. Love is really an emotional attachment, a sense of oneness with your good. You must be true to that which you love. You must be loyal to your purpose or to your ideal. We are not being true to the one we love when we are flirting or mentally entertaining other marriages with fear, doubt, worry, anxiety, or false beliefs. Love is a state of oneness, a state of fulfillment.

### December 7th

Ernest Holmes

I think sometimes we do not quite realize or recognize the absoluteness of law, and we do not recognize quite clearly enough that all law is cause and effect; nothing can happen in the outside unless there is something corresponding to it on the inside of life. Everything that comes to us comes through a law of attraction. You could not draw anything to you until there was first an avenue for that thing, through which that thing could flow toward you. You could not draw riches to you if you held the thought of poverty; you could only draw more of the same thing — more poverty. That is why Jesus said, "When you pray, believe that you have and you shall receive." They were to first provide within themselves the mental pattern of the thing prayed for. That person who can provide the best mental pattern — that is what we call realizing — that one who can do it the best, gets the best results. But we are all filled with some kind of a mental pattern. There is not a person who is not providing a consciousness about something. It may be an absence of the consciousness of the thing they want but it is a consciousness of the thing they get. And so, the only way to make a demonstration is to destroy in your consciousness everything that in any objective shape or manner supposes that that thing cannot be done. Before you can do that, you have got to stop looking for the thing you do not want. If you want to be well, don't look for sickness.

### December 8th

Orison Swett Marden

Your prosperity, your health, your happiness, your success, the fruition of your ambitions, all are in the great formless creative energy, ready to come into form when your thought does its part in starting the creative processes. Limitless wealth, inexhaustible supply to meet our needs, inventions, great productions of art and literature, music and drama, marvels in every field of human endeavor, are in the great cosmic intelligence waiting the contact, of man's thought to come into visible form on our earth. All the powers in the great cosmic intelligence are constantly working on the thoughts and desires of men. There is no favoritism in the unseen realities. The thoughts of the meanest man on earth are treated in precisely the same way as those of the noblest. Just as the sun and the rain, the wind and the dew give their potencies to the poor farmer and the good one alike, so the thief, the criminal, the murderer, the failure and the marplot have the same material to work in as the just man, the nobly successful, the great architects and artists, the great engineers, inventors, merchants, the great men and women in every field who are uplifting the race and making the world a better place to live in. In other words, the creative force of thought puts an invincible power into man's hands, makes him a creator, the molder of his life, his destiny, his fortunes. We cannot think without creating, for every thought is a seed planted in the universal substance; it will produce something like itself. You and I can sow in the invisible, constructive thoughts, beautiful thoughts, thoughts of love, of good will, of health, of prosperity, of happiness, of success in our chosen work; or we can sow destructive thoughts, ugly thoughts, thoughts of hatred and ill-will, of disease, of discord, of failure, of poverty, of all sorts of misery, and, one thing is certain, whatever we sow we shall reap. That is the law, and there is no escape from it..

## December 9th

Venice J. Bloodworth

Your true self is the spirit of you — and the spirit of you is forever complete and perfect. Spirit cannot know any lack, limit or disease; It is the conscious mind that places limits in accord with our education and environment training. There is no limit to our supply; the limitation is in our ability to receive. So we may broaden our conception of truth and enlarge our receiving powers by the use of affirmation, concentration, suggestion. You learn truth just as you would learn anything else — by study and practice. Affirmations are a wonderful help in establishing your knowledge of your real self, for you are healthy, young, beautiful, prosperous, and happy, but your conscious mind must be taught to know this fact. It is not necessary to use any set form of affirmation — just make any affirmation of anything or condition that YOU WISH TO SEE MADE MANIFEST. When you can truly believe that what you say is true, nothing on earth can keep it from you provided the quality of your thought is in accord with your affirmation. By which I mean that your intentions toward all men be good and your whole attitude one of loving kindness.

## December 10th

Robert Collier

If you want health, happiness, in your life, if you are seeking riches and success, attune your thoughts to these. BLESS the circumstances that surround you. Bless and praise those who come in contact with you. Bless even the difficulties you meet, for by blessing them, you can change them from discordant conditions to favorable ones, you can speed up their rate of activity to where they will bring you good instead of evil. It is only lack of RESPONSIVENESS to good that produces the lacks in your life. Good works on the plane of EXPANSION. Good revolves at a high rate of activity. You can key your activity to the same rate by an expectant confident state of mind. You can bring all your surroundings and circumstances up to that same level by BLESSING them, PRAISING the good in them. Remember, the basic magnet lies in your own thoughts. Upon the quality and activity of that magnet depend the good or evil that will be drawn to you. You are the Master of your fate. You are the architect who determines the materials that are to be used in making your life and your circumstances. You have the power of SELECTIVITY. How, then, shall we order our lives, to the end that we may have the good things we seek — riches and happiness, health and success? "Seek ye first the Kingdom of EXPANSION . . . and all things else shall be added unto you."

## December 11th

### Ernest Holmes

If you are a center of causation operating through the word, that word is every word you speak — every word. And every word you speak transcends law and creates law as fast as it goes along. There is a thing that is very hard to conceive. I took about two years studying that to see how that could be, that my word makes a new law and that new law will do a new thing. And since I am a center in causation and can think and say a word — and speak to it and it will create the law that will substantiate the word — that mighty concept of the vitality of the power behind the thing and within the thing will manifest as long as the word exists. If that is not true, all that is taught of metaphysics would be false. Since it is true, all that is taught is a practical application of law through the creative power within us or our spoken word audibly or inaudibly expressed. When you say "I am poor," you are creating the very thing that makes you poor. When you say "I am poor," you are using a word to make you poor. If you can awake to this truth, it will be the greatest truth you ever realized. When you say "I am not poor, I am perfect in expression," whatever it is you want your word to be it is. You are using a power that nothing can withstand outside of God. That concept is all that we need. Get the concept of the creative word flowing through us to such a degree that nothing can withstand it; and that individual who can appreciate it to the greatest extent is the one who believes it.

## December 12th

### Henry Thomas Hamblin

Thought control is a great assistance. Substituting a right or positive thought for a wrong one, will, in course of time, work wonders in the life. In the subconscious we have an illimitable power of extraordinary intelligence. According to our thoughts this wonderful power either builds up health, harmony and beauty in our life and body, or just the reverse. The power is good, the intelligence is apparently infinite, but it goes wherever our thoughts direct it. By our thinking, therefore, we either create or destroy, produce either good or evil. If, therefore, all our thoughts are good, positive and constructive, it follows that both our body and our life must become built up in harmony and perfection. The question is, can this be done? It can be done if we have the desire, and persevere in the face, often, of seeming failure.

## December 13th

Christian Larson

The discovery of the fact that man is as he thinks, has originated a number of strange ideas concerning the power of thought. One of the principal of these is the belief that thought is a domineering force to be used in controlling things and in compelling fate to come our way. But that this belief is unscientific in every sense of the term has been demonstrated any number of times. Those who have accepted this belief, and who have tried to use thought as a compelling force, have seemingly succeeded in the beginning, but later on have utterly failed, and the reason is that the very moment we proceed to apply thought in this manner, we place ourselves out of harmony with everything, both within ourselves and in our environment. The seeming success that such people have had in the beginning, or for a season, is due to the fact that a strong compelling force can cause the various elements of life to respond for a while, but the force that compels, weakens itself through the very act of compelling, and finally loses its power completely; and then, whatever has been gathered begins to slip away. This explains why thousands of ardent students of metaphysics have failed to secure the results desired, or have succeeded only in spurts. They have taken the wrong view of the power of thought, and therefore have caused their power to work against them during the greater part of the time. The power of thought is not a compelling force. It is a building force, and it is only when used in the latter sense that desirable results can be produced. The building capacity of thought, however, is practically unlimited. Therefore there is actually no end to what might be accomplished, so long as this power is employed intelligently. To apply the full building power of thought, we should proceed upon the principle that he can who thinks he can, and we should act in the full conviction that whatever man thinks he can do, he can do, because there is no limit to the power that such thinking can bring forth. The majority among intelligent minds admit that there is some truth in the statement that he can who thinks he can, but they do not, as a rule, believe it to be a very large truth. They admit that we gain more confidence in ourselves when we think that we can do what we have undertaken to do, and also that we become more determined, but aside from that, they see no further value in that particular attitude of mind. They do not realize that he who thinks he can, develops the power that can; but this is the truth, and it is one of the most important of all truths in the vast metaphysical domain.

## December 14th

### Wallace Wattles

Gratitude unifies the mind of man with the intelligence of substance, so that man's thoughts are received by the formless. A person can remain upon the creative plane only by uniting himself with the formless intelligence through a deep and continuous feeling of gratitude. A person must form a clear and definite mental image of the things he wishes to have, to do, or to become, and he must hold this mental image in his thoughts, while being deeply grateful to the supreme that all his desires are granted to him. The person who wishes to get rich must spend his leisure hours in contemplating his vision, and in earnest thanksgiving that the reality is being given to him. Too much stress cannot be laid on the importance of frequent contemplation of the mental image, coupled with unwavering faith and devout gratitude. This is the process by which the impression is given to the formless and the creative forces set in motion. The creative energy works through the established channels of natural growth, and of the industrial and social order. All that is included in his mental image will surely be brought to the person who follows the instructions given above, and whose faith does not waver.

## December 15th

Ernest Holmes

The reason we can make our requests known with thanksgiving is because we know from the beginning that we are to receive and therefore we cannot help being thankful. This grateful attitude to the Spirit puts us in very close touch with power and adds much to the reality of the thing that we are dealing with. Without it we can do but little. So let us cultivate all the gratitude that we can. In gratitude we will send our thoughts out into the world, and as it comes back it will come laden with the fruits of the Spirit.

## December 16th

Joseph Murphy

One of my class-students recently opened a restaurant. He phoned me, saying that he got married to a restaurant; he meant that he had made up his mind to be very successful, diligent, and persevering, and to see that his business prospered. This man's wife (mental) was his belief in the accomplishment of his desire or wish. Identify yourself with your aim in life, and cease mental marriages with criticism, self-condemnation, anger, fear, and worry. Give attention to your chosen ideal, being full of faith and confidence in the inevitable law of prosperity and success. You will accomplish nothing by loving your ideal one minute, and denying it the next minute; this is like mixing acid and alkali, and you will get an inert substance. In going along the Royal Road to Riches, you must be faithful to your chosen ideal (your wife).

## December 17th

Orison Swett Marden

We think we live in a material world, but in reality we live in a mental world, a world of externalized thought, a world controlled and guided by invisible forces. We contact with material things only at a few points in our lives. The corporal part of us is fed, warmed and clothed by material things, but we live, move, and have our being in the unseen. When we come to the reality of ourselves, the soul, the spirit of man, which is one with God, we live altogether in an invisible world. The real self is the unseen self. The man whose reflection we see in the mirror is but the shadow of the reality. The material body of flesh and blood that we see, and can touch with our hands, is not the real man. That is behind what we see and touch. It is back of the cell, back of the atoms, back of the electrons which make up the body. The new philosophy is going back of appearance and showing us the real man, the invisible man. It is revealing his hidden potencies and possibilities, and pointing the way to their development and use. It shows us that, the impotent, sickly, ailing man, the weakling, the discouraged, disconsolate, complaining being, the failure, the man full of discord, disease, inharmony, is not the man God made; that this is the unreal creature man himself has made. This is the being that wrong thinking, wrong living, and unfortunate motives have made, the being who is the victim of his passions, of his moods, of his ignorance of realities, the great eternal verities of life.

### December 18th

Uriel Buchanan

Are you dissatisfied with life, and disposed to blame fate and the injustice of social and commercial laws for your lack of achievement? The fault is not in the law; for unto every man is given the latent power and potentiality which he may make use of to the profit of a glorious success. If you feel the oppression of the world's indifference and coldness and are deprived of the sympathy and help you deserve, let your thoughts dwell on all that is beautiful in nature, and search with your aspirations for the light of high ideals. Though you may seem alone and neglected, and deprived of many things which make life beautiful and desirable, if you will listen to the monitor within you will receive help and guidance. You, as a part of the Infinite Power, may share all the riches and glory belonging to human existence. No man or set of men, no government or assigned authority, have the right to deprive you of freedom. For in the beginning of time it was ordained that you, an offspring of the Infinite, should inherit the riches belonging to universal life. Then, in the name of that power and that wisdom whose domain extends through all space and all time, reach up to the source of being and demand your rightful inheritance. There is no need to drift with the tide of adversity away from the source of your strength and your sustenance. You need only to go forth with the consciousness of your relationship to the eternal to demand from the world the recognition of your divine selfhood.

## December 19th

Ernest Holmes

We will always attract to us, in our lives and conditions, according to our thought. Things are but outer manifestations of inner mental concepts. Thought is not only power; it is also the form of all things. The conditions that we attract will correspond exactly to our mental pictures. It is quite necessary, then, that the successful business man should keep his mind on thoughts of happiness, which produce cheerfulness instead of depression; he should radiate joy, and should be filled with faith, hope and expectancy. These cheerful, hopeful attitudes of mind are indispensable to the one who really wants to do things in life. Put every negative thought out of your mind once and for all. Declare your freedom. Know that no matter what others may say, think or do, you are a success, now, and nothing can hinder you from accomplishing your good. All the power of the universe is with you; feel it, know it, and then act as though it were true. This mental attitude alone will draw people and things to you.

## December 20th

Mrs. Evelyn Lowes Wicker

Source of Energy. Out of the air we extract two very important elements for the sustaining of life. The first is energy. The medical profession has not in the past recognized this fact. This knowledge has come to us from the

Far East. It was a secret, and only given to those people who were privileged to study in the temples of the East. It was kept a secret because of the laws of caste as practiced by the Hindu. Little by little these secrets have seeped into the Western World. We have scientifically proven the truth of the Eastern philosophy of breath. It has become a part of the teaching of psychology. In the past we have been taught that our energy came from food. The result has been that whenever we feel worn out and innervated, we have been in the habit of trying to eat our way back to health. Through this ignorance we have shortened our life, instead of lengthening it. Man has eaten, and is today in the habit of eating, twice the amount of food necessary to sustain life. This fact is demonstrated and proven by psychologists and physiologists alike. Those who are practicing the principles as taught in psychology are living on a half or a third of the food that they ate when in the old thought. There is a law that the deeper you breathe the less you eat. Man is a fresh air animal.

## December 21st

Prentice Mulford

Three persons engaged in any form of gossip, tattle or scandal generate a force and send it from them of tattle, gossip and scandal. The thought they send into the air returns to them and does them injury to mind and body. It is far more profitable to talk with others of things which go to work out good. Every sentence you speak is a spiritual force to you and others for good or ill. Ten minutes spent in growling at your luck, or in growling at others because they have more luck than yourself, means ten minutes of your own force spent in making worse your own health and fortune. Every thought of envy or hatred sent another is a boomerang. It flies back to you and hurts you. The envy or dislike we may feel toward those who, as some express it, "put on airs." The ugly feeling we may have at seeing others riding in carriages and " rolling in wealth," represents just so much thought (i. e., force) most extravagantly expended, for in its expenditure we get not only unhappiness, but destroy future fortune and happiness. If this has been your common habit or mood of mind, do not expect to get out of it at once. Once convinced of the harm done you by such mood, and a new force has come to gradually remove the old mind and bring a new one. But all changes must be gradual. Your own private room is your chief workshop for generating your spiritual force and building yourself up. If it is kept in disorder, if things are flung recklessly about, and you cannot lay your bands instantly upon them, it is an indication that your mind is in the same condition, and therefore your mind as it works on others, in carrying out your projects, will work with less effect and result by reason of its disordered and disorganized condition. Ill temper or despondency is a disease. The mind subject to it in any degree is to that degree a sick mind. The sick mind makes the sick body. The great majority of the sick are not in bed. When you are peevish, remember your mind is sick. Demand then a well mind. When you say to yourself, " I am going to have a pleasant visit or a pleasant journey," you are literally sending elements and forces ahead of your body that will arrange things to make your visit or journey pleasant. When before the visit or the journey or the shopping trip you are in a bad humor, or fearful or apprehensive of something unpleasant, you are sending unseen agencies ahead of you which will make some kind of unpleasantness. Our thoughts, or in other words, our state of mind is ever at work "fixing up " things good or bad for us in advance.

## December 22nd

### Robert Collier

"I AM the Master of my fate." Until you have learned that, you will never attain life's full success. Your fate is in your own hands. You have the making of it. What you are going to be six months or a year from now depends upon what you think today. So make your choice now: Are you going to bow down to matter as the only power? Are you going to look upon your environment as something that has been wished upon you and for which you are in no way responsible? Or are you going to try to realize in your daily life that matter is merely an aggregation of protons and electrons subject entirely to the control of Mind, that your environment, your success, your happiness, are all of your own making, and that if you are not satisfied with conditions as they are, you have but to visualize them as you would have them be in order to change them? The former is the easier way right now — the easy way that leads to the hell of poverty and fear and old age. But the latter is the way that brings you to your Heart's Desire. And merely because this Power of Universal Mind is invisible, is that any reason to doubt it? The greatest powers of Nature are invisible. Love is invisible, but what greater power is there in life? Joy is invisible, happiness, peace, contentment. The radio is invisibles yet you hear it. It is a product of the law governing sound waves. Law is invisible, yet you see the manifestation of different laws every day. To run a locomotive, you study the law of applying power, and you apply that law when you make the locomotive go. These things are not the result of invention. The law has existed from the beginning. It merely waited for man to learn how to apply it. If man had known how to call upon Universal Mind to the right extent, he could have applied the law of sound waves, the law of steam, ages ago. Invention is merely a revelation and an unfoldment of Universal Wisdom.

### December 23rd

James Allen

Only by much searching and mining are gold and diamonds obtained, and man can find every truth connected with his being if he will dig deep into the mine of his soul. And that he is the maker of his character, the molder of his life, and the builder of his destiny, he may unerringly prove: if he will watch, control, and alter his thoughts, tracing their effects upon himself, upon others, and upon his life and circumstances; if he will link cause and effect by patient practice and investigation, utilizing his every experience, even to the most trivial, as a means of obtaining that knowledge of himself. In this direction, as in no other, is the law absolute that "He that seeketh findeth; and to him that knocketh it shall be opened"; for only by patience, practice, and ceaseless importunity can a man enter the Door of the Temple of Knowledge.

## December 24th

Ernest Holmes

Thinking back over the reason for things, you will find that you are surrounded by a mind, or law, that casts back at the thinker, manifested, everything that he thinks. If this were not true, man would not be an individual. Individuality can mean only the ability to think what we want to think. If that thought is to have power in our lives then there has to be something that will manifest it. Some are limited and bound by law through ignorance. This law is sometimes called "Karma," it is the law that binds the ignorant and gives freedom to the wise. We live in mind; and it can return to us only what we think into it. No matter what we may do, law will always obtain. If we are thinking of ourselves as poor and needy, then mind has no choice but to return what we have thought into it. At first this may be hard to realize, but the truth will reveal to the seeker that law could act in no other way. Whatever we think is the pattern, and mind is the builder.

## December 25th

Robert Collier

If I give help to the man whose desk is next to mine, it will come back to me multiplied, even if he apparently is a rival. What I give to him, I give to the firm, and the firm will value it, because it is teamwork in the organization that the firm primarily wants, not brilliant individual performance. If I have an enemy in the organization, the same rule holds; if I give him, with the purpose of helping him, something that will genuinely help him, I am giving service to the organization. Great corporations appreciate the peace-maker, for a prime requisite in their success is harmony among employees. If my boss is unappreciative, the same rule holds; if I give him more, in advance of appreciation, he cannot withhold his appreciation and keep his own job. "The more you think about this law, the deeper you will see it goes. It literally hands you a blank check, signed by the Maker of Universal Law, and leaves you to fill in the amount — and the kind — of payment you want! Mediocre successes are those that obey this law a little way — that fill in the check with a small amount — but that stop short of big vision in it. If every employee would only get the idea of this law firmly fixed in him as a principle, not subject to wavering with fluctuating moods, the success of the organization would be miraculous. One of my fears is apt to be that, by promoting the other fellow's success, I am side-tracking my own; but the exact opposite is the truth.

### December 26th

Joseph Murphy

The heart is called the subconscious mind in ancient allegories. The Egyptians knew that the heart was the subconscious mind, but they did not call it by that name. The Chaldeans and the Babylonians called it by different names. You can impress your subconscious mind, and your subconscious mind will express what is impressed upon it. Any idea that is emotionalized or felt as true will be accepted by your subconscious mind.

### December 27th

Christian Larson

Whatever we place in the hands of the subjective, the subjective will continue to hold until it is called upon to let go. Every cause that gains a foothold in the subjective will continue to produce its effects, until the subjective is directed to have it removed; and every impression that is formed upon the subjective will continue to act as a pattern for the creation of thought until a different impression is formed in its place. To know how to deal with the subjective is therefore one of the greatest essentials; and the reason why so few have the power to master their fate is because the conscious direction of the subjective is almost unknown. Mind has two sides, the outer and the inner; or the objective and the subjective. The objective is the conscious mind; the subjective is the subconscious mind. The objective acts; the subjective reacts. The objective mind gives orders; the subjective carries them out. The objective selects the seed and places that seed in the subjective; and the subjective causes that seed to grow and bear fruit after its kind. Whatever the objective desires to have done, the subjective has the power to do, and will do, if properly directed; though it must be properly and consciously directed. In the average mind the subjective is directed ignorantly and irregularly; sometimes for good, more frequently otherwise. Therefore, the results are as they are; uncertain, unsatisfactory and limited. However, when we learn to direct the subjective consciously and with method, we shall be able to produce any result desired, at any time desired. To direct the subjective, the will must be employed, as it must be in all forms of direction; and in the use of the will is where the real secret is found. The will must not act upon the external phase of any idea, desire or condition, but must intentionally act upon the internal side only.

## December 28th

Ernest Holmes

Each person is living in a world of his own making, and he should speak only such words and think only such thoughts as he wishes to see manifested in his life. We must not hear, think, speak, read or listen to limitation of any kind. There is no way under heaven whereby we can think two kinds of thought and get only one result; it is impossible, and the sooner we realize it the sooner we shall arrive. This does not mean that we must be afraid to think lest we create the wrong image, but it does mean that the way most people think can produce nothing but failure; that is why so few succeed. The person who is to succeed will never let his mind dwell on past mistakes. He will forgive the past in his life and in the lives of other people. If he makes a mistake he will at once forgive it. He will know that so long as he desires any good, there is nowhere in the universe anything that opposes him. God does not damn anyone or anything; man damns everyone and everything. God does not make things by comparing His power with some other power. God knows that when He speaks it done; and if we partake of the divine nature we must know the same thing in our lives that God knows in His.

## December 29th

### Venice J. Bloodworth

Time is not a prime factor in the building of our consciousness. One person may be able to get results quickly, while others will be months reaching any satisfaction, while some will be years learning the truth. You may learn more in ten minutes of intense concentration than you would in a month's ordinary thinking. Your progress depends on your ability to eject old ideas and set opinions. You are fortunate if you have no set opinions, for every generation brings a new set of scientific facts to set aside what everyone thought was the acme of wisdom. There can be no progress without change. So keep an open mind. Do not declare anything false just because you do not understand it. Dig in and find out what it is all about. Be up to date in worthwhile things and take a friendly interest in everything about you

## December 30th

### Christian Larson

Just Be Glad. All things respond to the call of rejoicing; all things gather where life is a song. This is the message of the new order, the new life and the new time. It is the golden text of the great gospel of human sunshine. It is the central truth of that sublime philosophy of existence, which declares that the greatest good is happiness, and that heaven is here and now. To live in the spirit of this wonderful message; to be a living example of this great gospel, to work out in everyday life the principle of this inspiring philosophy, the first and most important thing to do, is to lay aside our sorrows and glooms, and just be glad. Wherever you are, or whatever has happened, just be glad. Be glad because you are here. You are here in a beautiful world; and all that is beautiful may be found in this world. It is a world wherein all that is rich in life may be enjoyed beyond measure; a world wherein happiness may overflow eternally in every human heart; a world wherein all the dreams of life may be realized, and all the visions of the soul made true. Then why should we not be glad; first of all, that we are here; that we are in this world; that we may stay here for a long time if we so desire, and enjoy every minute to the full. The real truth is that this world is nothing less than a limitless sea of happiness, the vastness and glory of which we are just beginning to know. And life itself is a song, while time is one eternal symphony. To be in tune with life, therefore, and to be in harmony with the endless music of time, we must of necessity be glad. But after we have learned to be glad, under every circumstance, it is no longer a necessity; it is a privilege, and has become a part of our active, living, thinking self.

## December 31st

### Shirley Bell Hastings

It is remarkable and true that the thought or idea which you permit to live in you increases and, if persisted in, determines the trend of thinking and acts as a great attracting or repelling power which brings forth from within you your possibilities for producing the thing. At the same time it attracts to you all that can aid in producing and repels all contrary to it. Now think, think, think — plenty, opulence. Say the words; close the eyes; look and listen into mind. Plenty, opulence, richness, abundance, plenty. Say them over and over again. Say them until they are no longer just words. Say them until they grow into ideas in the mind. Keep thinking the ideas until they stay in the mind. Keep thinking them until they produce on the outer. You serve this God-force when you open to it. Give yourself to it and give to it an idea to work out. The more understandingly you do this, the more lovingly you do this, knowing that when you ask for riches the force of God all about, within, everywhere is the supply and is producing.

## Metaphysical / Law of Attraction Books

David Allen - The Power of I AM (2014), The Power of I AM - Volume 2 (2015) The Power of I AM - Volume 3 (2017)

David Allen - The Creative Power of Thought, Man's Greatest Discovery (2017)

David Allen - The Secrets, Mysteries & Powers of The Subconscious Mind (2017)

David Allen - The Money Bible - The Spiritual Secrets of Attracting Prosperity and Abundance (2017)

David Allen - Your Faith Is Your Fortune, Your Unlimited Power (2018)

The Neville Goddard Collection (All 10 of his books plus 2 Lecture series) (2016)

Neville Goddard - Assumptions Harden Into Facts: The Book (2016)

Neville Goddard - Imagination: The Redemptive Power in Man (2016)

Neville Goddard - The World is At Your Command - The Very Best of Neville Goddard (2017)

Neville Goddard - Imagining Creates Reality - 365 Mystical Daily Quotes (2017)

Neville Goddard's Interpretation of Scripture (2018)

The Definitive Christian D. Larson Collection (6 Volumes, 30 books) (2014)

David Allen - ASKffirmations (2018)

David Allen - The Creative Power of Man - Daily Meditations For A Better Life (2019)

All books are available online

www.ingramcontent.com/pod-product-compliance
Lightning Source LLC
Chambersburg PA
CBHW020418010526
**44118CB00010B/316**